Air Condi
Service Guide

By Michael Prokup

MW01352710

© Prokup Media 2011

ISBN: 978-0-615-92472-4

Prokup Media
227 Bucklin St
LaSalle IL, 61301

NOTE: This publication is general in nature and is intended for INSTRUCTIONAL PURPOSES ONLY. It is not to be used for equipment selection, application, installation or specific service procedures.

**Basic
Refrigeration Cycle**

**Basic
Refrigeration Cycle**

Chapter

The Basics of the Mechanical Refrigeration Cycle

Table Of Contents

Basic Refrigeration Cycle 2
- The Basic Refrigeration Cycle Drawing 2
- System Pressures and How Heat is Moved 2
- Converting Pressure to Saturation Temperature 4
- The Purpose of the Metering Device 6
- The Evaporator Circuit 6
- Superheating Suction Vapor 8
- The Suction Line and Pressure Loss 8
- The Compressor 9
- The Condenser Coil 9
- The Subcooling Process 10
- Liquid Line Pressure Loss 10
- A Summary of the Basic Refrigeration Cycle 11
- Pressure Ports 11
- Location of Pressure Ports 12
- Installing Pressure Ports 13
- Replacing Leaking Pressure Port Cores 13

Basic Refrigerant Circuit Components 14
- The Evaporator Coil and its Components 15
- Indoor Air Blower and its Components 17
- Suction Lines and Suction Line Driers 17
- Compressors and its Components 18
- Discharge Lines 20
- Condenser Coils and Circuits 21
- Condenser Fans and its Components 21
- Liquid Lines and Liquid Line Driers 22
- Metering Devices 22
- Expansion Valves 23

Field Service Guide: The Basics Of The Mechanical Refrigeration Cycle

Basic Refrigeration Cycle

The Basic Refrigeration Cycle Drawing

This illustration depicts a typical refrigeration system found in comfort cooling air conditioning systems. The system consists of a metering device, evaporator coil, suction line, compressor, hot gas line, condenser coil, and liquid line. The system uses refrigerant to transfer heat from the conditioned space (home) to the outdoor air. The operation of the system works because heat always flows from a warmer object to a colder object.

Notice the evaporator coil connects the refrigeration system to the heat source. The connection is between the refrigerant inside of the evaporator coil and the air that is passing across the surface of the evaporator coil. In the case of an air conditioning system, the heat from the home will flow into the cold refrigerant that is in the evaporator coil.

As the heat content of the air changes, it will have a profound affect upon the operation of the refrigeration system. In this chapter, we will learn how all of the components of the system integrate together.

System Pressures and How Heat is Moved

To move heat, a refrigerant is placed in the refrigeration system, and the refrigerant pressure is regulated from high to low. By changing the pressure in the system, the saturation temperature of the refrigerant can be changed. At high pressure, refrigerants have a high

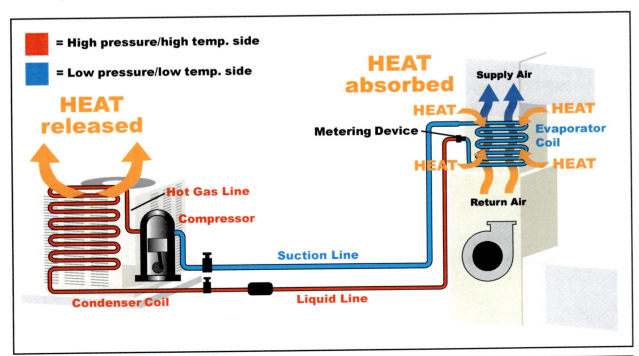

Field Service Guide: The Basics Of The Mechanical Refrigeration Cycle

saturation temperature, and at low pressure, they have a low saturation temperature.

In the refrigeration circuit, there is a high pressure high temperature side, and a low pressure low temperature side. The high pressure high temperature side of the system rejects heat, and the low pressure low temperature side of the system absorbs heat. The high pressure side of the system consists of the compressor, discharge line, condenser coil, and liquid line. The low side of the system consists of the evaporator coil and the suction line. The metering device is the pressure changing device that separates the two sides of the system.

To start our study of a basic refrigeration cycle, let's start the cycle at the evaporator coil where heat will be absorbed into the cold refrigerant. The metering device is in front of the evaporator coil circuiting. The metering device is simply a restriction that drops pressure. The metering device will drop the refrigerant pressure from a high pressure liquid to a low pressure cold saturated mix of refrigerant liquid and vapor.

Hot goes to cold, so heat will flow from the conditioned space air into the colder saturated refrigerant contained in the evaporator coil. As the refrigerant circulates through the evaporator coil circuiting, it continues to pick up heat. The amount of heat the refrigerant picks up is greatest when the refrigerant is in a cold saturated liquid state and is flashing or evaporating into vapor as it absorbs heat. As the liquid evaporates to vapor, the refrigerant now contains a lot of heat, yet the temperature of the vapor that flashes off the liquid refrigerant is the same temperature as the liquid. The liquid is using all of the heat energy simply to boil off to a vapor.

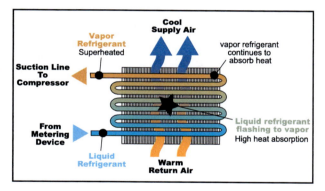

Eventually, all of the liquid will be boiled off and only vapor will remain. The vapor is still very cold and it too gathers up heat from the air. The amount of heat transfer will begin to fall as all changing of state has ceased. This phase of heat transfer in the evaporator coil now involves heat going into the vapor and raising the temperature of the vapor above the saturation temperature. This phase is called superheating.

Field Service Guide: The Basics Of The Mechanical Refrigeration Cycle

The air that leaves the evaporator now contains less heat than when it came in contact with the evaporator coil surface. The refrigerant leaving the evaporator coil now carries this heat in the suction vapor that is being directed to the compressor.

To reject the heat from the refrigerant, the mechanical refrigeration cycle must raise the pressure of the refrigerant so the saturation temperature of the refrigerant is above the temperature of the outdoor air. The compressor compresses the refrigerant to a high pressure, and corresponding high temperature. For example, if the system compressed the refrigerant to 300PSIG and the refrigerant is R-22, the saturation temperature of the refrigerant is now 131°F. With the saturation temperature of the refrigerant high, heat from the refrigerant can now flow to the cooler outdoor air circulated by the condenser fan assembly.

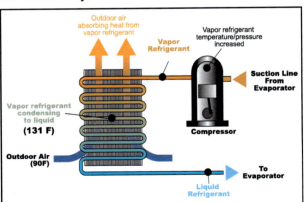

The relationship between pressure and temperature is what makes the refrigeration cycle work. Heat enters the cold low pressure vapor at the evaporator coil. The compressor compresses this low pressure vapor to high pressure to raise the saturation temperature to a level above the temperature of the outdoor air.

The compressor discharges the high temperature/high pressure hot gas to the condenser coil where the refrigerant gives up its heat to the cooler outdoor air.

Converting Pressure To Saturation Temperature

Temperature pressure tables are used to convert system pressure readings to saturation temperature.

R-410A PSIG	Saturation Temp. (F)	R-22 PSIG	R-410A PSIG	Saturation Temp. (F)	R-22 PSIG	R-410A PSIG	Saturation Temp. (F)	R-22 PSIG
12	-41	0	146	51	85	396	116	245
14	-36	2	154	54	90	400	117	250
16	-32	4	160	56	95	412	119	255
18	-28	6	168	59	100	416	120	260
22	-24	8	178	62	105	422	121	265
26	-20	10	184	64	110	434	123	270
30	-17	12	192	67	115	440	124	275
32	-14	14	198	69	120	450	126	280
36	-11	16	208	72	125	456	127	285
38	-8	18	216	74	130	462	128	290
42	-5	20	222	76	135	474	130	295
46	-2	22	230	78	140	482	131	300
48	0	24	240	81	145	494	133	310
50	2	26	248	83	150	512	136	320
54	5	28	256	85	155	526	138	330
58	7	30	262	87	160	544	141	340
60	9	32	270	89	165	560	143	350
64	11	34	280	91	170	572	145	360
68	13	36	288	93	175	596	148	370
70	15	38	292	94	180	608	150	380
74	17	40	300	96	185	624	152	390
78	19	42	308	98	190	640	154	400
80	21	44	318	100	195			
84	23	46	322	101	200			
86	24	48	330	103	205			
90	26	50	340	105	210			
98	30	55	346	106	215			
106	34	60	356	108	220			
114	38	65	364	110	225			
122	41	70	370	111	230			
128	44	75	380	113	235			
138	48	80	386	114	240			

When suction pressure is converted to saturation temperature, the saturation temperature of the refrigerant entering the evaporator circuit is found. When liquid pressure, or discharge pressure is converted to saturation temperature, the saturation temperature of the refrigerant that is condensing from a hot gas into a liquid in the condenser coil is determined. The use of these two saturation temperatures is critical to properly service an air conditioning system, because both saturation temperatures are used in the process of calculating superheat and subcooling levels.

Although R-22 and R-410A refrigerants operate at vastly different pressures, they operate in the system at the same saturation temperatures. In this temperature pressure table, both refrigerants can be compared at different pressure levels commonly encountered during service work.

In this example, we can see that an R-22 system operating with 85 PSIG of suction pressure would have an evaporator coil saturation temperature of about 51°F. An R-410A system operating at a suction pressure of 146 PSIG would also operate at an evaporator coil saturation temperature of 51°F.

The use of a temperature pressure table may not be necessary in the field as the table values are typically printed on the face of the refrigeration gauge. I find it to be a very good habit of simply reading the saturation temperature column on the gauge to quickly find saturation temperatures.

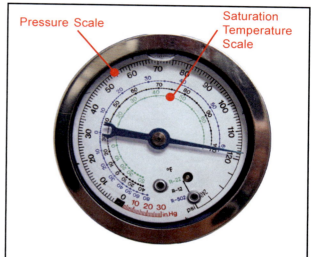

Refrigeration gauges display both the pressure and saturation temperature. This particular gauge shows the saturation temps for R-22, R-12, and R-502.

This is a good time to put to bed the idea that reading the temperature of a refrigeration pipe can tell you the pressure inside of the pipe. This is not true as the refrigerant in the pipe may be colder than saturation temperature (subcooled state) or warmer than saturation temperature (superheated state). The temperature of the pipe will have no relationship to the operating pressure as the refrigerants are not at saturation temperature.

R-410A PSIG	Saturation Temp. (F)	R-22 PSIG
146	51	85
154	54	90
160	56	95
168	59	100

Field Service Guide: The Basics Of The Mechanical Refrigeration Cycle

The Purpose Of The Metering Device

The metering device can be a simple piston that has a hole through its center, or a more complicated expansion valve. Regardless of what type of metering device is being used, the purpose of the metering device is to act as a pressure drop that separates the high temperature area of the refrigeration system from the low temperature area. Each type of metering device places a restriction in the liquid circuit between the liquid line and the evaporator coil circuiting.

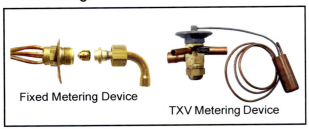

Fixed Metering Device

TXV Metering Device

When the high pressure warm liquid from the liquid line enters the restriction of the metering device, the warm liquid will use some of its own heat to turn into a low pressure cold saturated refrigerant mixture of liquid and vapor. The heat energy from the liquid is given up as some of the liquid turns into a vapor in the pressure drop area. This energy conversion returns heat not rejected at the condenser coil back into the refrigerant. This energy transfer is called the "Refrigerating Effect".

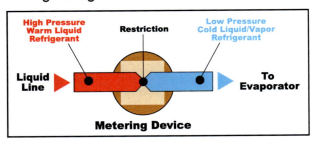

To maximize system capacity, the liquid line temperature should be kept to a minimum as hot liquid contains large amounts of heat which was not rejected at the condenser coil. A condition that can cause a hot liquid line is a dirty condenser coil. The system capacity will be low when the liquid line is hot, as the liquid contains heat that was not rejected from the refrigerant. The refrigerant cannot get rid of this heat and instead returns it to the evaporator coil.

The Evaporator Circuit

The evaporator coil is placed in direct contact with the warm air from a conditioned space. An indoor fan assembly will circulate the conditioned space's warm air through the cold evaporator coil.

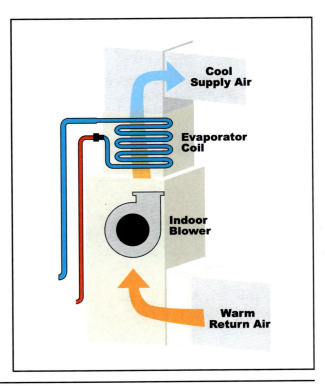

6

The refrigerant that enters the evaporator coil is in a saturated state and any addition of heat at saturation temperature will cause the refrigerant liquid to begin to flash off into a vapor as it travels through the evaporator coil circuiting. It is during this time in the evaporator cycle, that massive levels of heat are being transferred from the conditioned space's warm air into the cold saturated refrigerant. The massive heat transfer taking place is due to the large amount of thermal energy required for the cold liquid refrigerant to change its state from a liquid into a vapor. This process is the same process that makes ice such a good refrigerant!

In this example, we have a suction pressure of 130PSIG with R-410A refrigerant. The corresponding saturation temperature for R-410A at this pressure is 44°F. This is the temperature of the refrigerant as it flashes from a liquid to a vapor.

Assuming a properly working system, at some point in the evaporator coil circuit, all of the cold saturated liquid refrigerant will be boiled off and only vapor will remain. At this point in the evaporator coil, the changing of state process ends. The vapor that remains, is still at saturation temperature which in this example is 44°F.

When all of the saturated refrigerant liquid is used up in the evaporator circuiting, only vapor will remain in the circuit. This condition is created at the boiling off point. The remaining refrigerant vapor is still very cold. As the cold vapor travels through the remaining circuiting of the evaporator coil, it picks up heat from the warm air. Because there is no liquid left, the refrigerant vapor temperature begins to rise to a temperature above saturation temperature. Once the refrigerant vapor raises its temperature above saturation temperature, it is now called superheated. This heat added to the refrigerant vapor after all of the liquid has boiled off is called "Suction Vapor Superheat".

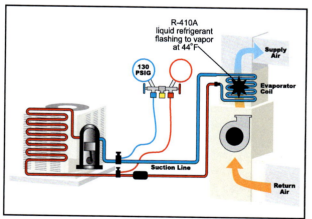

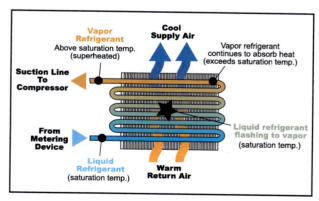

Superheating Suction Vapor

In our example, we have 44°F saturated refrigerant entering the evaporator circuiting. We know this temperature because we converted our 130PSIG suction pressure to saturation temperature. A digital temperature probe is placed at the suction line service gauge port and we measure 54°F. The temperature of the suction line is indicating that we have heated up the refrigerant vapor by 10 degrees, therefore the superheat level is 10°F.

Since no changing of state is taking place when the vapor is being superheated, the actual amount of cooling process declines in the evaporator circuiting where superheating occurs. At this point, the vapor temperature will rise very rapidly. Think of it as if the ice has all melted. The remaining cold water from the melted ice will produce very little refrigeration ability even though it's temperature is colder than the product being refrigerated.

Although superheating of the refrigerant vapor at the evaporator coil provides only minimal cooling benefits, it is needed. This way we are insured that no liquid refrigerant is leaving the evaporator circuit. It is necessary to prevent the escape of saturated refrigerant from the evaporator, because at saturation temperature both liquid and vapor refrigerant may be present, and compressors cannot pump liquid. If liquid is introduced into the compressor, damage to the compressor could occur.

The Suction Line And Pressure Loss

When the refrigerant leaves the evaporator coil, it enters the suction line. When the vapor travels through the suction line, it's pressure falls due to friction losses. The maximum allowable pressure drop from the outlet of the evaporator to the inlet to the compressor is 3 PSIG for R-22, and 5 PSIG for R-410A. If the pressure drop is greater, the capacity of the system falls to unacceptable levels. Causes of excessive suction line pressure loss include kinks in the line, long line sets, or undersized refrigerant piping.

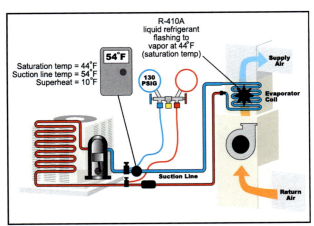

The Compressor

When the suction vapor is drawn from the suction line into the compressor, the cold refrigerant vapor absorbs heat from the compressor motor windings. If there is an adequate amount of vapor present, the compressor will receive adequate cooling. If there is a lack of enough vapor due to a condition such as an undercharge, the compressor will run very hot.

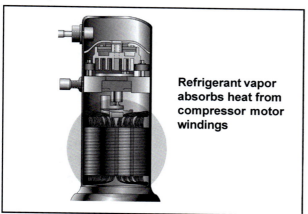

Refrigerant vapor absorbs heat from compressor motor windings

After cooling the motor, the vapor is compressed to a high pressure, and discharged into the hot gas line.

The Condenser Coil

At the condenser coil, the heat from the evaporator and compressor will be removed from the refrigerant by transferring the heat to the cooler outdoor air. When the hot gas enters the condenser coil, it is highly superheated, and at a high pressure and high temperature. The purpose of compression was to raise the pressure of the refrigerant so that it's corresponding saturation temperature is above the temperature of the outdoor air. In this example, we have a liquid pressure of 450 PSIG using R-410A refrigerant. The saturation temperature corresponding to 450PSIG with R-410A is 126°F.

The hot gas leaving the compressor is highly superheated so its actual temperature is going to be above the 126°F saturation temperature. The hot gas contains heat from the evaporator, compressor motor windings, and heat generated during the compression process. As the hot gas enters the condenser coil, it immediately begins to give up heat to the cooler outdoor air. The high pressure/high temperature gas travels through the condenser circuiting continually giving up heat until eventually enough heat is removed from the hot gas for it to reach its 126°F saturation temperature corresponding to the systems 450PSIG liquid pressure.

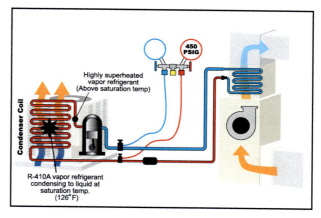

At saturation temperature, any removal of heat will cause a change of state. In the case of the hot gas, it begins to condense into a liquid. The liquid condensing is still at 126°F saturation temperature corresponding to the liquid pressure. As the hot gas condenses to a liquid, a massive amount of heat is transferred out of the refrigerant and into the cooler outdoor air being circulated by the condenser fan.

The Subcooling Process

At saturation temperature, refrigerants can be a mix of liquid and vapor. To ensure proper operation of the metering device, the refrigerant entering the metering device must be all liquid. To prevent the formation of vapor in the liquid line, the condenser coil must reject additional heat from the liquid until the liquid temperature is well below the saturation temperature corresponding to the liquid pressure. The process of removing heat from the refrigerant so that its temperature is below saturation temperature is called "Subcooling."

The subcooling process occurs in the condensing coil after all of the hot gas has condensed into a liquid. The liquid being condensed in the condenser coil continues to travel through the coil's circuiting where additional heat is removed from the liquid. This process drops the temperature of the liquid to a temperature that is below the corresponding saturation temperature for the liquid pressure.

In this example, the saturation temperature corresponding to liquid pressure is 126°F. A digital temperature probe placed on the liquid line at the outlet of the condenser coil reads 110°F. The liquid leaving the condenser coil is 16 degrees colder than saturation temperature. The system has a subcooling level in this example of 16°F.

Liquid Line Pressure Loss

When the liquid refrigerant exits the condenser coil, it is in a subcooled state. The reason it must be subcooled is to prevent the presence of vapor in the liquid line. If the refrigerant was allowed to leave the condenser at saturation temperature, there could be a mix of both liquid and vapor present.

The liquid that exits the condenser coil is moving at a very fast velocity down the liquid line. As it travels, friction between the refrigerant and piping causes the pressure of the liquid to fall. The further the liquid travels, the more pressure it loses. If the pressure falls to a level that is equivalent to the liquid line temperature at saturation, the liquid will begin to flash off to a vapor before it gets to the metering device.

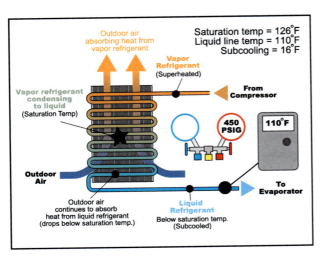

A Summary Of The Basic Refrigeration Cycle

The refrigerant cycle we have just covered is a sealed cycle, meaning that heat enters the refrigerant at the evaporator coil and exits the refrigerant at the condenser coil. For the system to operate properly, the following must be present:

- A properly sized metering piston installed at the metering device fitting
- A clean condenser and evaporator coil
- The proper charge of refrigerant in the system
- Heat load within acceptable ranges of minimum and maximum
- Properly sized refrigerant line set present
- A mechanically sound compressor present

In other sections of the book, diagnostic troubleshooting of system problems will be covered along with the necessary test procedures needed to make a diagnostic decision.

Pressure Ports

There are different types of pressure access valves used in residential air conditioning systems. Some access valves are simple copper tubes with an access port brazed onto the end of the tube. These are called "Service Tubes". Connecting to the tube will access system pressure.

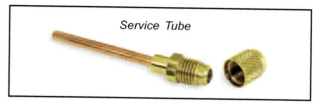

Service Tube

Other types of pressure ports are part of a valve called a "Service Valve". These types of valves can open or close the system to isolate the outdoor condensing unit from the refrigerant lines and the indoor evaporator coil. These valves are opened and closed using a hex wrench. When this type of valve is closed, the pressure port on the valve can still be used to read system pressure.

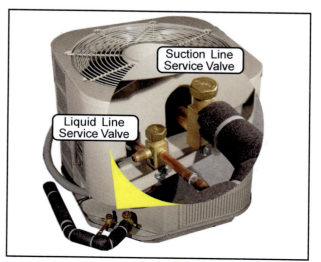

A special valve called a "King Valve" is also found on some air conditioning systems. This type of valve is a three way valve. There are three positions the valve can be in: They are back-seated, cracked, or front-seated.

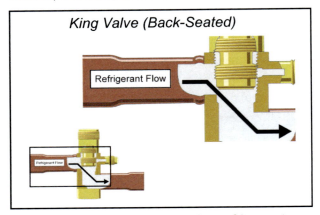
King Valve (Back-Seated)

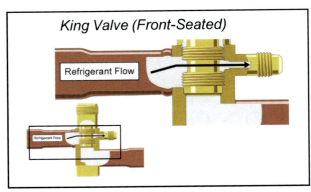
King Valve (Front-Seated)

In the back-seated position, the refrigerant can flow through the valve but the pressure port is shut off. When connecting or removing gauge hoses from the system, this is the position the valve should be in.

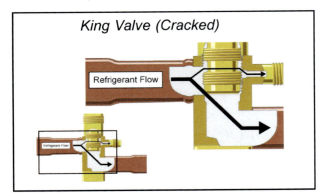
King Valve (Cracked)

When you wish to read the pressure, turn or crack the valve open a few turns and the gauge port will now be open to the system and pressure can be read. The valve will continue to allow refrigerant flow.

When the valve is front-seated, the refrigerant flow through the valve is blocked and the gauge access port is open to read system pressure.

Location of Pressure Ports

Residential air conditioning systems typically come with pressure access ports located at the outdoor unit service valves. These ports are used for charging and evacuation purposes and are located on the suction and liquid lines. In some cases, the system may have a high pressure port located on the compressor discharge line. This port is commonly found on heat pump systems.

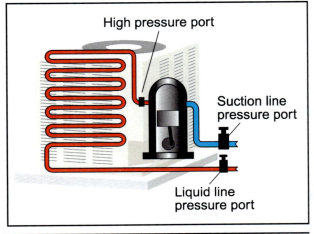

If the world were perfect, and you wished to have complete access to pressure at important diagnostic port positions, two additional pressure access ports should be added to the system. These ports should be installed in the liquid line about 1 foot in front of the metering device, and another pressure port on the suction line at the outlet of the evaporator coil. These two additional ports would allow you to measure the system pressure at the suction line outlet to the evaporator coil, and at the point where liquid is about to enter the metering device. Pressure at these ports would then be measured and compared against the pressure at the condensing unit service valves to detect excess pressure drop in the refrigerant lines.

The indicated ports are about one foot in distance from the evaporator coil and metering device as noted above.

Installing Pressure Ports

It is possible to add pressure ports to systems that are already installed and have been evacuated. There are special pressure access ports available that can be installed. These ports are comprised of a saddle fitting that fits to the copper refrigerant lines. The port is brazed to the refrigerant line, and then a special piercing piece is screwed down to make a hole in the line. These ports may be added to a system where flash gas problems exist, or where excessive suction line pressure drop is suspected.

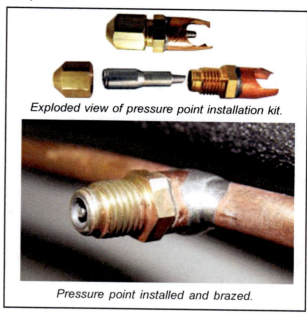

Exploded view of pressure point installation kit.

Pressure point installed and brazed.

Replacing Leaking Pressure Port Cores

The valve stem cores used in pressure ports can be damaged by heat, and then may leak refrigerant. The cap that covers the pressure port may prevent this leakage, or the refrigerant may leak from the system. In the event of a damaged core, it must be replaced.

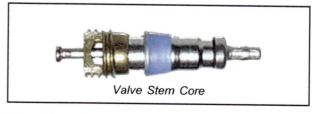

Valve Stem Core

Special tools called Valve Core Removal Tools can be used to remove the damaged stem and replace it with a new one without losing system charge. These core removal tools have a special

13

type screwdriver that removes the damaged core. The tool's ball valve is then shut to seal the refrigerant charge into the system. The damaged core is then replaced with a new core and screwed back into the system service valve.

Basic Refrigerant Circuit Components

Up to now, we have discussed the function of the mechanical refrigeration system as a whole, at this point we will identify the individual components that you will encounter when servicing systems. The components we will focus on are:

- The evaporator coil and its components
- Indoor air blowers and their components
- Suction lines and suction line driers
- Compressors and their components
- Discharge lines
- Condenser coils and circuits
- Condenser fans and their components
- Liquid lines and liquid line driers
- Metering devices

The Evaporator Coil and its Components

Evaporator coils are part of the low pressure side of the system. The coil is made from copper tubing that has been expanded to form a bond with aluminum heat transfer fins. When the tubing is expanded at the manufacturing facility, the tubing becomes extremely thin. Placing a brazing torch flame briefly on the copper tubing is likely to melt the copper if you are not careful. This makes repairing leaks extremely difficult for novices.

The copper tubing is stacked together in what are called circuits. The circuits channel the refrigerant into the coil so there is near uniform flow of refrigerant through all parts of the coil. The refrigerant enters the evaporator circuits from distributor tubes that are on the outlet side of the metering device. If there is an inlet, then there has to be an outlet to the coil. At the outlet, the individual circuits are piped together. The outlet of the coil circuiting is called the Suction Line.

The coil has cold saturated refrigerant in its circuits. The cold refrigerant absorbs heat from air passing across the surface of the coil. The evaporator coil also removes moisture from the air just like a cold glass of ice water will do on a humid day. The water that collects on the surface of the evaporator coil drains down into a drain pan that is called a Condensate Drain Pan. The drain pan has a fitting which is typically a threaded fitting where PVC plastic pipe is connected to carry the water to a convenient waste drain. This drain must be connected to the evaporator coil for proper draining of condensate to occur. If the drain becomes plugged, water will overflow the condensate pan and create a mess or cause damage to electrical components in the air handler or furnace. This is a common occurrence service technicians will deal with many times in their careers.

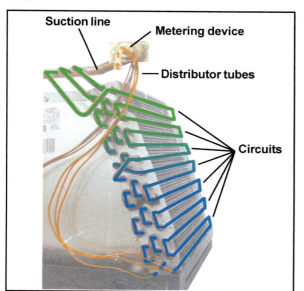

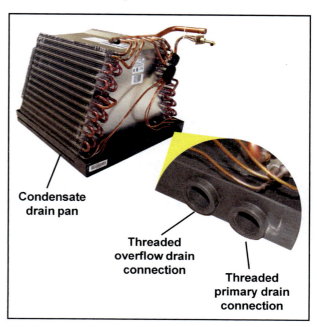

Field Service Guide: The Basics Of The Mechanical Refrigeration Cycle

Evaporator coils used in residential homes can come in either an "A" type or "slab" type coil configuration.

The "A" type coil is installed on the supply air outlet side of a gas furnace. Air from the furnace blower assembly blows into the bottom of the coil and out the top. This type of coil should never be installed on the inlet return air side of the furnace. The cold air would cause condensation on the furnace components.

Air handlers have coils installed internally within the air handler cabinet. These coils can be a single slab type or may be shaped like an "A" coil. The coil is installed on the return air side of the blower assembly.

Horizontal duct coils are coils that are installed in duct systems where they are not directly attached to the furnace like an "A" coil is. These types of coils can be slab shaped or "A" shaped. They are installed on the supply air outlet side of the furnace.

Finally, evaporator coils come in different capacity sizes. They are selected to match the size of the outdoor condensing unit. For example, if the outdoor condensing unit is a 2 ton model, a matching 2 ton evaporator coil size is usually selected. To get higher efficiency, some systems have evaporator coils that have a larger capacity size than the outdoor condensing unit. These coils will run with higher suction pressure and warmer evaporator saturation temperatures. The elevated evaporator temperature may not be a good choice for comfort yet it is good for efficiency.

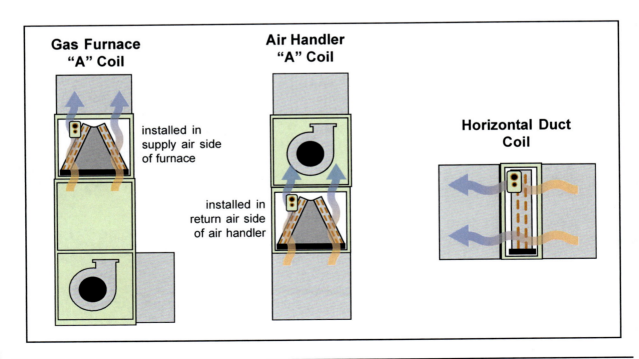

Indoor Air Blowers and their Components

Indoor air blowers consist of a blower wheel and housing that is attached to a motor. A mounting bracket holds the blower motor to the blower housing. Almost all residential furnaces made for use with air conditioning will have a direct drive motor. Direct drive means the blower wheel is attached directly to the motor shaft.

The blower motor type may be a PSC multi-speed motor with an associated run capacitor, or it may be a high performance ECM, Electronically Commutated Motor, that does not use a run capacitor.

When a call for cooling operation occurs, the indoor blower assembly will energize, and air will flow across the surface of the evaporator coil. Blowers come in different air delivery capability ratings (CFM). The amount of air that blows will be determined by how restrictive the duct system in the home is. If the duct system is restrictive, such as when it is sized incorrectly, (too small) the air volume will be lower than it should be. Properly sized duct systems will allow the blower to deliver the proper amount of air to the evaporator coil.

Suction Lines and Suction Line Driers

This line is part of the low pressure side of the system. The suction line is the refrigerant line that connects to the outlet of the evaporator coil, and to the suction line service valve on the outdoor condensing unit. The line is insulated because it is cold, which will cause it to attract heat from the outdoor air and other sources, and also to prevent condensate from forming on the line (sweating).

PSC Motor

Run Capacitor

ECM Motor

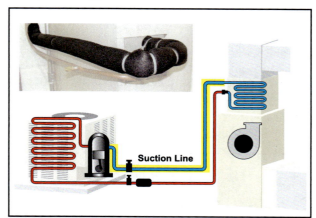

17

Field Service Guide: The Basics Of The Mechanical Refrigeration Cycle

Suction lines come in different size diameters. Typical sizes are 5/8", 3/4", 7/8", and 1 1/8". The size of the line will depend upon the capacity of the system. Larger tonnage systems require larger suction lines than smaller tonnage systems. The size will also be determined by how far the line must run, and by how many elbows are installed in the line.

Suction lines drop the pressure of the suction gas due to friction that occurs as the refrigerant vapor travels in the copper tubing. This pressure drop is bad for the system as it causes the capacity of the compressor to fall. This is due to the density or weight of the refrigerant vapor reducing as pressure reduces. The resulting lighter vapor causes the amount of pounds of refrigerant in the compressor cylinder to be reduced, and that is how the capacity is dropped. It is best to keep suction lines sized to drop no more than 3 PSIG for R-22 systems and 5 PSIG for R-410A systems. Both of these pressure drops reduce the system capacity by 3%. Not good, but physics rules.

At times, a suction line filter drier is placed in the suction line. This drier is never installed by the manufacturer of the system, but rather by a servicing technician. Suction line driers are used to clean up or remove contaminants from the refrigeration system after an electrical burn out of the compressor motor.

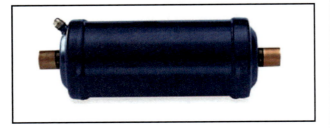

They have a pressure port on their shell so that the pressure can be measured at the inlet of the filter and compared against the pressure at the condensing unit suction line service valve pressure port. If the pressure drop across the filter is above allowable limits, the filter should be removed and replaced with a clean one. These filter driers come in different sizes based upon the capacity of the refrigeration system they must clean.

Compressors and their Components

The compressor is a vapor pump. The suction vapor enters the compressor where it is compressed to a high pressure high temperature discharge gas. Compressors found in residential split system units are typically either scroll models or reciprocating models. Scroll models have orbiting scrolls that compress the refrigerant vapor. Reciprocating models have a piston and cylinder just like a car engine. Regardless of the type of compressor present in the system, both types are vapor pumps.

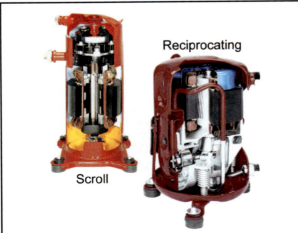

Scroll and Reciprocating Images Courtesy of Trane. Both are sealed and unable to be worked on by a servicing technician.

Field Service Guide: The Basics Of The Mechanical Refrigeration Cycle

The compressor has two refrigerant line connections. One connection is for the suction vapor and the other connection is the discharge line connection. These connections are typically brazed connections.

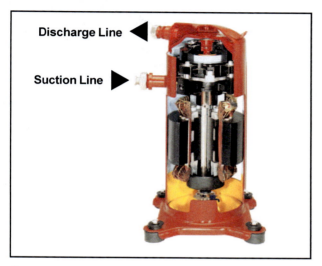

Compressors that are used in residential air conditioners are called hermetic compressors. Hermetic compressors are sealed compressors where internal components of the compressor cannot be accessed by servicing technicians.

Compressors have oil in them. The oil is a type that mixes with the refrigerant in the system. R-22 systems have mineral oil and R-410A systems have POE (Polyolester) oil. The oil lays in the bottom of the compressor shell and is circulated by internal oil lubricating components to critical bearing areas.

During normal operation, a small amount of this oil will circulate throughout the refrigeration circuit but the majority of the oil should remain in the compressor shell.

The temperature of the oil is critical to keeping compressor bearing wear to a minimum. If the oil is operated in a system that is running too hot, such as when the system is undercharged, the oil may break down and bearing damage may occur. This will not happen to systems that are operating at normal operating conditions.

There is a condition where liquid refrigerant may enter the compressor shell during periods where the air conditioning system is off. This condition is called liquid migration. When the liquid enters the compressor it mixes with the compressor oil. When the compressor is started, the heat from the compressor motor boils off the liquid. The boiling action of the refrigerant foams the oil and it mixes with the refrigerant and is carried out of the compressor shell. This is called an oil pump out. With no, or a low amount of oil in the shell, compressor bearing damage may occur.

To prevent liquid migration, a compressor electrical accessory called a crankcase heater is used.

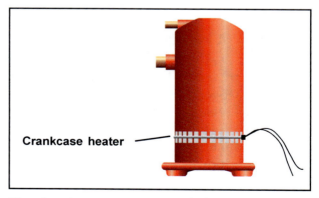

The heater wraps around the shell of the compressor and keeps the compressor shell warm, which prevents liquid refrigerant from mixing with the refrigerant oil during periods of time where the compressor is off. Crankcase

19

Field Service Guide: The Basics Of The Mechanical Refrigeration Cycle

heaters are sometimes installed by the manufacturer of the system, and in some cases are installed by smart service technicians.

Liquid can also enter compressors during run operation. This is due to overcharging the machine, or a lack of heat on the indoor coil such as when an air filter becomes plugged. The liquid will flood back to the compressor and cause an oil pump out. An accessory called an accumulator can be installed in front of the compressor to catch liquid before it gets to the compressor suction line connection. Accumulators are usually installed by the manufacturer of the system. They can also be installed by service technicians.

Fusite Plug

Discharge Lines

This is part of the high side of the refrigeration system. Discharge lines connect the compressor to the inlet of the condenser coil circuiting. This line is factory installed. Some systems will have a pressure port installed on the discharge line for charging purposes.

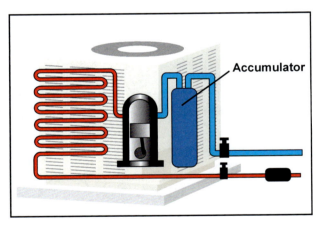

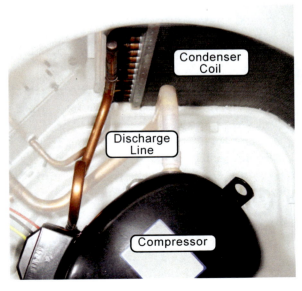

Compressors connect to the electrical circuit of the system with a special plug called a Fusite plug. This plug is located behind a protective cover that should never be removed if there is electrical power to the air conditioner. If a disconnect switch is used to disconnect power to the condensing unit, the cover can now be removed and the fusite plug electrical terminals accessed.

Condenser Coils and Circuits

This is part of the high side of the refrigeration system. Condenser coils are part of the outdoor condensing unit. The coil receives the hot discharge gas from the compressor and transfers heat from the hot refrigerant gas to the cooler outdoor air (In some cases water). The coil is usually a copper tube / aluminum fin type coil similar in construction to evaporator coils. There are also high efficient heat transfer condenser coils that are made from all aluminum and are tubing wound with spines of aluminum.

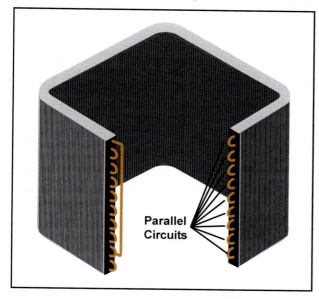

Condenser coils have individual parallel refrigeration circuits that spread the hot gas load across the area of the coil. The hot gas gives up its heat and condenses into a hot saturated liquid. The liquid flows in the circuits where it is subcooled to a cooler temperature than it condensed at. The subcooled liquid is gathered into a collection header assembly and is directed to the liquid line.

Condenser Fans and their Components

The condenser fan blows air across the surface of the condenser coil. The assembly consists of a fan motor mounted to the condensing unit cabinet and a fan blade that is attached to the shaft of the motor. Each assembly is unique for the design of a specific condensing unit. These assemblies are typically not interchangeable as they are designed to produce a specific amount of air flow across the surface of the condenser coil.

The motors used to drive the condenser fan blade are usually PSC single or two speed motors. They will have an associated run capacitor. In some super high efficiency models a variable speed ECM type motor is used to turn the condenser fan blade. This type of motor uses much less electricity than a PSC type motor.

Field Service Guide: The Basics Of The Mechanical Refrigeration Cycle

Liquid Lines and Liquid Line Driers

This is part of the high side of the refrigeration system. The liquid line connects the liquid line service valve to the inlet of the metering device.

Liquid Line Drier

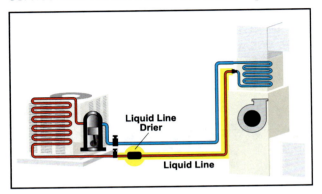

The line is not insulated unless it runs through hot spaces where it can pick up a lot of heat. Liquid lines come in different size diameters. Typical sizes are 5/16", 3/8", and 1/2". The size of the line will depend upon the capacity of the system. Larger tonnage systems require larger liquid lines than smaller tonnage systems. The size will also be determined by how far the line must run, how much vertical lift is present, and by how many elbows are installed in the line.

Liquid lines drop the pressure of the refrigerant liquid due to friction that occurs as the refrigerant liquid travels in the copper tubing. This pressure drop is bad for the system as it creates the potential for metering device problems. This pressure drop can be controlled by proper line sizing. Not good, but physics rules.

All liquid lines have a liquid line drier. The liquid line drier is either installed by the manufacturer of the system in the liquid circuit of the condenser coil, or it is field installed by the installing technician.

These driers collect debris and moisture that may be trapped in the system during manufacturing or installation. The size of the liquid line drier is determined by the capacity of the condensing unit. These driers may be brazed into the liquid line or may be connected using a flare fitting.

Metering Devices

The metering device is a pressure dropping device that separates the high pressure side of the system from the low pressure side of the system. Metering devices may be fixed piston type or expansion valve type. Piston types have a fitting that seats the piston against a piece of brass. This fitting allows liquid pressure to push the piston into a seat where it seals the liquid and prevents it from bypassing the piston's metering bore hole. A screen in the fitting catches debris that may have been missed by the filter drier.

Metering Piston

Expansion Valves

Expansion valves are typically factory installed. They have a sensing bulb that is mounted to the suction line at the outlet of the evaporator coil circuiting. There is a small copper tube called an equalizer line that connects to the expansion valve. This line allows the expansion valve to sense the pressure of the suction vapor that is leaving the evaporator coil.

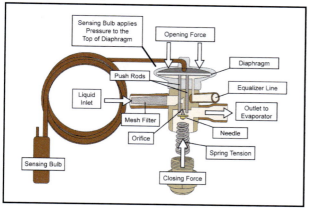

Both expansion valves and metering pistons are sized by the manufacturer of the system. It is hard if not impossible to have the wrong size expansion valve if the valve was sized by the manufacturer. On the other hand, pistons are changed depending upon the outdoor unit and indoor evaporator coil combinations. In many cases, the wrong size piston is installed in the evaporator coil.

Refrigerants
and Oils

Refrigerants and Oils

Field Service Guide: Refrigerants and Oils

Chapter

Refrigerants And Oils

Table of Contents

Refrigerants and Oils **3**
    Introduction 3
    How Refrigerants Flow Heat 3
    The Saturation Temperature Operating Ranges for R-22 and R-410A 3
    Using Pressure Gauges to find Refrigerant Saturation Temperature....................... 4
    What the Saturation Temperatures mean in terms of Operating Conditions of the
        Air Conditioning System 4
    Simple Chemistry - R-22 Versus R-410A 5
    Heat Transfer Ability - R-22 Versus R-410A 5
    Suction Vapor Weight Comparison - R-22 Versus R-410A 5
    Refrigerant Oil Compatibility 5
    Removing Mineral Oil from lines to be re-used with R-410A 6
NU-CALGON RX-11 FLUSH (Information courtesy of Nu-Calgon) **6**
        Nu-Calgon RX-11 FLUSH General Guidelines 7
To Flush a Line Set: Step By Step **7**
Detecting Mixed Refrigerants/Non-condensable Test **9**
Detecting Mixed Refrigerants Procedure: Step By Step **9**
    Non-condensable Gasses 10
    Moisture in Refrigeration Systems 11
    Moisture and POE Oil 11
    Driers and Moisture Removal 12
    Moisture Indicator Sight Glass 12
    Moisture and Hydrolysis 13
    Evacuating a System with a Vacuum Pump 13
        Micron Gauges 14
    Moisture Summary 14
    Sludge and Acid 14
PHASE III Test Kit (Information courtesy of Nu-Calgon) **15**
    How the PHASE III Test Kit Works 15
        Why use PHASE III Test Kit? 15
        Advantages 15
    Testing Oil with PHASE III Test Kit 15
PHASE III Test Kit Procedure: Step By Step **16**
    Using PHASE III Test Kit with Inhibited Oils 17
        Satisfactory for Use with PHASE III Test Kit 17
        Unsatisfactory for Use with PHASE III Test Kit 17
        Precautions 17
    Compressor Motor Burn-out 18

Field Service Guide: Refrigerants and Oils

Recovery of Refrigerants 18
R-22 Material Data Safety Sheet (Information courtesy of Honeywell) **19**
    Chemical Product and Company Identification 19
    Composition/Information on Ingredients 19
    Hazards Identification 19
    First Aid Measures 20
    Fire Fighting Measures 21
    Accidental Release Measures 22
    Handling and Storage 22
    Exposure Controls/Personal Protection 22
    Physical and Chemical Properties 23
    Stability and Reactivity 24
    Toxicological Information 25
    Ecological Information 25
    Disposal Considerations 25
    Transport Information 26
    Regulatory Information 26
    Other Information 28
R-410A Material Data Safety Sheet (Information courtesy of Honeywell) **29**
    Chemical Product and Company Identification 29
    Composition/Information on Ingredients 29
    Hazards Identification 29
    First Aid Measures 30
    Fire Fighting Measures 31
    Accidental Release Measures 32
    Handling and Storage 32
    Exposure Controls/Personal Protection 32
    Physical and Chemical Properties 34
    Stability and Reactivity 34
    Toxicological Information 35
    Ecological Information 35
    Disposal Considerations 36
    Transport Information 36
    Regulatory Information 36
    Other Information 38

Refrigerants and Oils

Introduction to Refrigerants and Oils

Refrigerants are special chemicals developed as heat transfer media for use in refrigeration systems. There are two refrigerants found in modern residential air conditioning systems, they are R-22 and R-410A. R-22 is an ozone depleting refrigerant. R-410A is a non-ozone depleting refrigerant.

How refrigerants flow heat

In nature, hot goes to cold. In other words, energy flows from high to low. Refrigerants, when hotter than air, will transfer their heat to the air. When the air is hotter than the refrigerant, the heat will flow from the air into the refrigerant.

Refrigerants have a special physical property that is called saturation temperature. A refrigerant that is at saturation temperature will be a mix of both liquid refrigerant and vapor refrigerant. Any addition or removal of heat from a saturated refrigerant will cause a change of state. The refrigerant may flash from a liquid to a vapor, or it may condense from a vapor to a liquid. These state changes occur when a heat exchange between the refrigerant and air takes place.

At saturation temperature the refrigerant exists as both a liquid and a vapor simultaneously.

A refrigerant at saturation temperature is a heat transfer animal that is at the edge of a significant event. When a refrigerant is at saturation temperature, any heat added to or removed from the refrigerant will cause the refrigerant to change state. The heat energy required to make a refrigerant change its state is very large. Therefore, when a refrigerant is at saturation temperature, and there is a source of heat that is warmer or cooler than the refrigerant, the refrigerant will either absorb or reject heat. The transfer of heat will cause the refrigerant to change from either a liquid to a vapor, or from a vapor to a liquid. The heat transfer does not change the temperature of the refrigerant, only the state!

If air gives up heat to a cold saturated refrigerant, the air will be colder than before the heat exchange. If hot refrigerant gives up heat to cooler outdoor air, the outdoor air will gain heat and the refrigerant will lose it. As this heat exchange occurs, the temperature of the refrigerant does not change.

R-410A can pick up much more heat than R-22 can. Pound for pound, R-410A is capable of exchanging about 40% more heat than R-22.

The saturation temperature operating ranges for R-22 and R-410A are identical

R-22 and R-410A operate at the same saturation temperature ranges. They differ by the pressure range they operate at. For example, R-22 at 50°F saturation temperature will have a gauge pressure of 84 PSIG. At 50°F saturation temperature, R-410A will have a gauge pressure of 144 PSIG.

Field Service Guide: Refrigerants and Oils

Using pressure gauges to find the refrigerant's saturation temperature

Taking a pressure reading with a refrigeration gauge will enable the service technician to determine what the saturation temperature of the refrigerant is. Many refrigeration gauges have a saturation temperature scale located on the gauge dial. Where the needle of the gauge intersects the temperature scale determines the saturation temperature of the refrigerant. Temperature pressure tables can also be referenced to find the saturation temperature for any measurable gauge pressure.

What the saturation temperatures mean in terms of operating conditions of the air conditioning system

The suction pressure reading when converted to saturation temperature is referenced to the refrigerant that is exiting the metering device. The refrigerant at that point in the system is saturated so it is a mix of liquid and vapor at a temperature corresponding to the suction pressure gauge. I call this temperature the "evaporator coil temperature."

The high pressure gauge reading corresponds to the temperature of the refrigerant that is condensing from a hot gas to a liquid in the condenser coil. I like to say "I am making liquid at a temperature of let's say 100°F." The condensing liquid is very unstable and the condensing temperature is an important temperature used in servicing.

Saturation temperature is defined in my world as the temperature of the refrigerant where all the heat transfer power exists.

R-410A PSIG	Saturation Temp. (F)	R-22 PSIG	R-410A PSIG	Saturation Temp. (F)	R-22 PSIG	R-410A PSIG	Saturation Temp. (F)	R-22 PSIG
12	-41	0	146	51	85	396	116	245
14	-36	2	154	54	90	400	117	250
16	-32	4	160	56	95	412	119	255
18	-28	6	168	59	100	416	120	260
22	-24	8	178	62	105	422	121	265
26	-20	10	184	64	110	434	123	270
30	-17	12	192	67	115	440	124	275
32	-14	14	198	69	120	450	126	280
36	-11	16	208	72	125	456	127	285
38	-8	18	216	74	130	462	128	290
42	-5	20	222	76	135	474	130	295
46	-2	22	230	78	140	482	131	300
48	0	24	240	81	145	494	133	310
50	2	26	248	83	150	512	136	320
54	5	28	256	85	155	526	138	330
58	7	30	262	87	160	544	141	340
60	9	32	270	89	165	560	143	350
64	11	34	280	91	170	572	145	360
68	13	36	288	93	175	596	148	370
70	15	38	292	94	180	608	150	380
74	17	40	300	96	185	624	152	390
78	19	42	308	98	190	640	154	400
80	21	44	318	100	195			
84	23	46	322	101	200			
86	24	48	330	103	205			
90	26	50	340	105	210			
98	30	55	346	106	215			
106	34	60	356	108	220			
114	38	65	364	110	225			
122	41	70	370	111	230			
128	44	75	380	113	235			
138	48	80	386	114	240			

Temperature/pressure tables are also published by refrigerant chemical companies that plot gauge pressure and saturation temperatures. Each refrigerant will have its own unique table. Here is an example of a combination R-22 and R-410A Temperature/Pressure Table.

R-22 requires different refrigeration gauges than R-410A. R-410A refrigeration hoses are heavier rated than R-22 gauge hoses. Make certain to use the proper refrigeration gauges and hoses for the two refrigerants.

4

Field Service Guide: Refrigerants and Oils

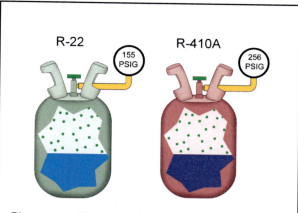

Place two refrigerant cylinders in a room that is 85°F and leave the cylinders sit until the temperature of the room air and the cylinders are equal. One cylinder is R-410A and the other R-22. Both cylinders will have a temperature of 85°F. The pressure in the cylinders will be equal to the corresponding saturation pressure that occurs at a temperature of 85°F.

Simple chemistry R-22 versus R-410A

R-22 is an HCFC refrigerant that will cause ozone depletion. R-410A is a non-ozone depleting HFC refrigerant. Both refrigerants may contribute to global warming and cannot be vented to the atmosphere.

R-22 is a single compound refrigerant. R-410A on the other hand is a blend of two refrigerants. The mixture is 50-50 HFC32 and HFC125. Although it is a mixture, the two refrigerants do not easily segregate in a system nor do they change composition when there is a leak. This behavior is called Azeotropic behavior and is highly desirable. When two refrigerants easily separate they are called a zeotropic blend. Because R-410A has a very stable composition, it is serviced in the same manner as R-22 systems.

Although the systems are serviced in similar manners, R-410A must be added to a refrigeration system as a liquid only. If the refrigerant is not added into the system as a saturated liquid, some separation of the two refrigerants may occur during charging.

Heat transfer ability - R-22 versus R-410A

R-410A carries more heat per pound of refrigerant vapor than R-22. For example, at 50°F saturation temperature in the evaporator coil, R-410A has about 124BTU/# versus 109BTU/# for R-22. Benefit is smaller coil sizes.

Suction vapor weight comparison - R-22 versus R-410A

R-410A is heavier per cubic foot of vapor than R-22. At 50°F saturation temperature R-410A weighs about 2.3 #/cubic foot versus 1.8#/cubic foot for R-22. Benefit is smaller compressor sizes.

Refrigerant oil compatibility

R-22 refrigerant based systems use mineral oil lubricant because the two mix together and form one liquid. The ability of two liquids to mix and form one liquid is called miscibility. R-410A refrigerant mixes well with Polyolester oil which is also called POE oil. If an R-410A system were to be mixed with mineral oil by mistake, two separate liquids would form and the compressor would experience oil loss.

Because of the inability of mineral oil and R-410A to mix well, care must be taken when replacing an R-22 system with an R-410A system where the refrigerant lines are to be re-used. The existing refrigerant lines should be flushed out with

5

Field Service Guide: Refrigerants and Oils

a cleaning solvent such as NU-CALGON RX-11-FLUSH. This solvent will remove all mineral oil from the line sets. If the mineral oil is not flushed out of the system, oil slugs will circulate and may cause compressor damage.

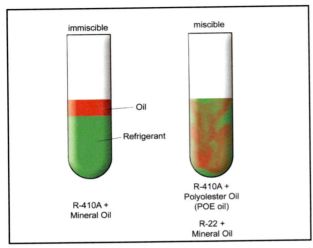

Not all manufacturers will approve of the use of additives in their systems so check with equipment suppliers prior to use of system additives.

Removing mineral oil from lines to be re-used with R-410A

Some manufacturers recommend blowing out the mineral oil with nitrogen. Other manufacturers say you can't reuse the lines. Well if the lines are buried in the walls of a building, odds are you need to reuse those lines.

One proven method of removing mineral oil from refrigerant lines is with a flush kit. These kits are also used to clean out systems after a compressor motor winding burn out. NU-CALGON offers a flush kit called RX11-FLUSH.

NU-CALGON RX-11 FLUSH

Required Equipment

The following equipment will be required for each flushing operation:

1. RX11-Flush

2. An Injection Tool (Part No. 4300-99) and standard refrigerant charging hose to inject the solvent into the AC/R system. The charging hose and injection tool should be dedicated and retained for future flushing.

4300-99

3. A small, resealable, waste container that will hold the solvent after it is flushed through the system. Ideally the solvent in the container must be visible so it can be inspected during the flushing process. This enables a technician to determine when the solvent begins to run clean, indicating that the system has been

Field Service Guide: Refrigerants and Oils

thoroughly purged.

4. A tank of clean compressed nitrogen, regulated to 120-150 psig. This tank should be equipped with a dispensing hose and will be used to purge the solvent from the system.

5. A vacuum pump with the appropriate hoses and clamps.

6. Safety equipment: Never flush a system without adequate face protection and rubber gloves. Convoluted piping in certain systems can cause momentary spikes in the solvent flow during the flushing process, resulting in erratic purges, which can splash into eyes and onto skin.

7. Adequate ventilation.

NU-CALGON RX-11 FLUSH General Guidelines

Use only the appropriate refrigerant, proper recovery equipment, component parts, tools and lubricants as established in the industry.

Do not inject the solvent into the compressor itself; only the supporting refrigeration system should be flushed.

Large systems or systems with unusual configurations that could trap the solvent should be disassembled and flushed section by section.

The exact amount of Rx11-flush required will vary by the internal design of the system, the nature of the system failure, the degree of contamination trapped in the system, and the temperatures at which the failure occurred.

If the system to be flushed includes larger components such as a receiver, we recommend a visual inspection. If these components appear to be contaminated, and are small enough to be flushed with Rx11-flush, then do so. If they are too large to economically flush with Rx11-flush, then the use of a traditional degreasing solvent, such as Degreasing Solvent ef (Part No. 4162-07) should be considered for them.

To Flush a Line Set

STEP 1

Establish one end of the line set as the exit point.

STEP 2

Crimp or restrict the exit point. This will increase the mass flow and contact time of Rx11-flush through the line.

STEP 3

For 3/8" tubing inject a 20-30 second burst of Rx11-flush through the line for every 50′

For 7/8" tubing send a 60-90 second burst of Rx11-flush through the line for every 50′

STEP 4

Follow the Rx11-flush with compressed nitrogen to increase mass flow for maximum cleaning power. The nitrogen will push the Rx11-flush along with the emulsified soils through the line.

STEP 5

Pull a vacuum on the line set to remove any residual solvent. Under vacuum, Rx11-flush rapidly boils off.

The line set will be clean and ready for service

Field Service Guide: Refrigerants and Oils

Information on RX-11 Flush Courtesy of Nu-Calgon

Tools
- Line Crimper
- Injection Tool
- Nitrogen Tank
- Safety Equipment
- Rx11-Flush
- Waste Container
- Vacuum Pump

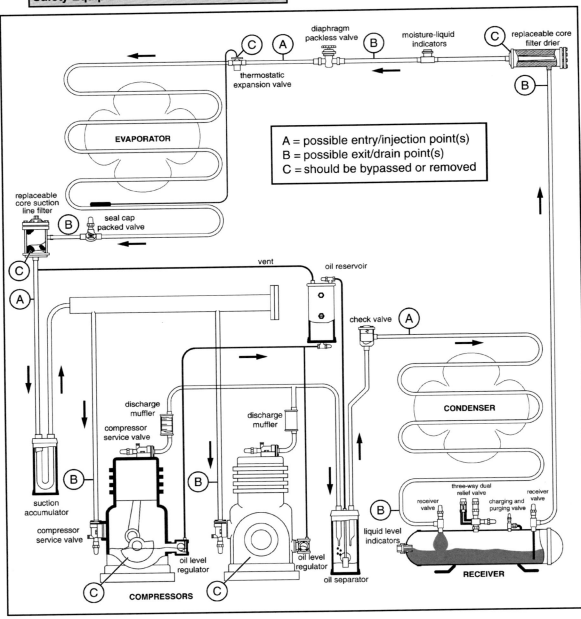

A = possible entry/injection point(s)
B = possible exit/drain point(s)
C = should be bypassed or removed

Field Service Guide: Refrigerants and Oils

Tools: Digital Temperature Probe, Refrigerant Gauges

Detecting Mixed Refrigerants/ Non-condensable Test

R-22 and R-410A should never be mixed or substituted for one another in a system. Metering device size, oil compatibility, compressor displacement, and coil surface area will all be incorrect. The result will be a system that operates at no level of reliability whatsoever.

Unfortunately, R-22 gauge hoses fit on R-410A systems and vice versa. Therefore, it is almost guaranteed that someone is going to add the wrong refrigerant into the system. Fortunately, there is a way to detect the problem.

If the system were to operate with a mixed refrigerant, there would be problems with system pressures and compressor operating performance. The reason for the problems is the two refrigerants are so dissimilar in their physical properties that neither the coils nor the compressor even come close to matching operating limits.

If you suspect the system has a mix of the two refrigerants, recover the charge and follow the steps shown here. This procedure will find both mixed refrigerants and non-condensable gasses. The test requires recovery of the total system charge into a clean recovery cylinder. The temperature of the cylinder is monitored and pressure of the cylinder measured. If the refrigerant is in the correct state, the pressure and temperature will follow temperature/pressure chart values.

Detecting Mixed Refrigerants Procedure

STEP 1

Start with an evacuated recovery cylinder and recover the system charge.

STEP 2

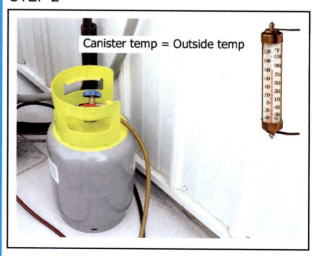

Allow the temperature of the recovery cylinder and air temperature to equalize.

9

Field Service Guide: Refrigerants and Oils

Step 3

Read the pressure in the refrigerant recovery cylinder.

Step 4

Measure the air temperature surrounding the recovery cylinder.

Step 5

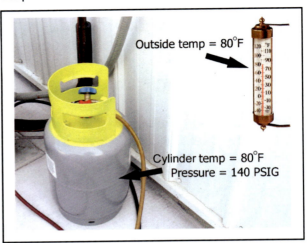

The cylinder pressure should be equal to the saturation pressure for the air temperature. If the pressure and temperature are not correctly matched for the type of refrigerant that should be in the system, mixed or incorrect refrigerant is present. In this example the recovery cylinder is at a pressure of 140 PSIG @ 80°F. These temperatures and pressures are correct for R-22. If the system were an R-410A machine, this would be an example of someone putting the wrong refrigerant into the system.

Non-condensable gasses

Non-condensable gasses found in residential systems consist of sources from air infiltration into the refrigeration circuit during installation and service, and when low side leaks introduce air into the machine. Those gasses include oxygen, nitrogen, and carbon dioxide. These gasses, when exposed to the pressure in the condenser, will not condense. They will simply reduce the effective area of the condenser and raise condensing pressure and temperature. Along with these gasses, systems that run hot can produce non-condensable gasses as the insulation in the compressor deteriorates due to high temperature. When the pressure in this test is too high, non-condensable gasses are likely to be present if the refrigerant is not a mixed blend.

Moisture in Refrigeration Systems

Since air contains moisture, moisture can get into the refrigeration systems when the systems are installed or the system is opened for service. Moisture, when mixed with refrigerants and refrigerant oils, can produce acid. Moisture contamination, if left untreated where acid has formed, can cause potential compressor failure due to corrosion inside the compressor, motor winding damage, and copper plating of compressor bearing areas.

When a system is operating in an acidic condition, the acid actually attacks copper surfaces in the refrigeration circuit. The copper is deposited on weight bearing areas within the compressor. The additional plating of copper on the weight bearing areas causes friction and reduces the area needing oil. Acid will also attack the compressor motor windings and can cause electrical failure of the compressor motor.

Image courtesy of Trane
This compressor damage was caused by copper plating due to excess moisture and acid formation in the system.

Moisture and POE Oil

R-410A systems use Polyolester oil which is a hydroscopic oil that will attract moisture at a far greater rate than mineral oil based systems. If water is absorbed into the oil in a large enough quantity, the oil will break down and form organic acid. The acid is highly corrosive and will cause damage to compressor components and internal refrigeration system surfaces.

When opening an R-410A system for servicing, moisture infiltration into the refrigerant oil must be minimized. One method used is to bleed a small amount of nitrogen into the system during repairs. The nitrogen will keep the system slightly above atmospheric pressure and minimize moisture contamination into the oil.

When servicing an R-410A system, do not allow the system to be open to atmospheric pressure for more than 15 minutes. If a system has been left open to atmosphere, such as when there is a leak and all charge is lost, it is best to remove the compressor from the system and replace the oil in the compressor.

Evacuation of the system will not separate the water from the POE oil. The only method of removing water from POE oil is through the use of a filter drier. Evacuation should always be performed when opening a system regardless of the fact that moisture in the oil cannot be separated from it.

Filter driers contain desiccants that can absorb moisture in the system and hold the moisture. They can not hold an indefinite amount of moisture and are rated for holding a specific amount of moisture drops. Therefore, installation of a filter drier may not stop acid formation if the water

Field Service Guide: Refrigerants and Oils

content in the system exceeds the capacity of the filter drier.

Driers and Moisture Removal

Filter driers contain special media that can absorb water, acid, and debris from circulating refrigerant. Driers are made for use in liquid lines and suction lines. Generally, liquid line driers remain permanently in the system until it is opened, when it is then replaced. Suction line driers should be removed from the system after about 48 hours of total operation.

Driers are sized to drop 1-2 PSIG of pressure when clean. If the drier is too small for the system, the pressure loss will be greater than 1-2 PSIG and will then contribute to flash gas problems if installed in the liquid line. When the drier loads up with moisture or debris, the pressure drop will increase.

At some point during the life of an air conditioner, the filter drier may become plugged with debris. Excessive pressure drop can be detected across a drier with a digital thermometer. Measure the temperature of the refrigerant entering the drier and then leaving the drier. If the temperature drop is in excess of 3°F, the pressure drop across the drier is at least 4 PSIG. The drier should be changed. The 3°F maximum temperature drop applies to both R-22 and R-410A driers.

Liquid Line Drier

3°F MAXIMUM TEMPERATURE DROP

Moisture Indicator Sight Glass

Color changing moisture indicators can be used to keep watch over potential problems due to moisture contamination. When the system contains too much moisture, the color of the indicator will change to indicate there is excessive moisture in the system. An acid test kit should be used on the system to determine if excessive acid is present.

Moisture Meter and Sight Glass

SEE•ALL SHOWS	MOISTURE CONTENT – PPM													
	REFRIGERANT 12		REFRIGERANT 22		REFRIGERANT 134a		REFRIGERANT 502		REFRIGERANT 404A & 507		REFRIGERANT 407C		REFRIGERANT 410A
	LIQUID LINE TEMPERATURE													
	75° F	100° F	75° F	100° F	75° F	100° F	75° F	100° F	75° F	100° F	75° F	75° F
Green - DRY	Below 5	Below 10	Below 30	Below 45	Below 50	Below 80	Below 10	Below 20	Below 15	Below 30	Below 120	Below 75
Chartreuse - CAUTION	5-15	10-30	30-90	45-130	50-200	80-225	10-45	20-65	15-90	30-140	120-280	75-150
Yellow - WET	Above 15	Above 30	Above 90	Above 130	Above 200	Above 225	Above 45	Above 65	Above 90	Above 140	Above 280	Above 150

Table courtesy of Sporlan

Field Service Guide: Refrigerants and Oils

Moisture and Hydrolysis

Ester oils such as POE oil are formed from organic acid and alcohol. When esters are exposed to moisture, they can change back into organic acids, alcohol, and water. This process is called Hydrolysis.

The acid that forms from the hydrolysis process now attacks internal components of the refrigeration circuit including copper surfaces and internal compressor parts.

Evacuating a System with a Vacuum Pump

When a refrigeration system has been opened to atmosphere, the water in the system needs to be removed. The best method of drying a system is to remove as much moisture as possible before installing a drier. To get water out of the system, the refrigeration system is pulled into a vacuum using a special pump called a vacuum pump. In a vacuum, water will boil off to water vapor at low temperatures. The vacuum pump then pumps the water vapor out of the system.

Vacuum pumps come in different sizes based upon how many cubic feet of air they can pump in a minute. (CFM) The greater the CFM rating of the pump, the quicker the evacuation process can be completed. It is good practice to purchase the most pump possible for your budget.

When evacuating a system with a vacuum pump, the pump should have fresh oil installed. If old oil is used, the oil will contain moisture that will make it very difficult to get the evacuation level deep enough to reach a 500 micron level.

Buy the best pump possible for maximum performance. Bigger CFM rating is good. 5-6 CFM best range for residential systems.

Remove the cores from pressure ports where hoses are installed to increase pump capacity.

Core removal tools allow a technician to remove the pressure port cores without losing refrigerant charge. Access for the pressure hoses is via a side port opening that is accessed by the core removal tool's ball valve.

Core Removal Tool

Field Service Guide: Refrigerants and Oils

Micron Gauges

When pressure is below atmospheric pressure, a special gauge called a micron gauge is used to measure the pressure. As the vacuum pump pulls down the refrigeration system pressure below atmospheric pressure, the micron level will fall. When the vacuum pump is shut off, the micron gauge will rise as water vapor boils off. The pump is started again and the process repeated until the vacuum level holds steady at 500 microns.

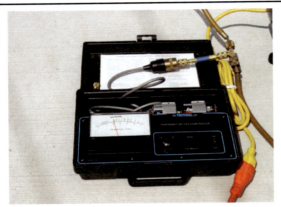

Gauge by Thermal

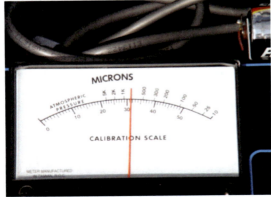

In this example, the pump needs to run longer in order to lower the MICRON level to 500.

Moisture Summary

Moisture can cause breakdown of refrigerant oils

POE oil can be broken down into organic acid and alcohol when exposed to moisture

Moisture indicators help warn of potential for damage

Driers should be installed on all systems

Driers will load with debris and will increase pressure drop

Evacuation to 500 microns is required whenever the system is opened

Use a good vacuum pump and change oil after every use.

Remove cores to speed evacuation process.

Sludge and Acid

Oil can break down and begin to form sludge when exposed to excess heat. The hottest spot in the refrigeration circuit is the compressor discharge line. The discharge gas will gain temperature when suction vapor superheat is high. Breakdown of the oil begins with extended compressor operation where the discharge line temperature is higher than 250°F.

Sludge can plug up metering devices and refrigerant driers and strainers. To prevent breakdown of the oil and limit the potential for sludge, moisture must be limited and proper air volume and charge level established. Acid can be detected in the system by taking an oil sample and testing the oil with an acid test kit such as NU-CALGON Phase III kits. If the kit detects acid, clean up measures will need to be taken. These measures will be covered shortly.

Information on Phase III Test Kit Courtesy of Nu-Calgon

PHASE III Test Kit

How the PHASE III Test Kit Works

The concentration of acid in refrigeration oil is expressed as an acid number in mg of KOH per gram of oil (milligrams of potassium hydroxide per gram of oil). The acid number is a measure of the amount of hydroxide solution needed to neutralize the acid in the oil. The more acid there is in the oil, the more potassium hydroxide is needed to neutralize it.

In the PHASE III test, an acid number of 0.05 mg KOH per gram of oil has been set as the maximum acceptable acid concentration in mineral oil and alkylbenzene oil. In polyolesters, the number is generally accepted as 0.16 mg. Mineral and alkylbenzene oils with an acid number less than 0.16 mg are acceptable and will cause no change in the color of the test kit's acid indicator. However, if the respective oils have an acid number greater than these limits, it will cause the acid indicator to change from purple to pink or clear indicating that the oil is contaminated.

Why use PHASE III Test Kit?

PHASE III is the universal acid test kit for oils

- •Use on mineral oils

- •Use it on alkylbenzene oils like Zerol

- •Use it on ICI EMKARATE RL and Mobil EAL Artic polyolesters.

Advantages

Simple - Phase separation makes it easy to see color changes in acid indicator.

Universal - Use one kit for mineral oil, alkylbenzenes, and POE's.

Precise - Only two bottles to work with. No glass to break open since bottles have screw caps.

Effect in the Presence of Dyes - Many systems will contain dyes, such as fluorescent colored dyes, for leak detection purposes.

These dyes render most acid test kits useless: not PHASE III. Because of its phase separation, PHASE III makes it easy to test such systems.

Handy Size - Several PHASE III Test Kits can be carried conveniently in a tool box.

Testing Oil with a PHASE III Test Kit

The PHASE III Test Kit consists of just two bottles which contain the precise amount of solutions required to conduct one test. The bottles have screw on caps, eliminating the need to break open glass.

Field Service Guide: Refrigerants and Oils

Information on Phase III Test Kit Courtesy of Nu-Calgon

PHASE III Test Kit Procedure

Tools: **PHASE III Test Kit**

STEP 1

Pour the solution from the small bottle into the large bottle. The bottom layer of this mixture will be purple.

STEP 2

Completely fill the small bottle with oil from the unit being tested. Do this immediately after the oil is removed from the crankcase since exposure to air will contaminate the oil and give a false test result.

STEP 3

Pour the oil into the large bottle and shake well. Then wait for two to three minutes.

STEP 4

A phase separation will develop as the oil rises to the top of the mixture and an aqueous layer forms on the bottom.

Field Service Guide: Refrigerants and Oils

Information on Phase III Test Kit Courtesy of Nu-Calgon

STEP 5

If the bottom layer:

Stays Purple - the oil is satisfactory
Turns Light Pink to Clear - the oil is contaminated

Using PHASE III with Inhibited Oils

Many inhibited oils contain additives or inhibitors that tend to react like an acid when tested with the PHASE III Test Kit. Even when these oils are new, the additives may cause the PHASE III Test Kit to indicate the oil has a higher acid number.

Unsatisfactory results found when testing inhibited oils with PHASE III do not necessarily mean that these oils are contaminated or unsuitable for use in refrigeration equipment. The results merely indicate that these oils may contain additives which react like an acid making the PHASE III Test Kit results invalid. Refer to the following list of oils to determine those which can or cannot be tested with the PHASE III Test Kit.

Satisfactory For Use With PHASE III Test Kit

Nu-Calgon C-3S	Calumet
Nu-Calgon C-4S	Calumet
Nu-Calgon C-5S	Calumet
Zerol® 150	Shrieve
Zerol 200TD	Shrieve
Zerol 300	Shrieve
Suniso 3GS	Witco
Suniso 4GS	Witco
Suniso 5GS	Witco
Texaco WF-32	Texaco
Texaco WF-68	Texaco
EMKARATE RL Series	ICI
EAL Arctic 22CC	Mobil

Unsatisfactory For Use With PHASE III Test Kit

Delvac 1120	Mobil Oil Company
DTE Heavy Medium	Mobil Oil Company
Ursa HD20	Texaco
Regal PC	Texaco
WS-5124	Exxon Company
WS-4672	Exxon Company
Teresso No. 52	Exxon Company
Rimula 54802	Shell Oil Company
Tellus 33	Shell Oil Company
Sunvis 620	Sun Oil Company
Sunvis 931	Sun Oil Company
Icematic	SW Series
American Industrial 31	Standard Oil (IN) Co.

PRECAUTIONS
DANGER-Flammable-Toxic.

The test solutions contain isopropanol, methanol, and toluene. Vapor harmful. Harmful if swallowed. Avoid breathing vapor. If swallowed, call a physician. Do not induce vomiting. Keep out of reach of children.

Compressor motor burn-out

If the compressor motor fails electrically and the motor insulation burns, sludge and acid may be produced. If the compressor failure took a period of time to fail, there is going to be a lot of this material circulated throughout the refrigeration circuit. The debris will find its way into driers, metering devices, coil circuits, and refrigerant line sets. If the compressor is going to be replaced, and the system repaired, the system must be cleaned up of the acid and sludge.

A flush kit can be used to clean the sludge out of the system. RX11-FLUSH was made for this purpose. Follow instructions provided with the flushing kit.

If the burnout was not severe, the refrigerant should be recovered and the compressor replaced.

The old liquid line drier should be replaced with one that is a size bigger than the original.

A suction line drier should be added to the suction line. Some suction line driers will have a pressure tap on the inlet side of the drier. If the drier you install does not, then install a pressure port on the suction line in front of the suction line drier. (Between the evaporator coil and the drier.)

Clean out any debris that may be at the metering device.

Evacuate and charge the system.

Run the system for 4-6 hours and monitor the pressure drop across the suction drier.

If the pressure drop in the suction line drier exceeds 4 PSIG, replace the drier. Keep monitoring drier pressure loss until the pressure drop is stable.

Remove the suction line drier after 48 hours.

Monitor the liquid line drier for excess pressure drop. Replace the drier if excess pressure drop is present.

Repeat drier changes as needed until drier pressure drop is stable.

Perform a final acid test on the new compressor oil to determine acid level of replacement compressor.

Recovery of refrigerants

R-22 is a Hydrochlorofluorocarbon refrigerant that has Chlorine atoms. Chlorine atoms can damage the Earth's ozone layer. This refrigerant is being phased out of production. Because it damages the ozone layer it must not be vented to atmosphere. Venting this refrigerant to atmosphere is a violation of law. This refrigerant must be recovered.

R-410A is a hydrofluorocarbon refrigerant that has no Chlorine atoms. It does not damage the ozone layer. It must also be recovered and cannot be vented to atmosphere.

Recovery is required for both R-22 and R-410A

Field Service Guide: Refrigerants and Oils

MSDS Courtesy of Honeywell

Material Safety Data Sheet Genetron® 22

1. CHEMICAL PRODUCT AND COMPANY IDENTIFICATION

PRODUCT NAME: Genetron® 22
OTHER/GENERIC NAMES: R-22, HCFC-22
PRODUCT USE: Refrigerant
MANUFACTURER: Honeywell
101 Columbia Road
Box 1053
Morristown, New Jersey 07962-1053

FOR MORE INFORMATION CALL:
(M-F, 9:00am-5:00pm)
1-800-522-8001

IN CASE OF EMERGENCY CALL:
(24 Hrs/Day, 7 Days/Wk)
Medical: 1-800-498-5701
Transportation: 1-800-424-9300 or 703-527-3887

2. COMPOSITION/INFORMATION ON INGREDIENTS

INGREDIENT NAME	CAS NUMBER	WEIGHT %
Chlorodifluoromethane	75-45-6	100

Trace impurities and additional material names not listed above may also appear in Section 15 toward the end of the MSDS. These materials may be listed for local "Right-To-Know" compliance and for other reasons.

3. HAZARDS IDENTIFICATION

EMERGENCY OVERVIEW: Colorless, volatile liquid with ethereal and faint sweetish odor. Non-flammable material. Overexposure may cause dizziness and loss of concentration. At higher levels, CNS depression and cardiac arrhythmia may result from exposure. Vapors displace air and can cause asphyxiation in confined spaces. At higher temperatures, (>250°C), decomposition products may include Hydrochloric Acid (HCl), Hydrofluoric Acid (HF) and carbonyl halides.

POTENTIAL HEALTH HAZARDS

SKIN: Irritation would result from a defatting action on tissue. Liquid contact could cause frostbite.

Field Service Guide: Refrigerants and Oils

MSDS Courtesy of Honeywell

EYES: Liquid contact can cause severe irritation and frostbite. Mist may irritate.

INHALATION: Genetron 22 is low in acute toxicity in animals. When oxygen levels in air are reduced to 12–14% by displacement, symptoms of asphyxiation, loss of coordination, increased pulse rate and deeper respiration will occur. At high levels, cardiac arrhythmia may occur.

INGESTION: Ingestion is unlikely because of the low boiling point of the material. Should it occur, discomfort in the gastrointestinal tract from rapid evaporation of the material and consequent evolution of gas would result. Some effects of inhalation and skin exposure would be expected.

DELAYED EFFECTS: None known

Ingredients found on one of the OSHA designated carcinogen lists are listed below.

INGREDIENT NAME	NTP STATUS	IARC STATUS	OSHA LIST
No ingredients listed in this section			

4. FIRST AID MEASURES

SKIN: Promptly flush skin with water until all chemical is removed. If there is evidence of frostbite, bathe (do not rub) with lukewarm (not hot) water. If water is not available, cover with a clean, soft cloth or similar covering. Get medical attention if symptoms persist.

EYES: Immediately flush eyes with large amounts of water for at least 15 minutes (in case of frostbite water should be lukewarm, not hot) lifting eyelids occasionally to facilitate irrigation. Get medical attention if symptoms persist.

INHALATION: Immediately remove to fresh air. If breathing has stopped, give artificial respiration. Use oxygen as required, provided a qualified operator is available. Get medical attention. Do not give epinephrine (adrenaline).

INGESTION: Ingestion is unlikely because of the physical properties and is not expected to be hazardous. Do not induce vomiting unless instructed to do so by a physician.

ADVICE TO PHYSICIAN:

Because of the possible disturbances of cardiac rhythm, catecholamine drugs, such as epinephrine, should be used with special caution and only in situations of

Field Service Guide: Refrigerants and Oils

MSDS Courtesy of Honeywell

emergency life support. Treatment of overexposure should be directed at the control of symptoms and the clinical conditions.

5. FIRE FIGHTING MEASURES

FLAMMABLE PROPERTIES

FLASH POINT:	Gas, not applicable per DOT regulations
FLASH POINT METHOD:	Not applicable
AUTOIGNITION TEMPERATURE:	Unknown
UPPER FLAME LIMIT (volume % in air):	None*
LOWER FLAME LIMIT (volume % in air):	None* *Based on ASHRAE Standard 34 with match ignition
FLAME PROPAGATION RATE (solids):	Not applicable
OSHA FLAMMABILITY CLASS:	Not applicable

EXTINGUISHING MEDIA:

Use any standard agent – choose the one most appropriate for type of surrounding fire (material itself is not flammable)

UNUSUAL FIRE AND EXPLOSION HAZARDS:

Genetron 22 is not flammable at ambient temperatures and atmospheric pressure. However, this material will become combustible when mixed with air under pressure and exposed to strong ignition sources.

Contact with certain reactive metals may result in formation of explosive or exothermic reactions under specific conditions (e.g. very high temperatures and/or appropriate pressures).

SPECIAL FIRE FIGHTING PRECAUTIONS/INSTRUCTIONS:

Firefighters should wear self-contained, NIOSH-approved breathing apparatus for protection against possible toxic decomposition products. Proper eye and skin protection should be provided. Use water spray to keep fire-exposed containers cool.

Field Service Guide: Refrigerants and Oils

MSDS Courtesy of Honeywell

6. ACCIDENTAL RELEASE MEASURES

IN CASE OF SPILL OR OTHER RELEASE: (Always wear recommended personal protective equipment.)

Evacuate unprotected personnel. Protected personnel should remove ignition sources and shut off leak, if without risk, and provide ventilation. Unprotected personnel should not return until air has been tested and determined safe, including low-lying areas.

Spills and releases may have to be reported to Federal and/or local authorities. See Section 15 regarding reporting requirements.

7. HANDLING AND STORAGE

NORMAL HANDLING: (Always wear recommended personal protective equipment.)

Avoid breathing vapors and liquid contact with eyes, skin or clothing. Do not puncture or drop cylinders, expose them to open flame or excessive heat. Use authorized cylinders only. Follow standard safety precautions for handling and use of compressed gas cylinders.
Genetron 22 should not be mixed with air above atmospheric pressure for leak testing or any other purpose. See Section 5: Unusual Fire and Explosion Hazards

STORAGE RECOMMENDATIONS:

Store in a cool, well-ventilated area of low fire risk and out of direct sunlight. Protect cylinder and its fittings from physical damage. Storage in subsurface locations should be avoided. Close valve tightly after use and when empty.

8. EXPOSURE CONTROLS/PERSONAL PROTECTION

ENGINEERING CONTROLS:

Provide local ventilation at filling zones and areas where leakage is probable. Mechanical (general) ventilation may be adequate for other operating and storage areas.

PERSONAL PROTECTIVE EQUIPMENT

SKIN PROTECTION:

Skin contact with refrigerant may cause frostbite. General work clothing and gloves (leather) should provide adequate protection. If prolonged contact with the liquid or gas is anticipated,

Field Service Guide: Refrigerants and Oils

MSDS Courtesy of Honeywell

insulated gloves constructed of PVA, neoprene or butyl rubber should be used. Any contaminated clothing should be promptly removed and washed before reuse.

EYE PROTECTION:

For normal conditions, wear safety glasses. Where there is reasonable probability of liquid contact, wear chemical safety goggles.

RESPIRATORY PROTECTION:

None generally required for adequately ventilated work situations. For accidental release or non-ventilated situations, or release into confined space, where the concentration may be above the PEL of 1,000 ppm, use a self-contained, NIOSH-approved breathing apparatus or supplied air respirator. For escape: use the former or a NIOSH-approved gas mask with organic vapor canister.

ADDITIONAL RECOMMENDATIONS:

Where contact with liquid is likely, such as in a spill or leak, impervious boots and clothing should be worn. High dose-level warning signs are recommended for areas of principle exposure. Provide eyewash stations and quick-drench shower facilities at convenient locations. For tank cleaning operations, see OSHA regulations, 29 CFR 1910.132 and 29 CFR 1910.133.

EXPOSURE GUIDELINES

INGREDIENT NAME	ACGIH TLV	OSHA PEL	OTHER LIMIT
Chlorodifluoromethane	1000 ppm TWA (8hr)	1000 ppm TWA (8hr)	None

* = Limit established by Honeywell.
** = Workplace Environmental Exposure Level (AIHA).
*** = Biological Exposure Index (ACGIH).

OTHER EXPOSURE LIMITS FOR POTENTIAL DECOMPOSITION PRODUCTS:
Hydrogen Fluoride: ACGIH TLV = 2 ppm ceiling, 0.5 ppm TLV-TWA

9. PHYSICAL AND CHEMICAL PROPERTIES

APPEARANCE: Clear, colorless liquid and vapor

PHYSICAL STATE: Gas at ambient temperatures

Field Service Guide: Refrigerants and Oils

MSDS Courtesy of Honeywell

MOLECULAR WEIGHT: 86.45

CHEMICAL FORMULA: $CHClF_2$

ODOR: Faint ethereal odor

SPECIFIC GRAVITY (water = 1.0): 1.21 @ 21.1°C (70°F)

SOLUBILITY IN WATER (weight %): 0.3 wt% @ 25°C and 1 atmosphere

pH: Neutral

BOILING POINT: -40.8°C (-41.40°F)

FREEZING POINT: -160°C (-256°F)

VAPOR PRESSURE: 136.1 psia @ 70°F 311.4 psia @ 130°F

VAPOR DENSITY (air = 1.0): 3.0

EVAPORATION RATE: >1   **COMPARED TO:** $CCl_4 = 1$

% VOLATILES: 100

FLASH POINT: Not applicable

(Flash point method and additional flammability data are found in Section 5.)

10. STABILITY AND REACTIVITY

NORMALLY STABLE? (CONDITIONS TO AVOID):

The product is stable.
Do not mix with oxygen or air above atmospheric pressure. Any source of high temperature, such as lighted cigarettes, flames, hot spots, or welding may yield toxic and/or corrosive decomposition products.

INCOMPATIBILITIES:

(Under specific conditions: e.g. very high temperatures and/or appropriate pressures) – Freshly abraded aluminum surfaces (may cause strong exothermic reaction). Chemically active metals:

Field Service Guide: Refrigerants and Oils

MSDS Courtesy of Honeywell

potassium, calcium, and powdered aluminum, magnesium and zinc.

HAZARDOUS DECOMPOSITION PRODUCTS:

Halogens, halogen acids and possibly carbonyl halides.

HAZARDOUS POLYMERIZATION:

Will not occur.

11. TOXICOLOGICAL INFORMATION

LC : 4hr. (rat) - $\geq$ 300,000 ppm
Cardiac Sensitization threshold (dog) - 50,000 ppm

DELAYED (SUBCHRONIC AND CHRONIC) EFFECTS:

Subchronic inhalation (rat) NOEL - 10,000 ppm
Not teratogenic
Not mutagenic in *in-vitro* or *in-vivo* tests

OTHER DATA:

Lifetime exposure of male rats was associated with a small increase in salivary gland fibrosarcomas.

12. ECOLOGICAL INFORMATION

Degradability (BOD):   Genetron 22 is a gas at room temperature; therefore, it is unlikely to remain in water.

Octanol Water Partition Coefficient: Unknown

13. DISPOSAL CONSIDERATIONS

RCRA

Is the unused product a RCRA hazardous waste if discarded?   Not a hazardous waste

If yes, the RCRA ID number is: Not applicable

Field Service Guide: Refrigerants and Oils

MSDS Courtesy of Honeywell

OTHER DISPOSAL CONSIDERATIONS:

Disposal must comply with federal, state, and local disposal or discharge laws. Genetron 22 is subject to U.S. Environmental Protection Agency Clean Air Act Regulations Section 608 in 40 CFR Part 82 regarding refrigerant recycling.

The information offered here is for the product as shipped. Use and/or alterations to the product such as mixing with other materials may significantly change the characteristics of the material and alter the RCRA classification and the proper disposal method.

14. TRANSPORT INFORMATION

US DOT HAZARD CLASS:
US DOT PROPER SHIPPING NAME: Chlorodifluoromethane
US DOT HAZARD CLASS: 2.2
US DOT PACKING GROUP: Not applicable

US DOT ID NUMBER: UN1018

For additional information on shipping regulations affecting this material, contact the information number found in Section 1.

15. REGULATORY INFORMATION

TOXIC SUBSTANCES CONTROL ACT (TSCA)

TSCA INVENTORY STATUS: Listed on the TSCA inventory
OTHER TSCA ISSUES: None

SARA TITLE III/CERCLA

"Reportable Quantities" (RQs) and/or "Threshold Planning Quantities" (TPQs) exist for the following ingredients.

INGREDIENT NAME	SARA/CERCLA RQ (lb.)	SARA EHS TPQ (lb.)
No ingredients listed in this section		

Spills or releases resulting in the loss of any ingredient at or above its RQ requires immediate notification to the National Response Center [(800) 424-8802] and to your Local Emergency Planning Committee.

Field Service Guide: Refrigerants and Oils

MSDS Courtesy of Honeywell

SECTION 311 HAZARD CLASS: IMMEDIATE
PRESSURE

SARA 313 TOXIC CHEMICALS:

The following ingredients are SARA 313 "Toxic Chemicals". CAS numbers and weight percents are found in Section 2.

INGREDIENT NAME	COMMENT
Chlorodifluoromethane (HCFC-22)	None

STATE RIGHT-TO-KNOW

In addition to the ingredients found in Section 2, the following are listed for state right-to-know purposes.

INGREDIENT NAME	WEIGHT %	COMMENT
No ingredients listed in this section		

ADDITIONAL REGULATORY INFORMATION:

Genetron 22 is subject to U.S. Environmental Protection Agency Clean Air Act Regulations at 40 CFR Part 82.

WARNING:
Do Not vent to the atmosphere. To comply with provisions of the U.S. Clean Air Act, any residual must be recovered.

Contains Chlorodifluoromethane, an HCFC substance which harms public health and the environment by destroying ozone in the upper atmosphere. Destruction of the ozone layer can lead to increased ultraviolet radiation which, with excess exposure to sunlight, can lead to an increase in skin cancer and eye cataracts.

WHMIS CLASSIFICATION (CANADA):

This product has been evaluated in accordance with the hazard criteria of the CPR and the MSDS contains all the information required by the CPR.

FOREIGN INVENTORY STATUS:
Canada – Listed on DSL
EU – EINECS # 2008719

Field Service Guide: Refrigerants and Oils

MSDS Courtesy of Honeywell

16. OTHER INFORMATION

CURRENT ISSUE DATE: December, 2005
PREVIOUS ISSUE DATE: January, 2004

CHANGES TO MSDS FROM PREVIOUS ISSUE DATE ARE DUE TO THE FOLLOWING:
Section 1: Updated medical emergency number
Section 8: Updated ACGIH-TLV for HF decomposition product

OTHER INFORMATION: HMIS Classification: Health – 1, Flammability – 1, Reactivity – 0
NFPA Classification: Health – 2, Flammability – 1, Reactivity – 0
ANSI/ASHRAE 34 Safety Group – A1
UL Classified

Regulatory Standards:
1. OSHA regulations for compressed gases: 29 CFR 1910.101
2. DOT classification per 49 CFR 172.10
3. Clean Air Act Class II Substance

MSDS Number: GTRN-0026

Field Service Guide: Refrigerants and Oils

MSDS Courtesy of Honeywell

Material Safety Data Sheet Genetron® AZ-20 (R-410A)

1. CHEMICAL PRODUCT AND COMPANY IDENTIFICATION

PRODUCT NAME: Genetron® AZ-20 (R-410A)
OTHER/GENERIC NAMES: R-410A
PRODUCT USE: Refrigerant
MANUFACTURER: Honeywell 101
Columbia Road
Box 1053
Morristown, New Jersey 07962-1053

FOR MORE INFORMATION CALL:
(Monday-Friday, 9:00am-5:00pm)
1-800-522-8001

IN CASE OF EMERGENCY CALL:
(24 Hours/Day, 7 Days/Week)
Medical: 1-800-498-5701
Transportation: 1-800-424-9300

2. COMPOSITION/INFORMATION ON INGREDIENTS

INGREDIENT NAME	CAS NUMBER	WEIGHT %
Difluoromethane	75-10-5	50
Pentafluoroethane	354-33-6	50

Trace impurities and additional material names not listed above may also appear in Section 15 toward the end of the MSDS. These materials may be listed for local "Right-To-Know" compliance and for other reasons.

3. HAZARDS IDENTIFICATION

EMERGENCY OVERVIEW: Colorless, volatile liquid with ethereal and faint sweetish odor. Non-flammable material. Overexposure may cause dizziness and loss of concentration. At higher levels, CNS depression and cardiac arrhythmia may result from exposure. Vapors displace air and can cause asphyxiation in confined spaces. At higher temperatures, (>250°C), decomposition products may include Hydrofluoric Acid (HF) and carbonyl halides

POTENTIAL HEALTH HAZARDS

SKIN: Irritation would result from a defatting action on tissue. Liquid contact could cause frostbite.

Field Service Guide: Refrigerants and Oils

MSDS Courtesy of Honeywell

EYES: Liquid contact can cause severe irritation and frostbite. Mist may irritate.

INHALATION: Genetron AZ-20 (R-410A) is low in acute toxicity in animals. When oxygen levels in air are reduced to 12–14% by displacement, symptoms of asphyxiation, loss of coordination, increased pulse rate and deeper respiration will occur. At high levels, cardiac arrhythmia may occur.

INGESTION: Ingestion is unlikely because of the low boiling point of the material. Should it occur, discomfort in the gastrointestinal tract from rapid evaporation of the material and consequent evolution of gas would result. Some effects of inhalation and skin exposure would be expected.

DELAYED EFFECTS: None known

Ingredients found on one of the OSHA designated carcinogen lists are listed below.

INGREDIENT NAME	NTP STATUS	IARC STATUS	OSHA LIST
No ingredients listed in this section			

4. FIRST AID MEASURES

SKIN: Promptly flush skin with water until all chemical is removed. If there is evidence of frostbite, bathe (do not rub) with lukewarm (not hot) water. If water is not available, cover with a clean, soft cloth or similar covering. Get medical attention if symptoms persist.

EYES: Immediately flush eyes with large amounts of water for at least 15 minutes (in case of frostbite water should be lukewarm, not hot) lifting eyelids occasionally to facilitate irrigation. Get medical attention if symptoms persist.

INHALATION: Immediately remove to fresh air. If breathing has stopped, give artificial respiration. Use oxygen as required, provided a qualified operator is available. Get medical attention. Do not give epinephrine (adrenaline).

INGESTION: Ingestion is unlikely because of the physical properties and is not expected to be hazardous. Do not induce vomiting unless instructed to do so by a physician.

ADVICE TO PHYSICIAN:

Field Service Guide: Refrigerants and Oils

MSDS Courtesy of Honeywell

Because of the possible disturbances of cardiac rhythm, catecholamine drugs, such as epinephrine, should be used with special caution and only in situations of emergency life support. Treatment of overexposure should be directed at the control of symptoms and the clinical conditions.

5. FIRE FIGHTING MEASURES

FLAMMABLE PROPERTIES

FLASH POINT:	Gas, not applicable per DOT regulations
FLASH POINT METHOD:	Not applicable
AUTOIGNITION TEMPERATURE:	>750°C
UPPER FLAME LIMIT (volume % in air):	None by ASTM D-56-82
LOWER FLAME LIMIT (volume % in air):	None by ASTM E-681
FLAME PROPAGATION RATE (solids):	Not applicable
OSHA FLAMMABILITY CLASS:	Not applicable

EXTINGUISHING MEDIA:

Use any standard agent – choose the one most appropriate for type of surrounding fire (material itself is not flammable) **MATERIAL SAFETY DATA SHEET** Genetron® AZ-20 (R-410A) MSDS Number: GTRN-0004 Page 3 of 7 Current Issue Date: December, 2005

UNUSUAL FIRE AND EXPLOSION HAZARDS:

Genetron AZ-20 (R-410A) is not flammable at ambient temperatures and atmospheric pressure. However, this material will become combustible when mixed with air under pressure and exposed to strong ignition sources.
Contact with certain reactive metals may result in formation of explosive or exothermic reactions under specific conditions (e.g. very high temperatures and/or appropriate pressures).

SPECIAL FIRE FIGHTING PRECAUTIONS/INSTRUCTIONS:

Firefighters should wear self-contained, NIOSH-approved breathing apparatus for protection

Field Service Guide: Refrigerants and Oils

MSDS Courtesy of Honeywell

against possible toxic decomposition products. Proper eye and skin protection should be provided. Use water spray to keep fire-exposed containers cool.

6. ACCIDENTAL RELEASE MEASURES

IN CASE OF SPILL OR OTHER RELEASE: (Always wear recommended personal protective equipment.)

Evacuate unprotected personnel. Protected personnel should remove ignition sources and shut off leak, if without risk, and provide ventilation. Unprotected personnel should not return until air has been tested and determined safe, including low-lying areas.

Spills and releases may have to be reported to Federal and/or local authorities. See Section 15 regarding reporting requirements.

7. HANDLING AND STORAGE

NORMAL HANDLING: (Always wear recommended personal protective equipment.)

Avoid breathing vapors and liquid contact with eyes, skin or clothing. Do not puncture or drop cylinders, expose them to open flame or excessive heat. Use authorized cylinders only. Follow standard safety precautions for handling and use of compressed gas cylinders. Genetron AZ-20 (R-410A) should not be mixed with air above atmospheric pressure for leak testing or any other purpose.

STORAGE RECOMMENDATIONS:

Store in a cool, well-ventilated area of low fire risk and out of direct sunlight. Protect cylinder and its fittings from physical damage. Storage in subsurface locations should be avoided. Close valve tightly after use and when empty.

8. EXPOSURE CONTROLS/PERSONAL PROTECTION

ENGINEERING CONTROLS:

Provide local ventilation at filling zones and areas where leakage is probable. Mechanical (general) ventilation may be adequate for other operating and storage areas.

PERSONAL PROTECTIVE EQUIPMENT

Field Service Guide: Refrigerants and Oils

MSDS Courtesy of Honeywell

SKIN PROTECTION:

Skin contact with refrigerant may cause frostbite. General work clothing and gloves (leather) should provide adequate protection. If prolonged contact with the liquid or gas is anticipated, insulated gloves constructed of PVA, neoprene or butyl rubber should be used. Any contaminated clothing should be promptly removed and washed before reuse. **MATERIAL SAFETY DATA SHEET** Genetron® AZ-20 (R-410A) MSDS Number: GTRN-0004 Page 4 of 7 Current Issue Date: December, 2005

EYE PROTECTION:

For normal conditions, wear safety glasses. Where there is reasonable probability of liquid contact, wear chemical safety goggles.

RESPIRATORY PROTECTION:

None generally required for adequately ventilated work situations. For accidental release or non-ventilated situations, or release into confined space, where the concentration may be above the PEL of 1,000 ppm, use a self-contained, NIOSH-approved breathing apparatus or supplied air respirator. For escape: use the former or a NIOSH-approved gas mask with organic vapor canister.

ADDITIONAL RECOMMENDATIONS:

Where contact with liquid is likely, such as in a spill or leak, impervious boots and clothing should be worn. High dose-level warning signs are recommended for areas of principle exposure. Provide eyewash stations and quick-drench shower facilities at convenient locations. For tank cleaning operations, see OSHA regulations, 29 CFR 1910.132 and 29 CFR 1910.133.

EXPOSURE GUIDELINES

INGREDIENT NAME	ACGIH TLV	OSHA PEL	OTHER LIMIT
Difluoromethane	None	None	*1000ppm TWA (8hr)
Pentafluoroethane	None None	None None	**1000 ppm TWA (8hr)

* = Limit established by AlliedSignal.
** = Workplace Environmental Exposure Level (AIHA).
*** = Biological Exposure Index (ACGIH).

Field Service Guide: Refrigerants and Oils

MSDS Courtesy of Honeywell

OTHER EXPOSURE LIMITS FOR POTENTIAL DECOMPOSITION PRODUCTS:

Hydrogen Fluoride: ACGIH TLV: 2 ppm ceiling, 0.5ppm TLV-TWA

9. PHYSICAL AND CHEMICAL PROPERTIES

APPEARANCE:	Clear, colorless liquid and vapor
PHYSICAL STATE:	Gas at ambient temperatures
MOLECULAR WEIGHT:	72.6
CHEMICAL FORMULA;	CHF_2CF_2
DOR:	Faint ethereal odor
SPECIFIC GRAVITY (water = 1.0):	1.08 @ 21.1°C (70°F)
SOLUBILITY IN WATER (weight %):	Unknown
pH:	Neutral
BOILING POINT:	-48.5°C (-55.4°F)
FREEZING POINT:	Not Determined
VAPOR PRESSURE:	215.3 psia @ 70°F 490.2 psia @ 130°F
VAPOR DENSITY (air = 1.0):	3.0
EVAPORATION RATE:	>1 **COMPARED TO:** CCl_4
% VOLATILES:	100
FLASH POINT:	Not applicable

(Flash point method and additional flammability data are found in Section 5.)

10. STABILITY AND REACTIVITY

Field Service Guide: Refrigerants and Oils

MSDS Courtesy of Honeywell

NORMALLY STABLE? (CONDITIONS TO AVOID):

The product is stable.
Do not mix with oxygen or air above atmospheric pressure. Any source of high temperature, such as lighted cigarettes, flames, hot spots, or welding may yield toxic and/or corrosive decomposition products.

INCOMPATIBILITIES:

(Under specific conditions: e.g. very high temperatures and/or appropriate pressures) – Freshly abraded aluminum surfaces (may cause strong exothermic reaction). Chemically active metals: potassium, calcium, and powdered aluminum, magnesium and zinc.

HAZARDOUS DECOMPOSITION PRODUCTS:

Halogens, halogen acids and possibly carbonyl halides.

HAZARDOUS POLYMERIZATION:

Will not occur.

11. TOXICOLOGICAL INFORMATION

IMMEDIATE (ACUTE) EFFECTS:

LC_{50} : 4 hr. (rat) - e"520,000 ppm (difluoromethane)
Cardiac Sensitization threshold (dog) e"100,000 ppm (pentafluoroethane)

DELAYED (SUBCHRONIC AND CHRONIC) EFFECTS:

Teratology - negative
Subchronic inhalation (rat) NOEL - 50,000 ppm

OTHER DATA:

Not active in four genetic studies

12. ECOLOGICAL INFORMATION

Degradability (BOD):   Genetron AZ-20 (R-410A) is a gas at room temperature; therefore, it is unlikely to remain in water.

Field Service Guide: Refrigerants and Oils

MSDS Courtesy of Honeywell

Octanol Water Partition Coefficient:

Log P_{OW} = 1.48 (pentafluoroethane), 0.21 (difluoromethane)

13. DISPOSAL CONSIDERATIONS

RCRA

Is the unused product a RCRA hazardous waste if discarded?   Not a hazardous waste

If yes, the RCRA ID number is: Not applicable

OTHER DISPOSAL CONSIDERATIONS:

Disposal must comply with federal, state, and local disposal or discharge laws. Genetron AZ-20 (R-410A) is subject to U.S. Environmental Protection Agency Clean Air Act Regulations Section 608 in 40 CFR Part 82 regarding refrigerant recycling.

The information offered here is for the product as shipped. Use and/or alterations to the product such as mixing with other materials may significantly change the characteristics of the material and alter the RCRA classification and the proper disposal method.

14. TRANSPORT INFORMATION

US DOT HAZARD CLASS:

US DOT PROPER SHIPPING NAME: Liquified gas, n.o.s.
(Pentafluoroethane, Difluoromethane)

US DOT HAZARD CLASS: 2.2
US DOT PACKING GROUP: Not applicable

US DOT ID NUMBER: UN3163

For additional information on shipping regulations affecting this material, contact the information number found in Section 1.

15. REGULATORY INFORMATION

TOXIC SUBSTANCES CONTROL ACT (TSCA)

Field Service Guide: Refrigerants and Oils

MSDS Courtesy of Honeywell

TSCA INVENTORY STATUS: Components listed on the TSCA inventory.

OTHER TSCA ISSUES: Subject to Section 12(b) export notification. May contain 0-10 ppm Ethane, 2-chloro-1,1,1-trifluoro, CAS# 75-88-7

SARA TITLE III/CERCLA

"Reportable Quantities" (RQs) and/or "Threshold Planning Quantities" (TPQs) exist for the following ingredients.

INGREDIENT NAME	SARA/CERCLA RQ (lb.)	SARA EHS TPQ (lb.)
No ingredients listed in this section		

Spills or releases resulting in the loss of any ingredient at or above its RQ requires immediate notification to the National Response Center [(800) 424-8802] and to your Local Emergency Planning Committee.

SECTION 311 HAZARD CLASS: IMMEDIATE
PRESSURE

SARA 313 TOXIC CHEMICALS:

The following ingredients are SARA 313 "Toxic Chemicals". CAS numbers and weight percents are found in Section 2.

INGREDIENT NAME	COMMENT
No ingredients listed in this section	

STATE RIGHT-TO-KNOW

In addition to the ingredients found in Section 2, the following are listed for state right-to-know purposes.

INGREDIENT NAME	WEIGHT %	COMMENT
No ingredients listed in this section		

ADDITIONAL REGULATORY INFORMATION:

Genetron AZ-20 (R-410A) is subject to U.S. Environmental Protection Agency Clean Air Act Regulations at 40 CFR Part 82.

Field Service Guide: Refrigerants and Oils

MSDS Courtesy of Honeywell

WARNING: Contains pentafluoroethane (HFC-125) and difluoromethane (HFC-32), greenhouse gases which may contribute to global warming

Do Not vent to the atmosphere. To comply with provisions of the U.S. Clean Air Act, any residual must be recovered.

WHMIS CLASSIFICATION (CANADA):

This product has been evaluated in accordance with the hazard criteria of the CPR and the MSDS contains all the information required by the CPR.

FOREIGN INVENTORY STATUS:

EU – EINECS # 2065578 (HFC-125)

16. OTHER INFORMATION

CURRENT ISSUE DATE: December, 2005

PREVIOUS ISSUE DATE: February, 2003

CHANGES TO MSDS FROM PREVIOUS ISSUE DATE ARE DUE TO THE FOLLOWING:

Section 1: Updated medical emergency number
Section 8: Updated ACGIH-TLV for HF decomposition product
Section 15: Updated TSCA information

OTHER INFORMATION: HMIS Classification: Health – 1, Flammability – 1, Reactivity – 0
NFPA Classification: Health – 2, Flammability – 1, Reactivity – 0
ANSI/ASHRAE 34 Safety Group – A1

Regulatory Standards:
1. OSHA regulations for compressed gases: 29 CFR 1910.101
2. DOT classification per 49 CFR 172.101

Toxicity information per PAFT Testing

MSDS Number GTRN-000400

Superheat and Subcooling

**Superheat
and Subcooling**

Field Service Guide: Superheat

Chapter
Superheat

Table of Contents

Suction Vapor Superheat..2
    Introduction..2
    How Superheat is used by Service Technicians...2
        Suction Vapor Superheat with a Totally Flooded Evaporator Coil...............3
        Suction Vapor Superheat Level with a Starved Evaporator Coil..................3
        Suction Vapor Superheat Level with a Low Heat Load on the Evaporator Coil...........4
        Suction Vapor Superheat Level with a High Heat Load on the Evaporator Coil.........4
    The Evaporator Circuit...4
    Superheating Suction Vapor..5
    What Affects Superheat Level 6
Thermostatic Expansion Valve..7
    Thermostatic Expansion Valve Overview 7
    Thermostatic Expansion Valve and Heat Load..8
    Thermostatic Expansion Valve and Outdoor Air Temperature 9
Measuring Suction Vapor Superheat: Step by Step..10
Evaporator Conditions -
      Fixed Metering Device..**12**
      TXV Metering Device..**14**

1

Field Service Guide: Superheat

Suction Vapor Superheat

Introduction

Suction vapor superheat is a measurement of the temperature gain in the refrigerant vapor that occurs in the evaporator coil. Another way to describe superheat is the temperature gain in the refrigerant after all of the cold liquid has boiled off in the evaporator circuiting.

Measuring superheat takes only a few moments to accomplish. Simply place a digital thermometer onto the suction line near the suction pressure port on the suction line service valve. Measure the suction pressure and convert it to saturation temperature. For example, if the refrigerant were R-22 operating at a suction pressure of 68 PSIG, the refrigerant saturation temperature is 40°F. The saturation temperature is the temperature of the refrigerant at the outlet of the metering device. Next, measure the suction line temperature. Let's say it is 55°F. The vapor is 15°F warmer than the refrigerant exiting the metering device. The superheat level is the temperature of the vapor above saturation temperature, therefore the superheat in this example is 15°F.

How Superheat is used by Service Technicians

Superheat is used by service technicians as a means to gauge whether the evaporator coil has the correct amount of refrigerant in its circuits. When the evaporator coil contains a lot of liquid, the liquid travels deep into the evaporator circuits and little area is left for heating up the vapor that formed from the liquid.

When the evaporator circuit lacks refrigerant, the evaporator quickly uses up the available liquid early in the circuits and the vapor travels a long distance through the circuiting. The greater the distance the vapor travels, the more heat it picks up.

By measuring the suction vapor superheat level, technicians can then compare their measured level against charts that indicate what the superheat should be. When the superheat is above the required level, the evaporator coil is either starving for refrigerant or has excessive heat load. When the superheat is below the required level, the evaporator coil is either flooded with too much refrigerant, or the coil lacks heat load.

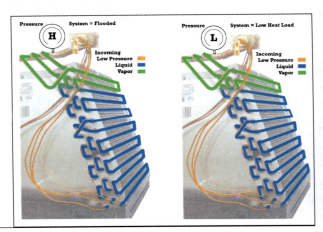

Suction Vapor Superheat with a Totally Flooded Evaporator Coil

With the coil totally flooded with cold liquid refrigerant at saturation temperature, every millimeter of the circuiting is boiling off cold liquid to cold vapor. The refrigerant in this example is R-22. The suction gauge indicates a pressure of 85 PSIG, which corresponds to a saturation temperature of 51°F. When the liquid boils to a vapor, the vapor contains a lot of heat that was used to change the liquid to vapor. The vapor temperature has not risen above 51°F, yet it contains massive amounts of heat.

A digital temperature probe is attached to the suction line at the outlet of the evaporator circuit. The suction line temperature is 51°F. Since the entering saturation temperature and leaving refrigerant temperature are the same, the vapor has not had a chance to travel through the circuit and pick up heat. This condition is producing maximum heat transfer in the evaporator but it is going to likely result in liquid flooding back to the compressor.

Suction Vapor Superheat Level with a Starved Evaporator Coil

The liquid flow through the metering device is low which results in a low suction pressure. The refrigerant is R-22 at a gauge pressure of only 49 PSIG. R-22 at this pressure has a corresponding saturation temperature of 25°F. The temperature of the vapor leaving this coil is 70°F which is 45°F warmer than the refrigerant saturation temperature at the outlet of the metering device. The large superheat level is a result of running out of liquid early in the coil circuiting which caused the vapor to travel an excessive distance in the evaporator coil circuiting.

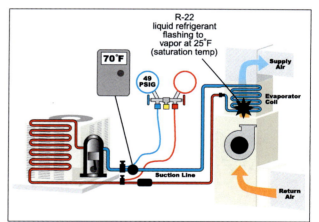

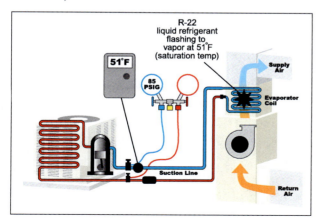

Field Service Guide: Superheat

Suction Vapor Superheat Level with a Low Heat Load on the Evaporator Coil

When the evaporator coil lacks heat, the refrigerant pressure will be below the charging chart requirement. The evaporator coil will have a hard time boiling off the cold liquid refrigerant. The liquid will travel at a low pressure deeper into the evaporator than it should. For example, let's say we had 60 PSIG suction pressure. The corresponding saturation temperature is 34°F out of the metering device. The temperature probe at the suction line outlet of the coil indicates a suction vapor temperature of only 36°F. There is only 2 degrees of superheat and the suction pressure is too low.

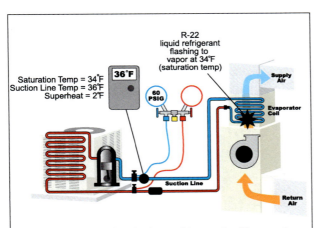

With a low heat load, the refrigerant will run at a lower pressure into the evaporator and will have low superheat.

Suction Vapor Superheat Level with a High Heat Load on the Evaporator Coil

When there is too much heat being absorbed into the refrigerant, pressures will be high and the system will run out of liquid early. In this example, the system suction pressure is all the way up to 88 PSIG. At 88 PSIG the saturation temperature of the refrigerant exiting the metering device is 53°F. The suction line temperature at the outlet of the evaporator coil is at a temperature of 83°F, which is 30 degrees warmer than saturation temperature. If the coil had too much refrigerant, the superheat would be low, but in this case, it is too high.

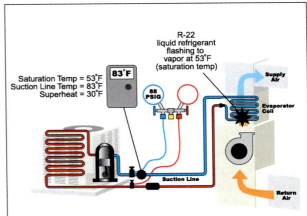

With a high heat load, the refrigerant will run at a higher pressure into the evaporator and will have a much higher superheat temperature.

The Evaporator Circuit

The evaporator coil is placed in direct contact with the warm air from a conditioned space. An indoor fan assembly will circulate the conditioned space's warm air through the cold evaporator coil.

The refrigerant that enters the evaporator coil is in a saturated state and any addition of heat at saturation temperature will cause the refrigerant liquid to begin to flash off into a vapor as it travels through the evaporator coil circuiting. It is during this time in the evaporator cycle that massive levels of heat are being transferred from the conditioned space's warm air into the cold saturated refrigerant. The massive heat transfer taking place is due to the large amount of thermal energy required for the cold liquid refrigerant to change its state from a liquid into a vapor. This process is the same process that makes ice such a good refrigerant!

In this example we have a suction pressure of 130PSIG with R-410A refrigerant. The corresponding saturation temperature for R-410A at this pressure is 44°F. This is the temperature of the refrigerant as it flashes from a liquid to a vapor.

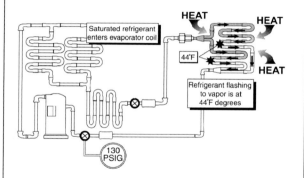

Assuming a proper charge and correct size metering piston, at some point in the evaporator coil circuit all of the cold saturated liquid refrigerant will be boiled off and only vapor will remain. At this point in the evaporator coil, the changing of state process ends.

Superheating Suction Vapor

When all of the saturated refrigerant liquid is used up in the evaporator circuiting, only vapor will remain in the circuit. This condition is created at the boiling off point. The remaining refrigerant vapor is still very cold. As the cold vapor travels through the remaining circuiting of the evaporator coil, it picks up heat from the warm return air. Because there is no liquid left, the refrigerant vapor temperature begins to rise to a temperature above saturation temperature. **Once the refrigerant vapor raises it's temperature above saturation temperature, it is now called superheated**. This heat added to the refrigerant vapor after all of the liquid has boiled off is called Suction Vapor Superheat.

In our example, we have 44°F saturated refrigerant entering the evaporator circuiting. We know this temperature because we converted our 130PSIG suction pressure to saturation temperature. A digital temperature probe is placed at the suction line service gauge port and we measure 54°F. The temperature of the suction line is indicating that we have heated up the refrigerant vapor by 10 degrees, therefore the superheat level is 10°F.

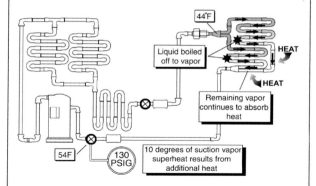

Since no changing of state is taking place when the vapor is being superheated, the actual amount of cooling process declines in the evaporator circuiting where superheating occurs. At this point, the vapor temperature will rise very rapidly. Think of it as if the ice has all melted. The remaining cold water from the melted ice will produce very little refrigeration ability even though its temperature is colder than the product being refrigerated.

Although superheating of the refrigerant vapor at the evaporator coil provides only minimal cooling benefits, it is needed. This way we are insured that no liquid refrigerant is leaving the evaporator circuit. It is necessary to prevent

Field Service Guide: Superheat

the escape of saturated refrigerant from the evaporator because at saturation temperature both liquid and vapor refrigerant may be present and compressors cannot pump liquid. If liquid is introduced into the compressor, damage to the compressor could occur.

What Affects Superheat Level

The position within the evaporator coil where all of the liquid is boiled off is determined by the amount of refrigerant entering the evaporator from the metering device and also by the amount of heat energy passing across the evaporator surface.

Fixed type metering devices allow the flow of refrigerant into the evaporator to be controlled by the amount of liquid pressure present at the end of the liquid line. The liquid pressure will vary with changes in outdoor air temperature and coil cleanliness. If the liquid pressure is high, the refrigerant flow through the metering device will be high and the evaporator will flood with refrigerant. If the pressure at the liquid line inlet is low, the refrigerant flow through the metering device will be low and the evaporator coil will be starved for refrigerant.

Because the fixed type metering device cannot reduce or increase the flow of refrigerant into the evaporator coil when the liquid pressure changes, the actual efficiency of the evaporator coil is affected both positively and adversely. On a cool day, the liquid pressure falls, causing the flow of refrigerant into the evaporator coil to decrease. Because the evaporator coil will lack adequate refrigerant flow, the liquid is boiled off early in the evaporator circuit. The remaining vapor travels through the evaporator circuiting and becomes highly superheated. This is not good for efficiency since no changing of state is taking place in a large area of the evaporator coil. During periods of high liquid pressure, the evaporator coil is flooded with cold refrigerant. The liquid boils off very late in the evaporator circuit, which leaves very little circuiting for superheating. In this state, the capacity of the evaporator is high since most of the coil circuit is being used to boil off cold liquid to a vapor.

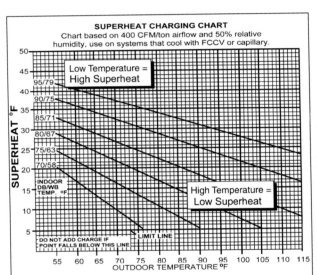

This chart is for instructional uses ONLY. Not for field use. Provided courtesy of The Trane Company

By studying charging charts, you will find good examples of how superheat changes with changes in the outdoor air temperature. On cold days, the superheat level will be high, and on hot days it will fall. At no time should it be allowed to fall below 5°F.

The other factor affecting the position at which all the cold liquid refrigerant is boiled off in the evaporator circuit is the amount of heat energy passing through the evaporator coil from the conditioned space. The amount of heat energy from the conditioned space includes the volume of air, the Sensible Heat of the air, and the

Latent Heat of the air. If the air volume or heat contained in the air is high, the liquid will boil off early in the evaporator circuit and the vapor will be highly superheated. If the air volume or heat contained in the air is low, the liquid will travel further into the evaporator coil before being boiled off to a vapor. In this case, there is very little circuiting left for superheating. In extreme cases, the refrigerant could leave the evaporator without being superheated.

It is typical for the indoor fan to deliver the air to the evaporator coil in a quantity from 350 to 450 Cubic Feet Per Minute (CFM) for every ton of cooling capacity present. For example, a 2-ton unit would need the air entering the evaporator coil to be anywhere from 700 to 900 CFM. If the system is to operate properly, the correct amount of indoor airflow must be present for the size of the cooling system.

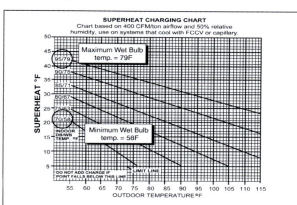

This chart is for instructional uses ONLY. Not for field use. Provided courtesy of The Trane Company

The heat contained in the air is plotted on the charging chart. The indoor heat load can be anywhere from 58° degree Wet Bulb (Total Heat Content) to 79° Wet Bulb. At levels below 58° or above 79° Wet Bulb, the heat is either too low or too high for proper operation of the system. The ranges for Dry Bulb temperature are used in the superheat chart. Refer to the chart for the minimum and maximum limits of temperature.

Thermostatic Expansion Valve

Thermostatic Expansion Valve Overview

A Thermostatic Expansion Valve (TXV) is a metering device that will attempt to maintain a constant level of suction vapor superheat over a wide range of heat load and outdoor air temperature range combinations. The superheat level maintained by the TXV is about 10-15°F. The TXV is able to maintain a constant superheat level by regulating the size of its internal orifice in response to changes in heat load and liquid pressure.

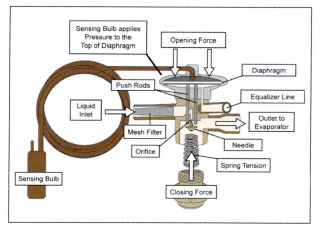

The size of the TXV orifice is controlled by an opening force and a closing force. The opening force consists of pressure from the TXV Sensing Bulb, which is placed to the top side of the TXV Diaphragm assembly. The closing force is internal spring tension pushing on the bottom of the orifice, and evaporator outlet pressure placed at the underside of the TXV Diaphragm via the Equalizer Line connection. The amount of spring tension determines how much superheat will be maintained by the expansion valve. *Typically,*

Field Service Guide: Superheat

this pressure is about 15 PSI which equals 10 degrees saturation temperature when working with R-22 systems.

The sensing bulb contains an internal charge of refrigerant. When the sensing bulb senses a warm suction line, the pressure in the sensing bulb rises. If the suction line temperature falls, the pressure in the sensing bulb will also fall. If the evaporator is starving for refrigerant, the suction line gets warm which raises the sensing bulb pressure. When the evaporator coil floods, the suction line gets cold, the sensing bulb pressure drops. This pressure is directed to the top of the Diaphragm assembly.

The operation of the valve is very simple. If the spring tension and evaporator outlet pressure are greater than the sensing bulb pressure, the orifice will go to a more closed position, thereby throttling back refrigerant flow. If the evaporator outlet pressure and spring tension are less than sensing bulb pressure, the orifice will move to a more open position, thereby increasing refrigerant flow. The two opposing forces allow the TXV to feed the proper amount of refrigerant into the evaporator coil as changes in suction line temperature occur. When the pressure on top of the diaphragm is greater than the evaporator outlet and spring tension, the orifice opens. When sensing bulb pressure is less than evaporator outlet and spring tension, the orifice closes.

There are some differences in the operation of a mechanical refrigeration system using an expansion valve metering device in place of a fixed type device. Differences in cycle operation include how the system reacts to changes in evaporator heat load, system charge, and changes in the outdoor air temperature.

A TXV will adjust to changes in heat load entering the refrigerant at the evaporator coil. If the heat load is very high, the suction pressure will rise and the saturated liquid entering the evaporator coil will be quickly boiled off early in the evaporator circuit. The vapor will be highly superheated due to the amount of circuiting it must travel through before exiting the evaporator coil. Because of the high suction pressure and superheat, the suction line will be warm.

At the outlet of the evaporator coil, the sensing bulb pressure will rise when it is exposed to the warm suction line. The sensing bulb pressure is directed to the top of the TXV Diaphragm. The diaphragm pushes against evaporator outlet pressure and spring tension to force the TXV orifice to a more open position.

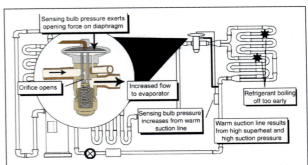

With the orifice in a more open position, the evaporator coil receives more refrigerant. With more refrigerant entering the evaporator coil, the suction pressure will rise and the superheat level will begin to drop.

If the heat load is excessively high, the TXV may not be able to maintain its design superheat level. In this state, there is simply not enough refrigerant in the system to keep up with the heat load requirement. In extreme cases where too much refrigerant is allowed into the evaporator

Thermostatic Expansion Valve and Heat Load

coil, the suction pressure could rise high enough to overload the compressor motor. This condition could exist due to infiltration air, excessive indoor airflow, new system start-up, or an undersized system.

In reverse, when the heat load is low, such as when the return air filter is dirty, the TXV will again try to maintain its design superheat. In this state, the suction pressure is low and the evaporator coil struggles to boil off all of the saturated liquid refrigerant.

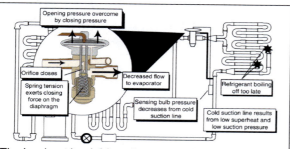

The low heat load drives the evaporator pressure and corresponding saturation temperature very low. As the cold saturated liquid travels through the evaporator circuiting, it will boil off very late in the circuit. Because of the low saturation temperature and late boil off point, there is little superheat and the suction vapor is very cold.

The TXV sensing bulb located at the suction line outlet of the evaporator coil senses the cold suction line and its internal pressure falls. The low sensing bulb pressure is directed to the top of the TXV diaphragm assembly. With very low sensing bulb pressure at the top of diaphragm, evaporator outlet pressure and spring tension push the orifice to a more closed position.

With less refrigerant entering the evaporator coil, the superheat level rises, and the suction pressure falls slightly.

Unfortunately, with inadequate airflow, the TXV will struggle in an attempt to reach a steady state of balance due to the lack of adequate suction pressure. The valve may hunt (alternately flood and starve the coil) in an attempt to maintain adequate superheat. The lack of suction pressure creates a very cold evaporator coil that may eventually develop a coating of ice.

Thermostatic Expansion Valve and Outdoor Air Temperature

With a Fixed Type Metering Device, the indoor coil receives less refrigerant as the outdoor air temperature drops. This condition is due to the loss of liquid pressure at lower outdoor air temperatures. Fixed type systems operating in this state lose some performance of the evaporator circuit due to a lack of refrigerant during these periods of operation. With decreased refrigerant flow, the suction vapor superheat level of Fixed Type Metering Devices can rise to significant levels during periods of cool outdoor air temperature operation.

Expansion Valve systems offer greater efficiency because they can adjust their orifice size to allow additional refrigerant into the evaporator coil at cooler outdoor air temperatures. With more refrigerant in the evaporator coil, the heat transfer process is enhanced and higher overall efficiency ratings are obtained.

When the system has low liquid pressure due to low outdoor air temperature, the flow of liquid refrigerant into the TXV decreases. With less refrigerant flowing through the TXV, the evaporator coil starves for refrigerant. The suction pressure will fall and the liquid is quickly boiled off early in the evaporator circuiting. The suction vapor superheat is high and the suction vapor leaving the evaporator is warm.

Field Service Guide: Superheat

The sensing bulb pressure rises in response to the warm suction line. The pressure at the top of the TXV Diaphragm assembly increases to a point greater than spring tension and evaporator outlet pressure. The orifice reacts to higher opening pressure by moving to a more open position and the evaporator coil receives more refrigerant.

With more refrigerant in the evaporator coil, the suction pressure rises and superheat falls. In this state, the TXV ensures that good use of the evaporator coil surface area is maintained despite the low liquid pressure.

The ability of the expansion valve to increase its orifice size to maintain a relatively low level of superheat has an effect upon the condenser coil. The condenser must give up some of its refrigerant charge to meet the refrigerant demand of the evaporator coil.

Cool Outdoor Air Temperature:

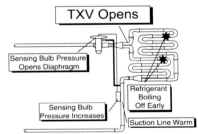

Warm Outdoor Air Temperature:

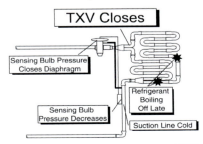

Tools | Digital Temperature Probe
Refrigerant Gauges

Measuring Suction Vapor Superheat

STEP 1

Run the air conditioner and allow system pressures and temperatures to stabilize.

STEP 2

Measure suction pressure and convert to saturation temperature.

Field Service Guide: Superheat

STEP 3

Measure suction line temperature near suction gauge pressure port. (Use a digital thermometer. DO NOT USE INFRARED TYPE THERMOMETERS.)

STEP 4

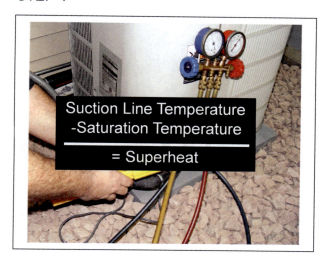

Subtract saturation temperature from suction line temperature. The difference is the amount of superheat.

STEP 5

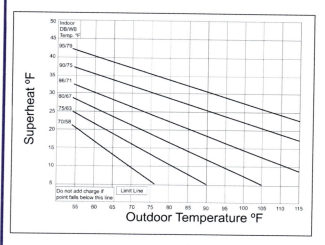

Compare actual superheat to the charging chart requirement. (Fixed metering) (TXV should be around 10°F with some exceptions as specified by Equipment Manufacturer)

NOTE:
Changing superheat level: (Fixed orifice metering only)

- Add refrigerant lowers superheat and raises pressure.
- Recover refrigerant raises superheat and lowers pressure.
- Increase air flow at evaporator coil raises superheat and raises pressure.
- Lower air flow at evaporator coil lowers superheat and lowers pressure.

Field Service Guide: Superheat

Evaporator Conditions (Fixed Metering Device)

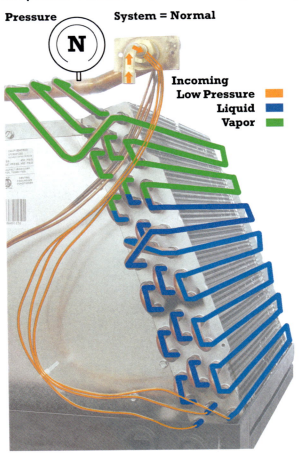

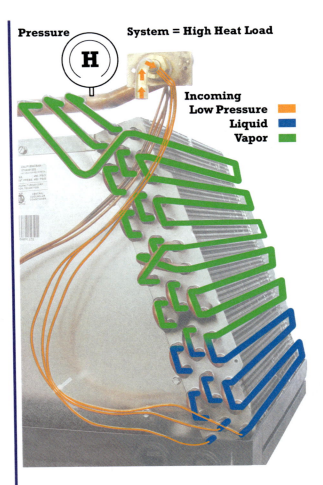

The coil is performing to factory specifications. The refrigerant liquid is boiling off at various points based upon the temperature of the outdoor air and indoor heat load.

The coil is running out of liquid refrigerant earlier in the circuit than it should. The coil is not undercharged because the suction pressure is high. The suction vapor superheat level will be higher than charging chart requirement.

This condition is caused by excess air volume or heat.

Field Service Guide: Superheat

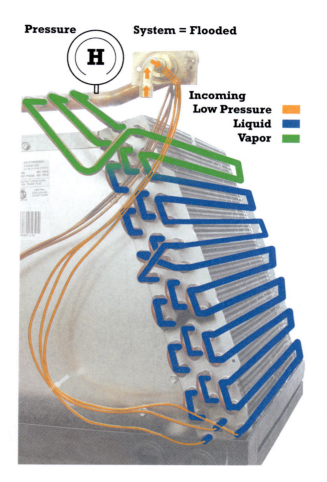

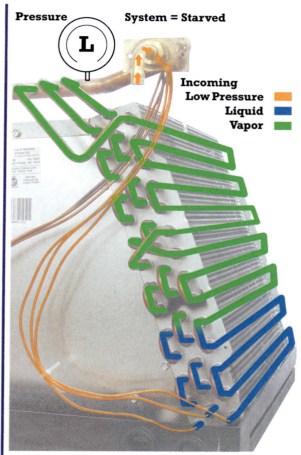

The coil is flooded with liquid refrigerant. The coil pressure is high and the liquid is present very late in the circuiting. If the system were operating at full load conditions, this may appear as a normal coil except for the fact that suction pressure is higher than it should be.

Causes include overcharging and oversizing of the metering piston.

The coil is lacking refrigerant. The saturated liquid is running out early in the circuit and the suction pressure is too low. Superheat is above the required chart value.

Causes include undercharging and liquid restrictions.

13

Field Service Guide: Superheat

Evaporator Conditions (TXV Metering Device)

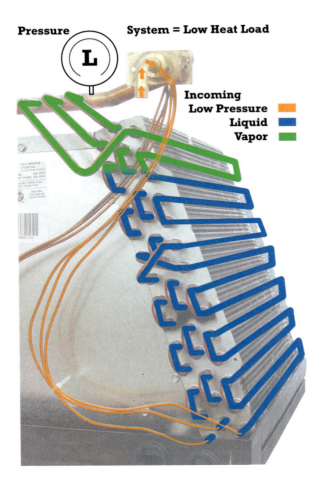

System = Low Heat Load

Pressure: **L**

Incoming Low Pressure — orange
Liquid — blue
Vapor — green

The coil is flooded with liquid refrigerant. The coil pressure is low. This can be due to low air volume or a lack of heat in the air.

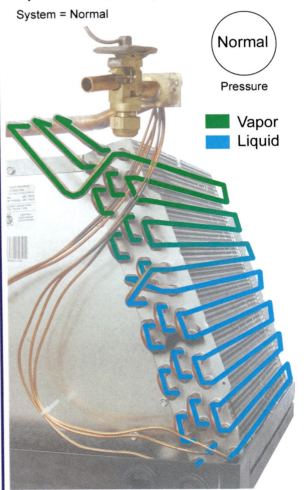

System = Normal

Normal Pressure

Vapor — green
Liquid — blue

Coils with TXV metering operate at 10°F of suction vapor superheat over a wide range of operating heat load and outdoor air temperatures.

Be aware that a TXV can mask undercharged conditions by maintaining normal evaporator conditions under certain combinations of indoor heat load and outdoor air temperature. The problem will appear intermittently.

Field Service Guide: Superheat

System = High Heat Load

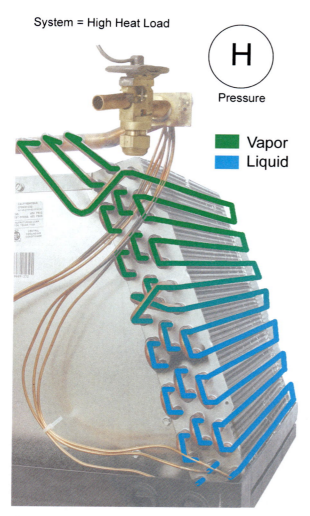

H Pressure

■ Vapor
■ Liquid

If the heat load on a TXV coil is excessive, the valve will open to try and maintain proper superheat. The suction pressure will be high. If the heat load is high enough, the TXV may not be able to maintain adequate superheat and the superheat will rise to a level above normal.

System = Flooded

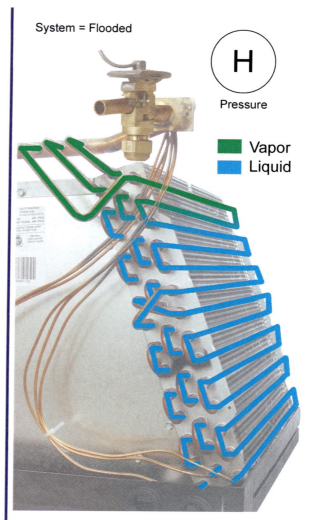

H Pressure

■ Vapor
■ Liquid

If the TXV over-feeds refrigerant into the circuiting, the suction pressure will be too high and the suction vapor superheat too low.

Causes include sensing bulbs that are not insulated, and improperly functioning TXV.

15

Field Service Guide: Superheat

System = Low Heat Load

Hunts
Pressure

Vapor
Liquid

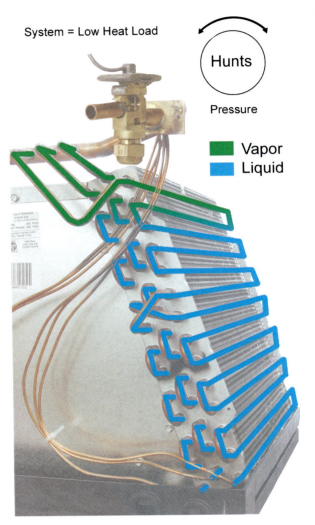

System = Starved

L
Pressure

Vapor
Liquid

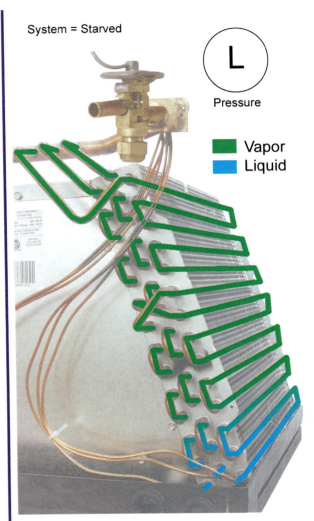

If the heat load on a TXV coil is too low, the TXV will struggle to maintain adequate superheat. The TXV will open and close as it tries to find a balance of refrigerant.

Causes are low air volume and low heat content in the air.

If the coil lacks refrigerant, the suction pressure will be low and the suction vapor superheat high.

Causes include low charge, refrigerant circuit restrictions, and failed TXV.

Field Service Guide: Subcooling and Condensers

Chapter

Subcooling and Condensers

Table of Contents

Function of the Condenser Coil 2
    Condensing Temperature and Liquid Subcooling Process 2
    How Subcooling Changes 4
    How Subcooling Changes w/Heat Load 4
    The Size of the Condenser Coil and Subcooling Design Levels 4
    Why Subcooling is Important 5
    Overcharging for more Subcooling may result in Abnormal Condensing Pressure 5
    Getting the right amount of Subcooling 6
Subcooling Measurement for Techs: Step By Step 7
Problems in the Condenser 8
    Dirt 8
    Non Condensable Gasses 8
Checking for Non Condensable Gasses: Step By Step 8
    Restrictions in Condenser Circuits 9
Checking for Restrictions in Condenser Circuits: Step By Step 10
    Summary 11

1

Field Service Guide: Subcooling and Condensers

Function of the Condenser Coil

In this illustration, the refrigerant circuiting of a typical condenser coil can be followed. Starting at the compressor discharge line, the hot gas enters a common header that directs the hot gas to the circuiting of the condenser coil. In this condenser, the hot gas is directed into two circuits. The refrigerant that exits the condenser circuits is collected and directed to a final circuit at the bottom of the coil. This circuit further cools condensed liquid refrigerant. A drier is located in the liquid line circuit to catch debris and absorb moisture

Condensing Temperature and Liquid Subcooling Process

The condensing temperature can be determined by measuring the pressure in the condenser coil. In the example shown below, the condenser is operating at a pressure of 250 PSIG and the refrigerant is R-22. From a saturated properties table, it can be determined that the saturation temperature for this example is 117°F.

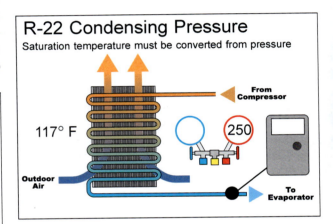

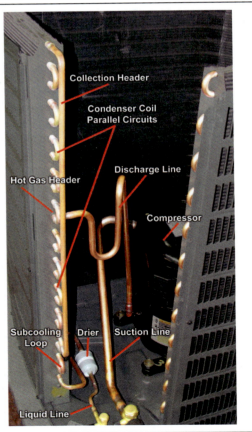

The condensing of hot gas into a hot saturated liquid refrigerant is a change of state operation that requires the transfer of a large amount of heat from the refrigerant. This large amount of heat transferred is due to the fact that a large amount of energy is needed to change the hot gas into a liquid. The saturated liquid refrigerant that forms in the initial circuits of the condenser coil is a mix of liquid and some refrigerant vapor. Both the liquid and vapor are at a temperature of 117°F.

The condensed saturated liquid then travels further into the condenser circuiting where it will begin to give up heat to the cooler outdoor air.

As the liquid travels, its temperature begins to drop below the temperature at which it condensed. (In this case, 117°F). When the liquid is at a temperature that is cooler than the condensing temperature, the liquid enters a state that is called subcooled.

<u>When a refrigerant liquid is subcooled, the refrigerant is pure liquid</u>. In other words, the vapor bubbles disappear.

The position where the subcooling begins is usually in the independent parallel circuits of the condenser coil. However, some coils have an additional circuit where the liquid circulates further, and more heat is removed from the liquid. This circuit is called a subcooling loop.

The liquid line in this example is 10 degrees cooler than the condensing temperature. This 10 degree difference in temperature is called liquid subcooling.

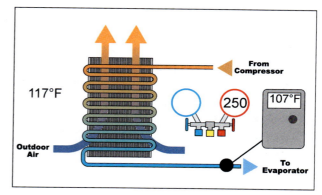

The coolest the liquid can be cooled to, is the temperature of the air surrounding the condenser coil. If refrigerant liquid leaves the condenser coil at a temperature that is colder than the air hitting the coil, there is a pressure drop in the coil that is causing the temperature of the refrigerant to fall. For example, if a drier were installed in the condensing unit, and the drier became plugged with debris, the temperature of the liquid at the outlet of the drier would be cold.

In the example shown below, a temperature probe has been attached to the liquid line at the outlet of the condenser coil circuiting. The temperature probe is measuring the temperature of the liquid line and in this case indicates 107°F. The high pressure gauge indicates a liquid line pressure of 250 PSIG with R-22 as the refrigerant. From our earlier discussion, R-22 has a saturation temperature of 117°F at 250 PSIG.

Field Service Guide: Subcooling and Condensers

How Subcooling Changes

The amount of subcooling that occurs in the condenser will depend upon the refrigerant level in the condenser coil. If the refrigerant level is high, the pressure in the condenser will be high and the amount of liquid condensing will be great. This liquid will travel further into the condenser circuiting and will be further cooled. If the refrigerant level is low in the condenser, the pressure will be low and the amount of liquid that forms from the discharge gas will be less. The liquid will then not travel as far into the condenser circuiting and will therefore not have its temperature reduced as much as when it travels a further distance. The subcooling level in this state will be lower than when the refrigerant level is high.

The refrigerant level in the condenser will vary by how much refrigerant charge is in the system. <u>At high charge levels the subcooling will be high and at low charge levels the subcooling will be lower.</u>

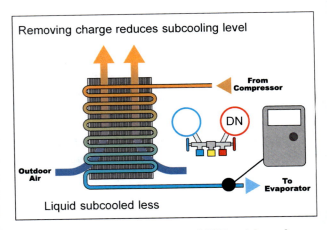

Removing charge reduces subcooling level

Liquid subcooled less

How Subcooling Changes W/Heat Load

If the metering device is a fixed piston type, changes in the indoor air heat load will also change the subcooling level. As heat load changes and suction pressure changes, the subcooling level will fluctuate. For example at low heat loads on the evaporator coil, the indoor coil will flood and the condenser will starve. The result will be low subcooling.

The Size of the Condenser Coil and Subcooling Design Levels

To get higher energy efficiencies, manufacturers of air conditioning systems need to keep the condensing pressure as low as possible without reducing liquid line pressure to a level that prevents the metering device from flowing adequate refrigerant into the evaporator circuiting. To lower condensing pressure, the size of the condenser coils is increased. The increase in size of the coils has resulted in higher levels of subcooling due to large charge levels in these systems. It is now common to see subcooling levels under normal charge being in a range of a minimum of around 10°F to a high of around 20°F. The subcooling requirements are typically printed on the condensing unit nameplate.

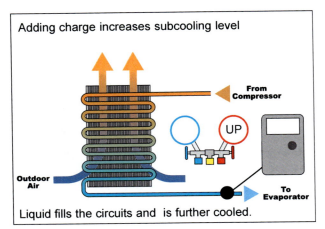

Adding charge increases subcooling level

Liquid fills the circuits and is further cooled.

Why Subcooling is Important

The liquid that exits the condenser coil must travel down the liquid line to the metering device. As the liquid travels down the line, its pressure keeps dropping due to friction between the moving liquid and pipe surface. There is also pressure loss that occurs when the liquid travels uphill to the evaporator coil. As the liquid pressure falls, the corresponding saturation temperature also drops.

This reduces the temperature difference between the saturation temperature and the liquid line temperature. In other words, the subcooling at the condenser coil outlet is greater than it is 20 feet down the liquid line.

In worst conditions, the liquid may reach a pressure where the saturation temperature for the pressure equals the temperature of the liquid. At that point, vapor will form along with the liquid. This is called flash gas.

The net affect of the flash gas will be poor refrigerant flow into the evaporator circuiting and wearing of the metering device orifice area.

To prevent this condition from occurring, it is important to charge systems so there is enough subcooling to overcome the pressure loss that occurs in liquid lines. The amount of subcooling that is needed will be determined by liquid line length, liquid lift, fittings, liquid line size, and overall condenser size.

R-22 liquid lines average maximum pressure loss is 30 PSIG. R-410A liquid line average maximum pressure loss is 50 PSIG. Systems need 10°F of subcooling to overcome these pressure losses.

Overcharging for more Subcooling may result in Abnormal Condensing Pressure

The condenser coil has only so much area for holding refrigerant. If the liquid line pressure drop is really large, adding charge to the system to increase the liquid subcooling level may in fact cause the condensing pressure to rise too high. The system will then operate with poor compressor performance and capacity.

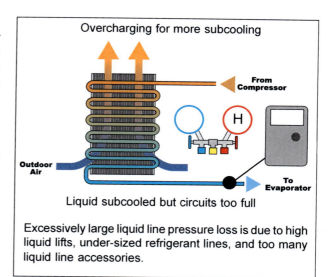

Overcharging for more subcooling

Liquid subcooled but circuits too full

Excessively large liquid line pressure loss is due to high liquid lifts, under-sized refrigerant lines, and too many liquid line accessories.

Field Service Guide: Subcooling and Condensers

Getting the right amount of Subcooling

Let's assume a system has a liquid subcooling level requirement of 10°F. The system uses R-22 refrigerant. The liquid line in this example has three pressure ports installed along its length. Each port will read lower pressure as the liquid travels down the liquid line. This is called pressure loss. In our example we did everything by the book. The liquid line pressure is operating at 220 PSIG at the condensing unit liquid service valve. This pressure has a corresponding saturation temperature of 108°F. The liquid temperature leaving the condenser coil is 98°F. Perfect. Now let's see if it works.

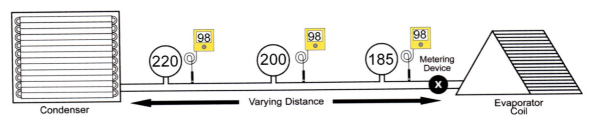

At the first gauge port on the liquid line the pressure is 220 PSIG with a liquid line temperature of 98°F. 220 PSIG = 108°F - 98°F = 10°F

At the second gauge port the pressure has dropped by 20 PSIG to 200 PSIG. The saturation temperature for 200 PSIG is 101°F. The liquid line is still 98°F. 101°F - 98°F = 3°F of subcooling.

Now the liquid goes to the last gauge port which has a pressure down to 185 PSIG. 185 PSIG has a saturation temperature of 96°F. The liquid is now 2 degrees above saturation temperature.

VAPOR WILL FORM IN THE LIQUID LINE. THINK OF REMOVING THE RADIATOR CAP ON A CAR. RELEASE PRESSURE AND IF THE WATER IS HOTTER THAN 212°F, WATER BOILS.

IN THIS EXAMPLE, SO WILL THE LIQUID REFRIGERANT.

The problem with this charge is the liquid line pressure is in excess of the maximum 30 PSIG R-22 limit for 10°F of subcooling. Solution is to add refrigerant. If condensing pressure goes way up, the capacity of the system will go way down. Better solution is to change the liquid line size to a larger size and reduce pressure drop.

R-410A PSIG	Saturation Temp. (F)	R-22 PSIG	R-410A PSIG	Saturation Temp. (F)	R-22 PSIG	R-410A PSIG	Saturation Temp. (F)	R-22 PSIG
12	-41	0	146	51	85	396	116	245
14	-36	2	154	54	90	400	117	250
16	-32	4	160	56	95	412	119	255
18	-28	6	168	59	100	416	120	260
22	-24	8	178	62	105	422	121	265
26	-20	10	184	64	110	434	123	270
30	-17	12	192	67	115	440	124	275
32	-14	14	198	69	120	450	126	280
36	-11	16	208	72	125	456	127	285
38	-8	18	216	74	130	462	128	290
42	-5	20	222	76	135	474	130	295
46	-2	22	230	78	140	482	131	300
48	0	24	240	81	145	494	133	310
50	2	26	248	83	150	512	136	320
54	5	28	256	85	155	526	138	330
58	7	30	262	87	160	544	141	340
60	9	32	270	89	165	560	143	350
64	11	34	280	91	170	572	145	360
68	13	36	288	93	175	596	148	370
70	15	38	292	94	180	608	150	380
74	17	40	300	96	185	624	152	390
78	19	42	308	98	190	640	154	400
80	21	44	318	100	195			
84	23	46	322	101	200			
86	24	48	330	103	205			
90	26	50	340	105	210			
98	30	55	346	106	215			
106	34	60	356	108	220			
114	38	65	364	110	225			
122	41	70	370	111	230			
128	44	75	380	113	235			
138	48	80	386	114	240			

Field Service Guide: Subcooling and Condensers

Subcooling Measurement for Techs

STEP 1

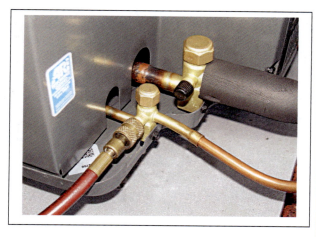

Attach high pressure gauge to the pressure port on the liquid line at the outdoor unit service valve.

STEP 2

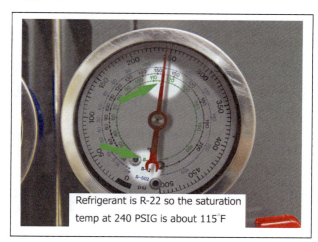

Refrigerant is R-22 so the saturation temp at 240 PSIG is about 115°F

Read the liquid line pressure and convert to saturation temperature. (Use the scale on the gauge or a temperature pressure table.)

STEP 3

Tools: **Digital Temperature Probe / Refrigerant Gauges**

Attach a digital temperature probe to the liquid line near the gauge port. Measure the temperature of the liquid line. It may take up to 20 minutes for the liquid line temperature to become stable following a change in charge level.

STEP 4

115.0°F (saturation temp found in step 2)
-102.7°F (temp of liquid line from step 3)
―――――――――――――――――――――――
12.3°F subcooling temp

Subtract the liquid line temperature from the saturation temperature corresponding to the liquid line pressure. The difference in temperature is the subcooling level.

Allow up to 20 minutes from charge changes to measure liquid subcooling.

7

Field Service Guide: Subcooling and Condensers

Problems in the Condenser

Dirt

The most common problem encountered with condenser coils is dirt and other airborne particles that become trapped on the surface of the condenser coil. The dirt insulates the refrigerant from the outdoor air and reduces the amount of heat that is rejected from the refrigerant. The pressure in the condenser will be elevated and the liquid line will be hot.

The excess condensing pressure and elevated liquid temperature will reduce the system capacity. The excess pressure reduces the volumetric efficiency of the compressor and the liquid carrying heat back to the evaporator circuit. The excess liquid heat may cause the formation of flash gas in the liquid line.

Specially formulated coil cleaners are used to clean off the debris from the coil. Some cleaners are acid based and others are environmentally friendly.

Non Condensable Gasses

Sometimes gasses that cannot be condensed at pressures found in the condenser are introduced into the system by accident. These gasses are typically nitrogen, oxygen, and carbon dioxide. When refrigerant charge is added to a system that contains these gasses, the non condensable gasses take up space inside the condenser coil circuiting. The condensing pressure will be high and heat transfer from the refrigerant to the outdoor air will be low. The liquid line will be hot and subcooling will be low.

Checking for Non Condensable Gasses

Tools | Digital Temperature Probe
Refrigerant Gauges
Recovery Cylinder

STEP 1

If non condensable gas is suspected in a system, the refrigerant charge should be recovered into an evacuated recovery cylinder.

Field Service Guide: Subcooling and Condensers

STEP 2

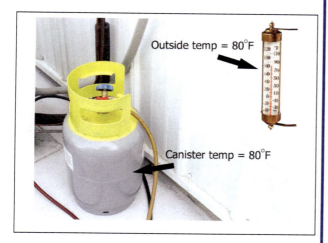

Let the cylinder sit until the cylinder temperature and the surrounding air temperature are equal.

STEP 3

Measure the pressure in the recovery cylinder. The pressure in the cylinder should be equal to the saturation temperature for the outdoor air temperature.

NOTE:
For example, if the refrigerant is R-22 and the outdoor air temperature is 100°F, the pressure should read 200 PSIG. If the pressure is higher, then non condensable gasses are in the recovery cylinder. If the pressure equals the corresponding outdoor air/saturation temperature, there are no non condensable gasses in the cylinder.

Restrictions in Condenser Circuits

It is very rare to ever have a refrigerant restriction in a condenser circuit. If a restriction were present, the compressor IPR (Internal Pressure Relief) valve would likely open or if a high pressure switch were on the unit, the switch would shut the system off. For example, if one of the two circuits (shown on the following page) had a restriction in it, the area of the condenser coil would be reduced and it is likely the system would go off on high condensing pressure.

To find a restriction in a condenser coil, the system must be operating. This may not be possible if the restriction is great enough to cause excessive discharge pressure.

Field Service Guide: Subcooling and Condensers

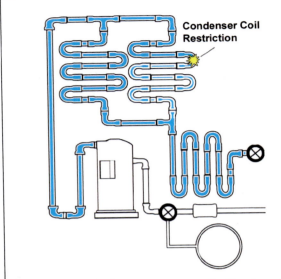

The restriction in the compressor coil will reduce surface area of the condenser. The restriction can be found with a digital thermometer.

Checking for Restrictions in Condenser Circuits

Tools: Digital Temperature Probe

STEP 1

Run the system.

STEP 2

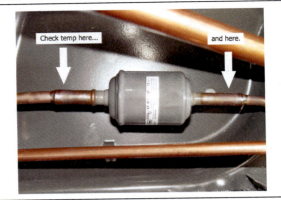

If there is a liquid line drier at the outlet of the subcooling loop, check the temperature of the liquid at the inlet and outlet of the drier. There should be no more than a 3°F drop in temperature across the drier. Replace the drier if needed. If there is no temperature drop detected, move to step 3.

STEP 3

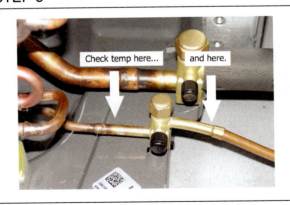

Check the temperature of the liquid as it enters and leaves the outdoor liquid line service valve. There should not be more than 3°F of temperature change if any at all. If excess temperature drop is detected, make sure the valve is open all of the way. If there is no excessive temperature drop, move to step 4.

Field Service Guide: Subcooling and Condensers

STEP 4

Measure the temperature of the refrigerant lines at the individual outlets of the condenser coil parallel circuits. The temperatures will vary based upon air flow pattern from the condenser fan. No outlet temperature should be cooler than the

outdoor air. If a low temperature is detected, there is a pressure drop in the circuit where the temperature drop is detected. Repair or replace the coil as needed. If no noticeable temperature drop is found, go to step 5.

STEP 5

If the condenser coil has a subcooling loop, check the temperature at the exit of the subcooling loop. The temperature of the liquid should not be colder than the outside air temperature. If it is, there is a pressure drop in the subcooling loop circuit. If no problem is found, condenser is OK.

Summary

Find the saturation temperature of the refrigerant based upon high pressure to determine the condensing temperature.

Subcooling makes liquid refrigerant pure liquid without bubbles.

The amount or level of subcooling needed will depend upon the condenser coil size and liquid line design.

The refrigerant leaving a condenser circuit should never be below the temperature of the air hitting the condenser coil.

**Suction and
Liquid Lines**

**Suction and
Liquid Lines**

Field Service Guide: Line Sets

Chapter
Suction and Liquid Line Audits

Table of Contents

Suction Lines 2
    Introduction to Suction Lines 2
    ASHRAE Recommended Limits for Suction Line Pressure Drop 2
    Piping Connection Size on Outdoor Unit Service Valves................................. 2
    Pipe Sizing Tables 3
    How to use the charts to audit the potential pressure drop in a suction line 4
    R-410A Suction Line Performance Versus R-22 Systems................................ 6
    Identifying a pressure drop in the suction line that is caused by a kink 8
    Buried Suction Lines... 8
If Improper Suction Line Sizing is Detected Beware of the Charge....................... 8
    If Improper Suction Line Sizing is Detected Beware of Compressor Liquid Migration........... 9
    R-410A Versus R-22 Suction Line Capacity 9
    Un-insulated Lines 9
    R-410A systems can be used on existing line sets to increase capacity.............. 9
    Placing a pressure tap in the suction line at the outlet of the evaporator circuit.......... 9
    Suction Line Audit Worksheet... 10
    Suction Line Summary.. 11
    Section Quiz 11
Auditing Liquid Lines.. 12
    Introduction 12
    Subcooled liquid and its role in proper system operation 12
    Causes of flash gas formation 12
    How the liquid line can cause flash gas to form.. 13
    Subcooling requirement versus liquid line pressure drop 14
    Pressure Drop Allowances... 14
    Flash Gas With Proper Charge... 14
    Pressure loss in liquid lines 14
    How to audit liquid lines for proper size 15
    Now let's plot the job onto the R-410A Piping Chart...................................... 18
    R-410A Liquid Line Performance Summary 19
    Tapping the liquid line at the end of the liquid line to confirm subcooling 19
    Systems operating with flash gas present 19
    Liquid Line Summary 19
    Section Quiz 20
    R-22 Liquid Line Sizing Worksheet.. 21
    R-410A Liquid Line Sizing Worksheet 22

Field Service Guide: Line Sets

Suction Lines

Introduction to suction lines

Suction lines connect the evaporator outlet to the inlet of the compressor. The line carries the suction vapor and compressor oil back to the compressor. Improperly sized suction lines can lead to low system capacity, improper charge and poor oil return to the compressor. Technicians working on split system heat pumps and air conditioning systems need to know how to audit the suction line to ensure it is properly sized.

The importance of recognizing a potential pressure drop problem with a suction line prior to charging the system cannot be overstated. Since the suction pressure port is at the outdoor

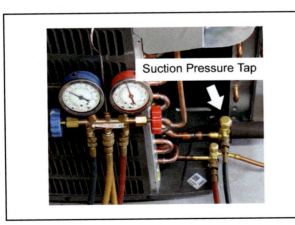
Suction Pressure Tap

condensing unit location, the servicing technician may in fact be charging downstream from a large pressure drop caused by an undersized line or a possible kink in the line. If the technician does not identify the problem, he will tend to overcharge the system in an attempt to achieve proper suction pressure.

ASHRAE Recommended Limits for Suction Line Pressure Drop

ASHRAE standards for suctions lines recommend a maximum pressure drop of 3 PSIG for R-22 systems and a maximum of 5 PSIG for R-410A systems. These pressure drop allowances if followed will limit the capacity loss of either type system to a maximum of 3% of its rated cooling capacity.

(R-22 loses 1% capacity for every 1 PSIG of suction pressure drop. R-410A loses .6% capacity for every 1 PSIG of suction pressure drop.)

Piping Connection Size on Outdoor Unit Service Valves

The connection size on the outdoor condensing unit is not always used to select the suction line size. The connection size is for a standard line length of 25 feet used during the certification testing for the condensing unit. If the suction line length is longer than 25 feet, and the standard connection size is used, the pressure loss in the line may be excessive. To properly determine what line size should be used when the outdoor unit and indoor evaporator coil distance exceeds 25 feet, special pipe sizing charts are used.

Field Service Guide: Line Sets

Pipe Sizing Tables

Here are two pipe sizing tables courtesy of The Trane Company. The table on the right is used for sizing R-22 suction lines and the chart on the left is used for sizing R-410A suction lines. The charts list the system capacity, suction line size, and how much pressure the line will drop at 100 equivalent feet of pipe. Equivalent feet of piping is the sum of the linear length of the pipe and the equivalent feet of each fitting used in the line. (See Table 3) At the pipe size combinations shown on these tables, proper oil return can be maintained to the compressor.

Table 1

R-410A Suction Line Sizing Table		
Tons	Tube Size Inches	PD/100ft Equiv.
1.5	1/2 5/8 3/4	10.8 3.1 1.2
2.0	5/8 3/4 7/8	5.4 2.0 .9
2.5	5/8 3/4 7/8	8.2 3.0 1.3
3	5/8 3/4 7/8	11.7 4.3 1.9
3.5	3/4 7/8	5.8 2.5
4.0	3/4 7/8 1-1/8	7.4 3.2 .9
5.0	3/4 7/8 1-1/8	11.5 4.9 1.3

Courtesy of The Trane Company

Table 2

R-22 Suction Line Sizing Table		
Tons	Tube Size Inches	PD/100ft Equiv.
1.5	5/8 3/4	4.7 1.8
2.0	5/8 3/4 7/8	8.1 3.0 1.3
2.5	5/8 3/4 7/8	12.7 4.6 2.0
3	3/4 7/8	6.5 2.8
3.5	3/4 7/8 1-1/8	8.8 3.8 1.0
4.0	7/8 1-1/8	4.9 1.3
5.0	7/8 1-1/8 1-3/8	7.5 2.0 .7

Courtesy of The Trane Company

Table 3

Equivalent Length Brazed Elbows (Feet)		
OD Tube (In.)	Short Radius	Long Radius
5/8	5.7	3.9
3/4	6.5	4.5
7/8	7.3	5.3
1-1/8	2.7	1.9
1-3/8	---	---

Use Table 3 to determine how many feet of pipe each elbow equals. Next add the linear length of pipe to the equivalent elbow distance. The result is the Total Equivalent Feet of the suction line. It highly unlikely the result will equal 100 feet but it will equal a % of 100 feet. Take the length of the line for example, 65 feet and divide that number by 100. The result if less than 100 feet will look like this: .65. To determine the total pressure drop, multiply the PD/100 ft value times .65 for example: .65 X 11.7 = 7.6 PSIG loss.

3

Field Service Guide: Line Sets

How to use the charts to audit the potential pressure drop in a suction line

The charts are very easy to use and will calculate an approximate pressure drop that will occur at peak system performance. This audit procedure should be performed on all service calls to confirm there is not an excessive pressure drop in the suction line prior to charging of the system.

Step 1	Identify the type of refrigerant used in the system and select the proper chart.	*Let's assume the system is an R-22 unit that has been installed for a few years. We would select the R-22 Suction Line Sizing chart to begin the audit.*
Step 2	Identify the line size and tonnage of the system. Use the table to determine the pressure drop PD that would occur at 100 equivalent feet of suction line.	*If the system were a 2 ton system and the line size installed was 5/8 the chart indicates that a pressure drop of 8.1 PSIG would occur at 100 equivalent feet of piping.*

R-22 Suction Line Sizing Table

Tons	Tube Size Inches	PD/100ft Equiv.
1.5	5/8	4.7
	3/4	1.8
2.0	5/8	8.1
	3/4	3.0
	7/8	1.3
2.5	5/8	12.7
	3/4	4.6
	7/8	2.0
3	3/4	6.5
	7/8	2.8
3.5	3/4	8.8
	7/8	3.8
	1-1/8	1.0
4.0	7/8	4.9
	1-1/8	1.3
5.0	7/8	7.5
	1-1/8	2.0
	1-3/8	.7

Courtesy of The Trane Company

Step 3	Measure the linear length of the suction line.	*In this example let's say the line length is 40 feet long. This length is not the equivalent length, it is the linear length.*

Field Service Guide: Line Sets

Step 4	Count the number of elbows in the line and identify whether they are short radius or long radius elbows.	*In this example, the line has 6 short radius 90 degree elbows installed between the evaporator coil and the outdoor condensing unit.*
Step 5	Reference the Equivalent Length Fitting Table to determine how many feet in pipe each fitting is equal to.	*(table below)*

Equivalent Length Brazed Elbows (Feet)

OD Tube (In.)	Short Radius	Long Radius
5/8	5.7	3.9
3/4	6.5	4.5
7/8	7.3	5.3
1-1/8	2.7	1.9
1-3/8	---	---

Each 90 degree short radius elbow is worth 5.7 feet of pipe.

Step 6	Add up the total length of piping that all of the fittings equal.	*There are 6 elbows in the line. 5.7 feet X 6 elbows = 34.2 feet*
Step 7	Add the total linear length of pipe to the total length of pie due to fittings. The sum is the total equivalent length of the suction line.	*40 linear feet of copper pipe + 34.2 feet due to fittings = 74.2 equivalent feet of pipe*
Step 8	Divide the equivalent length of the line by 100 to determine the multiplier to use in Step 9.	*74.2/100 = .742*
Step 9	From Step 2 find the Pressure Drop PD per 100 feet of pipe for the system. Multiply this value by the multiplier calculated in Step 8. The result is the approximate pressure drop that will occur when system capacity is max.	*In our example we had 8.1 Pressure drop per 100 feet of pipe from Step 2.* *We multiply .742 X 8.1 which equals **6 PSIG of pressure loss.**_*
Step 10	If the pressure drop is within ASHRAE standards, the capacity loss caused by the line is within acceptable limits.	*ASHRAE standards recommend a maximum 3 PSIG of pressure loss in the suction line for R-22 systems. The estimated pressure drop in this example is way above this limit and will cause a **6%** loss of system capacity.* *If operating costs are excessive, or there is a lack of cooling complaint, the line will need to be replaced.*

Field Service Guide: Line Sets

R-410A Suction Line Performance Versus R-22 Systems

Let's re-audit the line set we just checked with R-22 and see what would have happened if the system had used R-410A refrigerant.

Step 1	Identify the type of refrigerant used in the system and select the proper chart.	*With R-410A systems we have a maximum pressure drop allowance of 5 PSIG and would use this chart.*
Step 2	Identify the line size and tonnage of the system. Use the table to determine the pressure drop PD that would occur at 100 equivalent feet of suction line.	*Let's compare the same job only this time we will use R-410A as the system refrigerant. The line is 5/8 and fthe table, the PD/100 feet is now 5.4 PSIG.*

R-410A Suction Line Sizing Table

Tons	Tube Size Inches	PD/100ft Equiv.
1.5	1/2	10.8
	5/8	3.1
	3/4	1.2
2.0	5/8	5.4
	3/4	2.0
	7/8	.9
2.5	5/8	8.2
	3/4	3.0
	7/8	1.3
3	5/8	11.7
	3/4	4.3
	7/8	1.9
3.5	3/4	5.8
	7/8	2.5
4.0	3/4	7.4
	7/8	3.2
	1-1/8	.9
5.0	3/4	11.5
	7/8	4.9
	1-1/8	1.3

Courtesy of The Trane Company

Step 3	Measure the linear length of the suction line.	*The line length is 40 feet long. This length is not the equivalent length, it is the linear length.*

Step 4	Count the number of elbows in the line and identify whether they are short radius or long radius elbows.	*In this example, the line has 6 short radius 90 degree elbows installed between the evaporator coil and the outdoor condensing unit.*
Step 5	Reference the Equivalent Length Fitting Table to determine how many feet in pipe each fitting is equal to.	(see table below)

Equivalent Length Brazed Elbows (Feet)

OD Tube (In.)	Short Radius	Long Radius
5/8	5.7	3.9
3/4	6.5	4.5
7/8	7.3	5.3
1-1/8	2.7	1.9
1-3/8	---	---

Each 90 degree short radius elbow is worth 5.7 feet of pipe.

Step 6	Add up the total length of piping that all of the fittings equal.	*There are 6 elbows in the line. 5.7 feet X 6 elbows = 34.2 feet*
Step 7	Add the total linear length of pipe to the total length of pie due to fittings. The sum is the total equivalent length of the suction line.	*40 linear feet of copper pipe + 34.2 feet due to fittings = 74.2 equivalent feet of pipe*
Step 8	Divide the equivalent length of the line by 100 to determine the multiplier to use in Step 9.	*74.2/100 = .742*
Step 9	From Step 2 find the Pressure Drop PD per 100 feet of pipe for the system. Multiply this value by the multiplier calculated in Step 8. The result is the approximate pressure drop that will occur when system capacity is max.	*In our example we had 5.4 PSIG Pressure drop per 100 feet of pipe from Step 2.* *We multiply .742 X 5.4 which equals **4 PSIG of pressure loss.***
Step 10	If the pressure drop is within ASHRAE standards, the capacity loss caused by the line is within acceptable limits.	*ASHRAE standards recommend a maximum 5 PSIG of pressure loss in the suction line for R-410A systems. The estimated pressure drop in this example is well below this limit and will cause around a 2% loss of system capacity.*

Field Service Guide: Line Sets

Identifying a pressure drop in the suction line that is caused by a kink

At times, an installer may fold over a suction line during an installation as he attempts to bend the pipe. Most attempts at correcting the kink in the copper tubing involve the use of Channel Lock pliers crimping the tubing to try and round it off. The result is a pressure drop in the pipe.

Since refrigerants drop temperature as they drop their pressure, a touch type thermometer can be used to find a potential pressure drop by checking for a temperature drop across the suspected kink. A temperature drop that is 2F across the kink indicates a pressure drop that is 3 PSIG for R-22 and 5 PSIG for R-410A.

Without taking into account piping pressure drop, the kink at this temperature drop uses up all of the allowable pressure drop allowance for the line and will drop the system capacity by at least 3%. So in summary, a temperature drop across a kink that is 2F or greater is excessive and should be corrected.

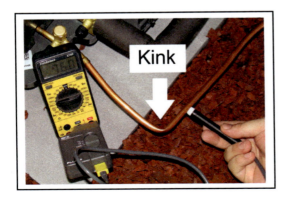

Restricted suction line driers will also cause a suction line pressure drop.

Buried Suction Lines

Refrigerant will migrate to the coldest point of the system during off cycle shut down. If the suction line is buried in the ground or concrete floor, refrigerant liquid will migrate to the buried portion of the line. When the compressor is started, the compressor will receive a slug of liquid refrigerant courtesy of the suction line.

If this problem is pre-existing, it is likely that compressor bearing wear is occurring due to liquid refrigerant floodback during start mode. The compressor may also experience starting problems.

The addition of a suction line accumulator at the outdoor unit will help prevent further damage to the system. The accumulator will try to catch the liquid as it slugs back to the condensing unit from the buried suction line.

If Improper Suction Line Sizing is Detected Beware of the Charge

When servicing a system where the suction line is determined to have excessive pressure loss, it is likely that someone may have added refrigerant in an attempt to set the suction pressure to the proper level. The overcharged condition will need to be corrected. When the line is undersized and is causing excessive pressure loss, adding a line tap on the suction line at the outlet of the evaporator coil to check system evaporator superheat may be necessary to acheive normal evaporator superheat level.

Field Service Guide: Line Sets

If Improper Suction Line Sizing is Detected Beware of Compressor Liquid Migration

Excessive charge requires the addition of a crankcase heater at the compressor. Systems that operate with small suction lines tend to be overcharged in an attempt to make the pressures look better to the technician attempting a charge. Excess charge may cause scroll compressors to flood during early morning starts due to liquid migration during off cycle periods. Adding a crankcase heater to the compressor will help prevent liquid refrigerant from migrating into the compressor shell during off cycle periods.

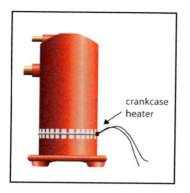
crankcase heater

R-410A Versus R-22 Suction Line Capacity

It is pretty obvious that R-410A systems have better performance in suction lines when compared to R-22 systems. In some cases, informed technicians can recommend changing out an existing R-22 system to R-410A when it is impractical to change out the line sets due to excessive run length, lack of accessibility or economics.

Un-insulated Lines

Refrigerant lines that are lacking pipe insulation will pick up heat into the cold suction vapor This heat, if obtained from outdoor air, will decrease the capacity of the system and will contribute to excessive compressor heat.

R-410A systems can be used on existing line sets to increase capacity

In some cases, it may be possible to correct system capacity problems by changing out R-22 systems and replacing them with an R-410A system when the capacity drop is due to excessive suction line pressure loss. Re-using existing line sets by clearing out the mineral oil left in the line can be accomplished with flush kits that are available at local wholesalers. A very popular flush kit called RX11 Flush is marketed by Nu-Calgon and sold at many HVAC wholesalers. Always check with your equipment supplier to ensure the manufacturer of the air conditioning system approves the use of flush solvents in their systems prior to using.

Placing a pressure tap in the suction line at the outlet of the evaporator circuit

When excessive pressure drop is present, a pressure tap should be installed at the outlet of the evaporator circuit. Measure the suction pressure at this port and then compare it to the suction pressure at the outdoor unit service valve. In situations where the suction line size problem cannot be corrected, it is best to charge the system at the indoor pressure tap port if using the superheat method. This will ensure the system is charged using the true evaporator superheat conditions.

Field Service Guide: Line Sets

Suction Line Audit Worksheet

Refrigerant Type: R-22   R-410A   System Tons: _____   Line Size: _____   *PD/100 Feet:* ____ *PSIG*

Fitting and refrigerant line Information

Line Linear Length: _____ ft.
Number of Short Radius Elbows: ____   Equivalent ft each: ____Ft X Total Equivalent Feet = _____ft.
Number of Long Radius Elbows: ____   Equivalent ft each: ____Ft X Total Equivalent Feet = _____ft.
Total Equivalent Feet Elbows Plus Linear Feet of line   =   Total Equivalent Line Length of _____ft.

Total Pressure Drop Calculation

Total Equivalent Line Length (_____ / 100 = _____) X   PD/100 ft _____ = _____ PSIG DROP

Capacity Loss Calculation

R-410A   PSIG DROP X .6 = Capacity Loss
R-22   PSIG DROP X   1 = Capacity Loss

PSIG DROP _____   X ____ = _____%

R-410A Suction Line Sizing Table

Tons	Tube Size Inches	PD/100ft Equiv.
1.5	1/2	10.8
	5/8	3.1
	3/4	1.2
2.0	5/8	5.4
	3/4	2.0
	7/8	.9
2.5	5/8	8.2
	3/4	3.0
	7/8	1.3
3	5/8	11.7
	3/4	4.3
	7/8	1.9
3.5	3/4	5.8
	7/8	2.5
4.0	3/4	7.4
	7/8	3.2
	1-1/8	.9
5.0	3/4	11.5
	7/8	4.9
	1-1/8	1.3

Courtesy of The Trane Company

R-22 Suction Line Sizing Table

Tons	Tube Size Inches	PD/100ft Equiv.
1.5	5/8	4.7
	3/4	1.8
2.0	5/8	8.1
	3/4	3.0
	7/8	1.3
2.5	5/8	12.7
	3/4	4.6
	7/8	2.0
3	3/4	6.5
	7/8	2.8
3.5	3/4	8.8
	7/8	3.8
	1-1/8	1.0
4.0	7/8	4.9
	1-1/8	1.3
5.0	7/8	7.5
	1-1/8	2.0
	1-3/8	.7

Courtesy of The Trane Company

Equivalent Length Brazed Elbows (Feet)

OD Tube (In.)	Short Radius	Long Radius
5/8	5.7	3.9
3/4	6.5	4.5
7/8	7.3	5.3
1-1/8	2.7	1.9
1-3/8	---	---

Courtesy of The Trane Company

Suction Line Summary

Suction lines drop pressure. For R-22 systems, every 1 PSIG of pressure drop results in 1% capacity loss. R-410A loses .6% capacity for ever 1 PSIG of suction line pressure drop.

3% is about the maximum a system should lose. Some systems may slightly exceed this value. It is then a decision of economy as to whether to leave the system as is or make a change.

R-410A has better performance in suction lines when compared against R-22 performance.

Suction lines can be re-used when changing from one refrigerant to another. The lines should be cleaned to remove any residual oils and other contaminants.

Kinks cause pressure drop. Check for excessive temperature drop across deformations in a suction line tube. A 2F temperature drop indicates a pressure loss that is equal to the total recommended loss of the line itself.

Section Quiz

1. An R-22 3 ton system has a 3/4 inch suction line. The line is 40 feet long and has 6 short radius elbows. Using the Suction Line Audit Worksheet, determine the total pressure loss of the line and the capacity loss that will occur due to suction line pressure drop.

2. An R-410A 5 ton system has a 7/8 inch suction line. The line is 65 feet long and has 4 long radius elbows. Using the Suction line Audit Worksheet determine the total pressure loss of the line and the capacity loss that will occur due to suction line pressure drop.

3. An R-410A 2 ton system has a 5/8 inch suction line. The line is 30 feet long and has 5 long radius elbows. Using the Suction line Audit Worksheet determine the total pressure loss of the line and the capacity loss that will occur due to suction line pressure drop.

4. An R-22 5 ton system has a 7/8 inch suction line. The line is 80 feet long and has 7 long radius elbows. Using the Suction line Audit Worksheet determine the total pressure loss of the line and the capacity loss that will occur due to suction line pressure drop.

Next, calculate the performance of the line using an R-410A system and determine the total pressure drop and capacity loss that would occur if the line had an R-410A system installed.

5. An R-22 2.5 ton system has a 3/4 inch suction line. The line is 50 feet long. There are 6 short radius elbows installed in the line. Is the line performance within ASHRAE standards?

END

Answers:

Field Service Guide: Line Sets

Auditing Liquid Lines

Introduction

The liquid line connects the condensing unit to the inlet of the metering device. The liquid line flows refrigerant at high pressure and the line is quite small. The small line size and the high pressure cause a high pressure drop to be present between the outdoor unit and inlet to the metering device. If the pressure drop is excessive, due to improper line sizing, the system may experience low capacity, compressor failure and potential damage to the metering device.

Technicians who are investigating poor system performance or compressor failures, should know how to inspect and audit the liquid line circuit to rule out any potential problem caused by the line.

Subcooled liquid and its role in proper system operation

The role of subcooled liquid and the liquid line are extremely important to overall system performance and reliability. In a subcooled state, the refrigerant is colder than the saturation temperature for a given pressure and is pure liquid. Subcooling should occur late in the condenser coil circuiting and should be present all the way from the condensing unit outlet to the inlet of the metering device. If the refrigerant at the inlet to the metering device is saturated, or superheated, vapor will be present in the liquid line and the metering device will not feed adequate refrigerant volume to the evaporator. This condition is called flash gas. The presence of flash gas will result in a system that is operating with a starved evaporator coil.

Symptoms of flash gas include noisy liquid lines, overheating compressors, high superheat, low system capacity and intermittent comfort complaints.

Causes of flash gas formation

Flash gas can form from an undercharged system where there is inadequate subcooling. Inadequate subcooling means there is not enough of it to overcome the pressure drop of the liquid line.

Flash gas can also form when the pressure drop in the liquid line is greater than the amount of pressure drop that can be overcome by the amount of liquid subcooling present. This means that even if the system is properly charged, if the liquid line is too small, or has too many pressure dropping components, flash gas will still form.

Flash gas can also form from an uninsulated liquid line running through hot spaces or in direct sunlight where the line is heated and subcooling lost. Let's take a closer look at subcooling and the liquid line to gain a better understanding.

Field Service Guide: Line Sets

How the liquid line can cause flash gas to form
The liquid line receives a subcooled liquid

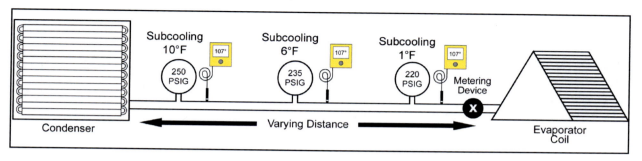

from the condensing coil. The pressure at the inlet of the line is let's say 250 PSIG with R-22 pressure. At 250 PSIG, R-22 is at a condensing temperature of 117F. In this example, the liquid line is 107F which is 10F cooler than the saturation temperature of 117F. The liquid at this pressure port is therefore subcooled by 10 degrees and is in a pure liquid form.

A second pressure port is approached by the liquid. At this pressure port the liquid line pressure has dropped to 235 PSIG. At 235 PSIG, R-22 is at a saturation temperature of 113F, the 107F liquid reaches this port and the subcooling has now dropped to 6F. Since the liquid is still cooler than the corresponding condensing temperature at the second gauge port, the refrigerant is still in a subcooled state and is pure liquid.

Now the 107F liquid reaches a third gauge port at the end of the liquid line. The pressure at this gauge port is 220 PSIG. At 220 PSIG, R-22 is at a saturation temperature of 108F. The refrigerant at this point is still subcooled by 1 degree and will remain pure liquid. If the line pressure at the last port were to drop below 220 PSIG due to improper (too small) of liquid line sizing, the refrigerant would flash partially to vapor.

If the liquid line were not insulated and were running through a hot attic, the heat from the attic could increase the refrigerant temperature above 107F which would return the refrigerant to a saturated state where vapor would form in the line.

In this example you can see that the amount of subcooling that is measured at the condensing unit is not the amount of subcooling that is present at the end of the liquid line. In many cases, sight glasses are improperly installed at the outdoor condensing unit. Other than a moisture indicator, the glass provides no information as to the condition of the liquid as it gets to the end of the line. It is best to install a sight glass at the end of the liquid line to get a look at the condition of the liquid as it enters the metering device.

Field Service Guide: Line Sets

Subcooling requirement versus liquid line pressure drop

The relationship between the amount of subcooling in the condenser and the liquid line pressure drop show that 10 degrees of subcooling with R-22 refrigerant can run down a liquid line that drops a maximum of 30 PSIG. This relationship is standard for R-22 liquid lines. Systems that can subcool by 12F can run down a larger pressure drop of up to 35 PSIG. In summary, the more the condenser can subcool the liquid, the greater the amount of liquid line pressure loss allowed.

Pressure Drop Allowances

The piping tables in this chapter are courtesy of The Trane Company. These tables are based upon the following charging criteria:

R-22 @ 10F subcooling = 30 PSIG Max.
R-22 @ 12F Subcooling = 35 PSIG Max.
R-410A @ 10F Subcooling = 50 PSIG Max.

Flash Gas With Proper Charge

From our example it should be clear that if the charge is properly set by the technician using the subcooling method, yet the liquid line is undersized, the system will still malfunction and form flash gas. The charge level of subcooling establishes the maximum amount of pressure the liquid line can drop. If the charge is low, and the liquid line is properly sized, flash gas will occur. If the charge is normal, and the liquid line is too small, flash gas will form. When flash gas is present, system capacity is low and the compressor will run hot. Auditing the liquid line will confirm if the liquid line is capable of delivering pure liquid to the TXV.

Pressure loss in liquid lines

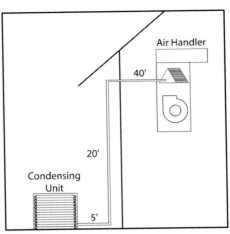

The pressure drop that takes place in the liquid line is due to friction loss, accessories and liquid line lift. (Lift is when the condenser is located below the evaporator coil.) When auditing the estimated pressure drop in the line, all of these factors must be taken into consideration. For example, a properly sized liquid line drier when new, dry, and clean will drop 1 PSIG. Once the drier loads with debris the pressure drop will increase.

The pressure drop due to liquid lift is calculated by pounds of drop per foot of lift. R-22 systems will drop .5 PSIG for every 1 foot of liquid lift. R-410A systems will drop .43 PSIG for every 1 foot of liquid lift.

The pressure drop due to friction can be calculated using special piping tables. The table shown here is courtesy of The Trane Company. In these tables, the equivalent length of the line is calculated and then plotted onto the table to determine the estimated pressure drop of the line. If the pressure loss is greater than the subcooling charge can overcome, the line must be re-sized.

Field Service Guide: Line Sets

How to audit liquid lines for proper size

To audit the liquid line to ensure proper line sizing, Liquid Line Pipe Sizing Tables are used. The table below is used for auditing R-22 and liquid lines used with residential systems. This chapter contains both this table and another table for auditing R-410A liquid lines. The tables give you the maximum allowable pressure drop allowance based upon the subcooling capability of the condensing unit and then plots the liquid line equivalent length against line size and capacity to determine the estimated total pressure loss of the line. If the loss exceeds the Maximum Allowable Drop, the line is either too small, there are too many fittings in the line or the lift is too high.

In the next few pages we will use these tables to audit the liquid line on both an R-22 system and then an R-410A system.

R-22 Liquid Line Sizing Table

Maximum Allowable Pressure Drop
 10F Subcooling = 30 PSIG
 12F Subcooling = 35 PSIG
 Subtract From Maximum Allowable Any Lift Pressure Drop .50 PSIG X _____Ft. of lift = _____LOSS
 Total Available PSIG After any Lift Loss = _____PSIG Maximum piping pressure drop

Tube OD	Rated BTUH	20'	40'	60'	80'	100'	120'	140'	160'	180'	200'	220'	240'
1/4"	18000	6.0	12.0	18.1	24.1	30.1	-	-	-	-	-	-	-
	24000	10.2	20.3	30.5	-	-	-	-	-	-	-	-	-
5/16"	18000	1.6	3.2	4.7	6.3	7.9	9.5	11.1	12.6	14.2	15.8	17.4	19.0
	24000	2.7	5.3	8.0	10.6	13.3	16.0	18.6	21.3	23.9	26.6	29.3	31.9
	30000	4.0	8.0	11.9	15.9	19.9	23.9	27.9	31.8	-	-	-	-
	36000	5.5	11.1	16.6	22.2	27.7	33.2	-	-	-	-	-	-
	42000	7.3	14.6	22.0	29.3	-	-	-	-	-	-	-	-
3/8"	18000	0.6	1.1	1.7	2.2	2.8	3.4	3.9	4.5	5.0	5.6	6.2	6.7
	24000	0.9	1.9	2.8	3.8	4.7	5.6	6.6	7.5	8.5	9.4	10.3	11.3
	30000	1.4	2.8	4.2	5.6	7.0	8.4	9.8	11.2	12.6	14.0	15.4	16.8
	36000	1.9	3.9	5.8	7.8	9.7	11.6	13.6	15.5	17.5	19.4	21.3	23.3
	42000	2.6	5.1	7.7	10.2	12.8	15.4	17.9	20.5	23.0	25.6	28.2	30.7
	48000	3.3	6.5	9.8	13.0	16.3	19.6	2.8	26.1	29.3	32.6	-	-
	60000	4.9	9.8	14.7	19.6	24.5	29.4	34.3	-	-	-	-	-
1/2"	36000	0.4	0.8	1.2	1.6	2.0	2.4	2.8	3.2	3.6	4.0	4.4	4.8
	42000	0.5	1.0	1.6	2.1	2.6	3.1	3.6	4.2	4.7	5.2	5.7	6.2
	48000	0.7	1.3	2.0	2.6	3.3	4.0	4.6	5.3	5.9	6.6	7.3	7.9
	60000	1.0	2.0	3.0	4.0	5.0	6.0	7.0	8.0	9.0	10.0	11.3	12.0

Courtesy of The Trane Company

Field Service Guide: Line Sets

How to audit liquid lines for proper size

Step 1	Determine which type of refrigerant is being used and select the proper liquid line sizing table. Measure the operating subcooling of the system.	*Let's say the system is R-22 and operates with 10F subcooling. We will use the table on page 17 for our example. It is the R-22 Liquid Line Sizing Table.*
Step 2	Measure the length of the liquid line. Take note of the pipe size and capacity of the system.	*The line size in this example is a 5/16" line and the capacity of the system is 42,000BTUH. The line is 65 feet long.*
Step 3	Count the number of elbow fittings and solenoid valves on the line.	*The line has 6 long radius elbows with no liquid line solenoid valve or drier.*
Step 4	Determine the equivalent length of copper for all fittings in the line using the Equivalent length table for fittings. (Note the table is for brazed fittings. Error on the safe side and use these lengths for copper bends.)	*There are 6 long radius elbows that equal from our chart 3.1 ft. of pipe each. 3.1 ft. X 6 = about 18.6 feet of piping. Let's round this off to 19 feet.*
Step 5	Add the linear pipe length to the equivalent length of fittings to determine the total equivalent length of the liquid line.	*65 feet of linear line + 19 feet for fittings = 84 equivalent feet of piping.*
Step 6	Determine if there is liquid lift. Multiply the lift length X the multiplier on the piping table. This will determine how much pressure is lost in the lift process. <u>This pressure loss must be subtracted from the allowable maximum liquid line loss.</u> The pressure that remains after subtracting the lift pressure loss is the maximum the line can lose due to friction drop and any additional liquid line components such as liquid line filter driers.	*There is 20 feet of lift at the job. From our chart each foot of lift will cost .5 PSIG of our allowance. 20 X .5 = 10 PSIG* *In our example, we have 10F of subcooling so we can overcome up to 30 PSIG of liquid line pressure drop. Of the 30 PSIG, we will lose 8.6 in the lift. 30 PSIG – 10 = 20 PSIG of loss allowance for the liquid line friction.*
Step 7	Using the liquid line pipe sizing table, plot the total equivalent length of line onto the data on the table. If the pressure drop is in excess of the allowance and the condenser is not able to take any additional refrigerant without raising head pressure above the desired level, the liquid line size is too small. If the pressure drop falls below the maximum allowance, the liquid line is properly sized.	*On the table plot the 5/16 line size @ 42,000 BTUH and cross over to 80 ft. At 80 feet the line will drop 29.3 PSIG which is well above the allowance of 20 PSIG. The line is too small for an R-22 system that has a subcooling capability of 10F. The line will need to be replaced with a larger line or if the line cannot be removed or changed, the system may need to be changed out to one that will work with the line. To see if the line can perform with an R-410A system, plot the line information onto the piping table for R-410A.*

Field Service Guide: Line Sets

STEP 1
R-22 Liquid Line Sizing Table

Maximum Allowable Pressure Drop
10F Subcooling = 30 PSIG
12F Subcooling = 35 PSIG

STEP 6

Subtract From Maximum Allowable Any Lift Pressure Drop .50 PSIG X __20__ Ft. of lift = __10 PSIG__ LOSS
Total Available PSIG After any Lift Loss = __20__ PSIG Maximum piping pressure drop

Tube OD	Rated BTUH	20'	40'	60'	80'	100'	120'	140'	160'	180'	200'	220'	240'
1/4"	18000	6.0	12.0	18.1	24.1	30.1	-	-	-	-	-	-	-
STEP 2	24000	10.2	20.3	30.5	-	-	-	-	-	-	-	-	-
5/16"	18000	1.6	3.2	4.7	6.3	7.9	9.5	11.1	12.6	14.2	15.8	17.4	19.0
	24000	2.7	5.3	8.0	10.6	13.3	16.0	18.6	21.3	23.9	26.6	29.3	31.9
	30000	4.0	8.0	11.9	15.9	19.9	23.9	27.9	31.8	-	-	-	-
	36000	5.5	11.1	16.6	22.2	27.7	33.2	-	-	-	-	-	-
STEP 7	42000	7.3	14.6	22.0	29.3	-	-	-	-	-	-	-	-
3/8"	18000	0.6	1.1	1.7	2.2	2.8	3.4	3.9	4.5	5.0	5.6	6.2	6.7
	24000	0.9	1.9	2.8	3.8	4.7	5.6	6.6	7.5	8.5	9.4	10.3	11.3
	30000	1.4	2.8	4.2	5.6	7.0	8.4	9.8	11.2	12.6	14.0	15.4	16.8
	36000	1.9	3.9	5.8	7.8	9.7	11.6	13.6	15.5	17.5	19.4	21.3	23.3
	42000	2.6	5.1	7.7	10.2	12.8	15.4	17.9	20.5	23.0	25.6	28.2	30.7
	48000	3.3	6.5	9.8	13.0	16.3	19.6	2.8	26.1	29.3	32.6	-	-
	60000	4.9	9.8	14.7	19.6	24.5	29.4	34.3	-	-	-	-	-
1/2"	36000	0.4	0.8	1.2	1.6	2.0	2.4	2.8	3.2	3.6	4.0	4.4	4.8
	42000	0.5	1.0	1.6	2.1	2.6	3.1	3.6	4.2	4.7	5.2	5.7	6.2
	48000	0.7	1.3	2.0	2.6	3.3	4.0	4.6	5.3	5.9	6.6	7.3	7.9
	60000	1.0	2.0	3.0	4.0	5.0	6.0	7.0	8.0	9.0	10.0	11.3	12.0

Courtesy of The Trane Company

Liquid LIne Brazed Fitting Equivalent Lengths

OD Line Size (in.)	45 Degree ELL	Short Radius ELL	Long Radius ELL	Solenoid Value	Sight Glass
1/4"	2	4.6	3.1	17	1.2
5/16"	2.1	4.6	3.1	20	1.4
3/8"	2.2	4.7	3.2	22	1.6
1/2"	2.4	4.7	3.2	24	1.7

STEP 3

STEP 4
Fitting Length Each __3.1__ X __6__ Number = __19__ ft.
STEP 5
Linear Length __65__ ft. + __19__ Fitting ft. = __84__ ft.

Field Service Guide: Line Sets

Now let's plot the job onto the R-410A Piping Chart (See Chart Opposite Page)

To begin, 10F subcooling can overcome up to 50 PSIG of liquid line pressure drop. The job lift is 20 feet of pipe. R-410A will burn .43 PSIG per foot of lift. 20 X .43 = 8.6 PSIG of loss. Let's round that off to 9 PSIG of pressure drop due to liquid line lift.

Subtract 9 PSIG from the available 50 PSIG Maximum allowance which leaves 41 PSIG for friction loss in the piping.

Plot the 5/16 inch piping @ 42,000 BTUH onto the piping chart and move over to 80 total equivalent feet of pipe. The table indicates a loss of 30.7 PSIG. We have slightly more pipe @ 84 feet but looking at the 100 ft. column we are well within tolerance.

R-410A Liquid Line Sizing Table

Maximum Allowable Pressure Drop
10F Subcooling = 50 PSIG
Subtract From Maximum Allowable Any Lift Pressure Drop   .43 PSIG X _____Ft. of lift = _____LOSS
Total Available PSIG After any Lift Loss = _____PSIG Maximum piping pressure drop

Tube OD	Rated BTUH	20'	40'	60'	80'	100'	120'	140'	160'	180'	200'	220'	240'
1/4"	18000	6.3	12.6	18.8	25.1	31.4	37.7	44.0	-	-	-	-	-
5/16"	18000	1.6	3.3	4.9	6.6	8.2	9.8	11.5	13.1	14.8	16.4	18.0	19.7
	24000	2.8	5.5	8.3	11.0	13.8	16.6	19.3	22.1	24.8	27.6	30.4	33.1
	30000	4.1	8.3	12.4	16.6	20.7	24.8	29.0	33.1	37.3	41.4	45.5	49.7
	36000	5.8	11.6	17.3	23.1	28.9	34.7	40.5	46.2				
	42000	7.7	15.4	23.0	30.7	38.4	16.1						
3/8"	24000	1.0	1.9	2.9	3.8	4.8	5.8	6.7	7.7	8.6	9.6	10.6	11.5
	30000	0.4	2.9	4.3	5.8	7.2	8.6	10.1	11.5	13.0	14.4	15.8	17.3
	36000	2.0	4.0	6.1	8.1	10.1	12.1	14.1	16.2	18.2	20.2	22.2	24.2
	42000	2.7	5.3	8.0	10.6	13.3	16.0	18.6	21.3	23.9	26.6	29.3	31.9
	48000	3.4	6.8	10.2	13.6	17.0	20.4	23.8	27.2	30.6	34.0	37.4	40.8
	60000	5.1	10.3	15.4	20.6	25.7	30.8	36.0	41.1	46.3			
1/2"	42000	0.5	1.1	1.6	2.2	2.7	3.2	3.8	4.3	4.9	5.4	5.9	6.5
	48000	0.7	1.4	2.0	2.7	3.4	4.1	4.8	5.4	6.1	6.8	7.5	8.2
	60000	1.0	2.1	3.1	4.2	5.2	6.2	7.3	8.3	9.4	10.4	11.4	12.5

R-410A Liquid Line Performance Summary

In summary, an R-410A system would perform properly on this liquid line yet an R-22 system will not. Upgrading the system and re-using the piping if allowed by the equipment manufacturer is a great way to deliver customer satisfaction, performance, and system reliability.

When line sets are converted from R-22 to R-410A, residual mineral oil should be removed from the system. Flush kits such as Nu-Calgon RX11 Flush are recommended for use.

Tapping the liquid line at the end of the liquid line to confirm subcooling

A line pressure tap such as a Bullet valve can be added to the liquid line to create a pressure port at the end of the liquid line. This port can be used to take  a liquid subcooling measurement at the end of the liquid line to confirm proper liquid line performance. Bullet valves are a very cheap way of gaining access to the refrigerant circuit for pressure tapping without having to recover and recharge the system.

Systems operating with flash gas present

When flash gas is present in the liquid line, the liquid line may sound like there is air inside of the line. The evaporator coil may be noisy as the refrigerant mix or vapor leaves the TXV. The suction gauge may shake and suction vapor superheat will be high. The compressor may experience hot operation.

Liquid Line Summary

Liquid lines drop pressure. This pressure drop if excessive can overcome the subcooling level and cause flash gas formation in the liquid line.

R-410A has better pressure drop tolerance than R-22.

Liquid lift burns up available liquid line pressure.

Proper charge and incorrect line sizing can cause flash gas formation.

Flash gas can lead to overheating compressors.

Audit line sets to confirm they are capable of working with the available subcooling.

Field Service Guide: Line Sets

Section Quiz

1. An R-22 liquid line is 50 ft. long. The line has 6 long radius elbows and is 3/8". The system has no lift and is a 5 ton system. The subcooling limit is 10F. Will the system be capable of delivering subcooled liquid to the TXV?

2. An R-22 liquid line is 40 ft. long. The line has 8 long radius elbows and is 3/8". The system has 20 feet of lift and is a 4 ton system. The subcooling limit is 10F. WIll the system be capable of delivering subcooled liquid to the TXV?

3. An R-22 liquid line is 25 feet long. The line has 6 long radius elbows and is 1/4". The system has 10 feet of lift and is a 1.5 ton system. The subcooling capability is 10F. Will the system be capable of delivering subcooled liquid to the TXV?

4. An R-410A liquid line is 70 feet long. The line has 10 long radius elbows and is 3/8". The system has 20 feet of lift and is a 5 ton system. The subcooling capability is 10F. WIll the system be capable of delivering subcooled liquid to the TXV?

5. An R410A liquid line is 50 feet long. The line has 6 long radius elbows and is 3/8". The system has 30 feet of lift and is a 3 ton system. Will the system be capable of delivering subcooled liquid to the TXV?

Field Service Guide: Line Sets

R-22 Liquid Line Sizing Worksheet

R-22 Liquid Line Sizing Table

Maximum Allowable Pressure Drop
 10F Subcooling = 30 PSIG
 12F Subcooling = 35 PSIG
 Subtract From Maximum Allowable Any Lift Pressure Drop   .50 PSIG X _____Ft. of lift = _____LOSS
 Total Available PSIG After any Lift Loss = _____PSIG Maximum piping pressure drop

Tube OD	Rated BTUH	20'	40'	60'	80'	100'	120'	140'	160'	180'	200'	220'	240'
1/4"	18000	6.0	12.0	18.1	24.1	30.1	-	-	-	-	-	-	-
	24000	10.2	20.3	30.5	-	-	-	-	-	-	-	-	-
5/16"	18000	1.6	3.2	4.7	6.3	7.9	9.5	11.1	12.6	14.2	15.8	17.4	19.0
	24000	2.7	5.3	8.0	10.6	13.3	16.0	18.6	21.3	23.9	26.6	29.3	31.9
	30000	4.0	8.0	11.9	15.9	19.9	23.9	27.9	31.8	-	-	-	-
	36000	5.5	11.1	16.6	22.2	27.7	33.2	-	-	-	-	-	-
	42000	7.3	14.6	22.0	29.3	-	-	-	-	-	-	-	-
3/8"	18000	0.6	1.1	1.7	2.2	2.8	3.4	3.9	4.5	5.0	5.6	6.2	6.7
	24000	0.9	1.9	2.8	3.8	4.7	5.6	6.6	7.5	8.5	9.4	10.3	11.3
	30000	1.4	2.8	4.2	5.6	7.0	8.4	9.8	11.2	12.6	14.0	15.4	16.8
	36000	1.9	3.9	5.8	7.8	9.7	11.6	13.6	15.5	17.5	19.4	21.3	23.3
	42000	2.6	5.1	7.7	10.2	12.8	15.4	17.9	20.5	23.0	25.6	28.2	30.7
	48000	3.3	6.5	9.8	13.0	16.3	19.6	2.8	26.1	29.3	32.6	-	-
	60000	4.9	9.8	14.7	19.6	24.5	29.4	34.3	-	-	-	-	-
1/2"	36000	0.4	0.8	1.2	1.6	2.0	2.4	2.8	3.2	3.6	4.0	4.4	4.8
	42000	0.5	1.0	1.6	2.1	2.6	3.1	3.6	4.2	4.7	5.2	5.7	6.2
	48000	0.7	1.3	2.0	2.6	3.3	4.0	4.6	5.3	5.9	6.6	7.3	7.9
	60000	1.0	2.0	3.0	4.0	5.0	6.0	7.0	8.0	9.0	10.0	11.3	12.0

Courtesy of The Trane Company

Liquid LIne Brazed Fitting Equivalent Lengths

OD Line Size (in.)	45 Degree ELL	Short Radius ELL	Long Radius ELL	Solenoid Value	Sight Glass
1/4"	2	4.6	3.1	17	1.2
5/16"	2.1	4.6	3.1	20	1.4
3/8"	2.2	4.7	3.2	22	1.6
1/2"	2.4	4.7	3.2	24	1.7

Fitting Length Each _____ X _____Number = ____ft.

Linear Length _____ft. + _____Fitting ft. = _____ft.

Field Service Guide: Line Sets

R-410A Liquid Line Sizing Worksheet

R-410A Liquid Line Sizing Table

Maximum Allowable Pressure Drop
10F Subcooling = 50 PSIG
Subtract From Maximum Allowable Any Lift Pressure Drop   .43 PSIG X _____Ft. of lift = _____LOSS
Total Available PSIG After any Lift Loss = _____PSIG Maximum piping pressure drop

Tube OD	Rated BTUH	20'	40'	60'	80'	100'	120'	140'	160'	180'	200'	220'	240'
1/4"	18000	6.3	12.6	18.8	25.1	31.4	37.7	44.0	-	-	-	-	-
5/16"	18000	1.6	3.3	4.9	6.6	8.2	9.8	11.5	13.1	14.8	16.4	18.0	19.7
	24000	2.8	5.5	8.3	11.0	13.8	16.6	19.3	22.1	24.8	27.6	30.4	33.1
	30000	4.1	8.3	12.4	16.6	20.7	24.8	29.0	33.1	37.3	41.4	45.5	49.7
	36000	5.8	11.6	17.3	23.1	28.9	34.7	40.5	46.2				
	42000	7.7	15.4	23.0	30.7	38.4	16.1						
3/8"	24000	1.0	1.9	2.9	3.8	4.8	5.8	6.7	7.7	8.6	9.6	10.6	11.5
	30000	0.4	2.9	4.3	5.8	7.2	8.6	10.1	11.5	13.0	14.4	15.8	17.3
	36000	2.0	4.0	6.1	8.1	10.1	12.1	14.1	16.2	18.2	20.2	22.2	24.2
	42000	2.7	5.3	8.0	10.6	13.3	16.0	18.6	21.3	23.9	26.6	29.3	31.9
	48000	3.4	6.8	10.2	13.6	17.0	20.4	23.8	27.2	30.6	34.0	37.4	40.8
	60000	5.1	10.3	15.4	20.6	25.7	30.8	36.0	41.1	46.3			
1/2"	42000	0.5	1.1	1.6	2.2	2.7	3.2	3.8	4.3	4.9	5.4	5.9	6.5
	48000	0.7	1.4	2.0	2.7	3.4	4.1	4.8	5.4	6.1	6.8	7.5	8.2
	60000	1.0	2.1	3.1	4.2	5.2	6.2	7.3	8.3	9.4	10.4	11.4	12.5

Liquid LIne Brazed Fitting Equivalent Lengths

OD Line Size (in.)	45 Degree ELL	Short Radius ELL	Long Radius ELL	Solenoid Value	Sight Glass
1/4"	2	4.6	3.1	17	1.2
5/16"	2.1	4.6	3.1	20	1.4
3/8"	2.2	4.7	3.2	22	1.6
1/2"	2.4	4.7	3.2	24	1.7

Fitting Length Each _____ X _____Number = ____ft.

Linear Length _____ft. + _____Fitting ft. = _____ft.

Charging
Procedures

Charging
Procedures

Field Service Guide: Charging Procedures

Chapter
Charging Procedures for Fixed Metering and Expansion Valve Systems

Table of Contents

Fixed Metering Charging Procedure..**2**
    Introduction 2
    Fixed Metering Systems and Superheat.. 2
    Suction Vapor Superheat and Heat Load 4
    Heat load and Superheat Charging Chart 5
    Suction Vapor Superheat Levels at Proper Charge Level 6
    Determining Suction Vapor Superheat Requirement using a Superheat Charging Chart 7
    System Suction Pressure 8
    Suction Pressure Charts.. 8
    Suction Pressure and Capacity 8
    Fixed Metering Evaporator Coil Operation at Proper Charge Level 9
    Superheat and Suction Pressure Changes when Charge is Increased........................... 10
    Liquid Pressure... 11
    Liquid Pressure versus Piston Bore Size... 11
    Conditions with Improper Piston Size and Charging Attempt 12
    Liquid Subcooling at Proper Charge Levels (Fixed Metering Device) 13
    Compressor Operation at Proper Charge Levels 13
    Undercharged Systems 14
    Overcharged Systems 15
Fixed metering Charging Procedure: Step By Step **16**
Generic Fixed Metering Superheat Charging Chart.....................................**19**
TXV Charging Procedure **20**
    Introduction 20
    Liquid Condition at the Entrance to the TXV... 20
    Liquid Subcooling Charging Method... 20
    TXV Metering Overview... 21
    TXV Metering and Evaporator Heat Load... 21
    About High Heat Load on Evaporator Coils.. 22
    TXV Metering and Changes in the Outdoor Air Temperature 22
    Condenser Coils and Subcooling 23
    Charge Level and Subcooling... 24
    System Subcooling Level Requirements 24
    Liquid Subcooling Levels as Charge is Added.. 25
    Subcooling Charts 25
    When the System is Properly Charged.. 27
    When the System is Undercharged 28
    When the System is Overcharged 28
TXV Charging Procedure: Step By Step...**29**

Field Service Guide: Charging Procedures

Fixed Metering Charging Procedure

Introduction: Fixed Metering Procedure

In this chapter proper charging procedures for air conditioning systems using a fixed piston type metering device will be covered.

Example of a piston type metering device.

Fixed piston type metering devices are nothing more than a hole in a piece of brass. These type of metering devices are the cheapest to produce and have limited control over the flow of refrigerant into the evaporator coil circuiting. Refrigerant flow into the evaporator is determined by liquid line pressure and indoor heat levels.

Since indoor heat load and liquid pressure are constantly changing, the amount of refrigerant entering the evaporator circuiting is constantly changing. This changing flow of refrigerant into the evaporator circuiting causes suction vapor superheat levels to fluctuate. In other words, the operating pressures and suction vapor superheat are constantly fluctuating in response to changes in the outdoor air temperature/liquid line pressure and indoor air temperature.

Since the fundamental operating characteristic of these systems is a constantly fluctuating flow of refrigerant into the evaporator circuiting, these systems are charged using the *superheat charging method*.

Fixed Metering Systems and Superheat

Fixed type metering devices are dependent upon liquid line pressure. When high pressure liquid enters the hole, the pressure at the outlet of the piston is much lower than the pressure of the liquid at the front of the piston. The amount of refrigerant that flows through the piston is affected by the pressure at the front of the piston. (Liquid line pressure.)

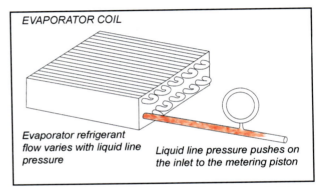

Liquid pressure pushes on the front of the metering device.

The operation of a fixed metering piston is very similar to the operation of a garden hose with an attached nozzle. When the pressure on the hose is high, the flow out of the nozzle is also high. When the pressure is reduced, the flow is reduced. Fixed metering pistons operate in a similar manner with changes in liquid line pressure. At high liquid line pressure levels, the flow is high. When the liquid line pressure is low, the flow out of the piston is reduced.

The resulting change in flow out of the piston results in fluctuations of refrigerant level in the evaporator coil circuiting. In other words, the evaporator coil will flood and starve based upon the pressure on the liquid line.

Because a fixed type metering device allows for changing flow of refrigerant into the evaporator coil when the liquid pressure changes, the actual efficiency of the evaporator coil is affected both positively and adversely.

On a cool day, the liquid pressure falls, which causes the flow of refrigerant into the evaporator coil to decrease. Because the evaporator coil will lack adequate refrigerant flow, the liquid is boiled off early in the evaporator circuit. The remaining vapor travels through the evaporator circuiting and becomes highly superheated. This is not good for efficiency since no changing of state is taking place in a large area of the evaporator coil.

During periods of high liquid pressure, the evaporator coil is flooded with cold refrigerant. The liquid boils off very late in the evaporator circuit, which leaves very little circuiting for superheating. In this state, the capacity of the evaporator is high since most of the coil circuit is being used to boil off cold liquid to a vapor. Both evaporator coil conditions are illustrated below:

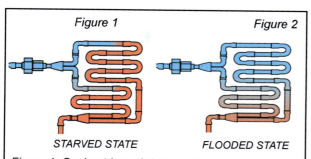

Figure 1   Figure 2

STARVED STATE   FLOODED STATE

Figure 1: Cool outdoor air temperature drops the head pressure and corresponding liquid pressure. The corresponding evaporator condition is illustrated.

Figure 2: Hot outdoor air temperature increases the condensing pressure and corresponding liquid pressure. The corresponding evaporator condition is illustrated.

The major cause of liquid pressure change is a change in outdoor air temperature. Superheat charging tables illustrate good examples of how superheat changes with changes in the outdoor air temperature. These tables are used to determine how much superheat should be present when operating with proper charge.

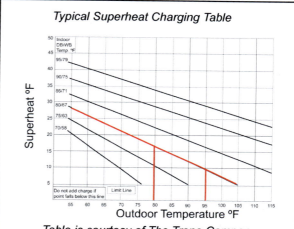

Typical Superheat Charging Table

Table is courtesy of The Trane Company

In this superheat table chart, the 80°/67° indoor air temperature line has been highlighted. This line will be used to illustrate how outdoor air temperature affects the superheat level requirement on the chart.

The first example shows that at an outdoor air temperature of 95°F, the suction vapor superheat requirement is 10°F.

At 80°F outdoor air temperature, the superheat requirement is 17°F.

The superheat requirement is rising as the outdoor air temperature is dropping.

From our examples and explanation, it is clear that outdoor air temperature must be measured and then plotted onto a superheat charging table to determine how much superheat should be present when the system is operating with proper charge.

Field Service Guide: Charging Procedures

Suction Vapor Superheat and Heat Load

The amount of heat that comes in contact with the surface of the evaporator coil has an impact upon the superheat level. At high heat load levels the superheat will be high, and at low heat load levels the superheat will be low.

Heat load is a combination of two factors, how much heat the air contains, and the amount of air being delivered by the indoor fan. The combination of the two factors is defined here as the heat load. Both factors must be measured to ensure they are set properly before attempting to adjust the refrigerant charge.

The air volume is measured in cubic feet per minute of air delivered across the surface of the evaporator coil. The system was engineered to operate at a specific air volume level. The capacity and efficiency tables published for the system were generated at these air volume levels. If the system is to operate as specified, the air volume must be set to the level that was specified by the manufacturer. In the event the information is not available on either the charging chart or installation information, adjust the air volume to 400 CFM of air per 1 ton of cooling capacity. *(See Air Volume Measurement Chapter.)*

The heat contained in the air can be referenced to the wet bulb temperature of the air returning to the evaporator coil. The relationship between heat content of air, and the wet bulb temperature of the return air, are plotted on charging charts by the engineering staff of the system manufacturer.

Think of heat load as square 1 cubic foot blocks of air passing over the surface of the evaporator coil. Each block contains heat. If the number of blocks are reduced, the amount of heat available drops. If the amount of heat contained in each block is reduced, the heat available also drops.

A tool called a sling psychrometer is used to measure the wet bulb temperature of the air. Sling psychrometers come in both mechanical and digital models. Both types of meters provide an acceptable means of measuring the wet bulb temperature of the air in the home.

Sling Psychrometer

When possible, measure the wet bulb temperature of the air directly at the return air filter rack in or near the air handler/furnace. When the reading is taken at this point, any infiltration air that may have entered the return air ducting is now measured as part of the total heat load. If the wet bulb temperature was measured in the conditioned space and heat was infiltrating into the return air ducting between the conditioned space and the filter rack, the true wet bulb temperature of the air would not be known. The result would be the use of the wrong wet bulb temperature being plotted onto the charging chart. Incorrect charging would result.

Estimating or shortcutting the process by not measuring indoor air volume will also result in improper charge. For example, if the air volume is too low, the charging technician will add excess refrigerant in an attempt to raise pressure when in fact the system needed more heat.

Heat Load and the Superheat Charging Chart

In this example of a superheat charging chart, the heat load is represented on the diagonal dry bulb/wet bulb temperature lines. Notice the increase in superheat required as the wet bulb temperature of the air increases. For example, at an outdoor air temperature of 90°F and a return air temperature of 75° dry bulb/63° wet bulb, the superheat under proper charge should be about 5 °F. When the temperature of the air in the home increases to 80°F dry bulb/67°F wet bulb, the superheat will rise to around 12°F.

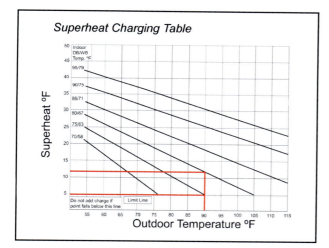

Note that these charts assume the air volume being delivered by the indoor blower motor has been properly set or established. If the air volume is improper, and the wet bulb temp is measured, the actual heat coming in contact with the evaporator coil will not be correct. The result will be improper superheat and improper adjustment of refrigerant charge as the refrigerant level is adjusted to compensate for the wrong amount of heat coming in contact with the surface of the evaporator coil.

From our example it is clear that as the temperature of the air in the home falls, the suction vapor superheat falls. When the air temperature in the home rises, the suction vapor superheat also rises. Therefore, when the thermostat first calls for cooling operation, the superheat will be higher than when the thermostat is satisfied and the system shuts off.

An important observation can be made by studying the superheat charging table. Notice at an outdoor air temperature of 95°F, and a return air temperature of 80°F dry bulb and 67°F wet bulb, the evaporator coil under proper charge will have a superheat level of about 10°F. When the return air temperature reaches 75°F dry bulb and 63°F wet bulb, the superheat is all the way down to 5°F.

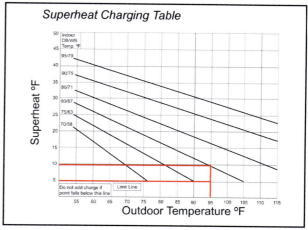

This is a really good illustration of how critical it is to properly charge a fixed piston system. At 5 degrees of superheat, the system is very close to the potential for saturated refrigerant entering the suction line back to the compressor. At saturation temperature, refrigerant is a mix of liquid and vapor. Compressors can be damaged by liquid floodback.

Field Service Guide: Charging Procedures

Suction Vapor Superheat Levels at Proper Charge Level (Fixed Metering Systems)

When the evaporator coil is operating at the proper charge, the refrigerant flow into the evaporator coil will fluctuate from a starved state to a flooded state. During periods where the air conditioning system is operated at cool outdoor air temperatures, the evaporator coil will starve and high suction vapor superheat will be present. During periods where the air conditioning system is operating at hot outdoor air temperatures, OAT, the evaporator coil will flood and low superheat levels will be present.

Indoor air heat load fluctuations will also affect the suction vapor superheat level. When the heat load is low, the evaporator coil will flood and the superheat level will drop. When the heat load is high, the evaporator coil will starve and the superheat level will rise.

With the system charge set properly, during flooded state operation like on a hot day, a minimum level of suction vapor superheat will be maintained. The minimum level of suction vapor superheat will ensure that liquid floodback to the compressor does not occur.

When the evaporator circuit is operating in a starved state due to low outdoor air temperature, and charge is set properly, the compressor will operate within acceptable temperature ranges. Compressors will overheat when excessive suction vapor superheat levels are present. The overheating may open the compressor internal temperature overload, or it may cause oil breakdown and potential bearing damage. Proper charging eliminates the potential for these problems.

Important Conditions Of Components

Evaporator Coil Circuits

Flooded State

Low Heat Load
High OAT
Overcharge
Oversized Metering Piston

Starved State

High Heat Load
Low OAT
Undercharge
Restrictions

Heat Load And Superheat

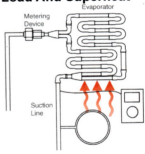

Low Heat Load will cause low superheat.

High Heat Load will cause high superheat.

Compressors and superheat

High superheat will cause the compressor to run hot.

Floodback of liquid may cause compressor damage.

Determining Suction Vapor Superheat Requirement using a Superheat Charging Chart

There are different styles of superheat charging charts. Some charts are plotted on slide rules and others reference suction line temperature requirements at given suction pressures. Regardless of the type of chart used, they all plot the same information to determine the required superheat. That information is that the outdoor air temperature must be known, and the indoor air wet bulb temperature must be known. The two required temperatures are plotted and the required suction vapor superheat level is determined.

The next step is to measure the actual suction vapor superheat level of the system being charged. The superheat level is then compared to the charging chart required superheat. If they are the same, then charge adjustment is not required. If the required superheat level and actual superheat level are different, an adjustment in refrigerant charge is made.

If the superheat level is too high, ADD REFRIGERANT. If the superheat level is too low, RECOVER REFRIGERANT. Remember that adjustment of refrigerant charge should only be done after confirming proper air volume, suction line size and condition, and if necessary, piston bore size.

Example of determining suction vapor superheat requirements for charging:

An R-22 air conditioning system is operating at a suction pressure of 68 PSIG. The suction line temperature is 55°F.

The outdoor air temperature is 90°F and the indoor air wet bulb temperature is 63°F. The air volume has been properly adjusted.

The first step to determine is, how much superheat the system requires under proper charge. We do this by plotting the outdoor air temperature and indoor wet bulb temperature onto the superheat charging table. In our example, we require 5°F of superheat.

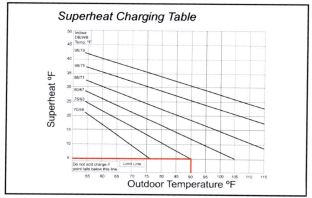

Next, we determine how much superheat the system is currently operating at. In our case, we have a suction pressure of 68 PSIG. By referring to a Pressure/Temperature table for R-22 we would find that this pressure equals a saturation temperature of 40°F at the evaporator circuiting.

The suction line temperature is 55°F which is 15°F warmer than the saturation temperature. Therefore we have a superheat level of 15°F.

The superheat we measure is higher than it should be so we must add refrigerant to the system and then re-measure pressure and suction line temperature. Repeat the superheat calculation until the suction vapor superheat level falls to 5°F.

Field Service Guide: Charging Procedures

System Suction Pressure

The suction pressure of the system will fluctuate with changes in flow rate of liquid into the evaporator coil circuiting and by the heat load that is being absorbed by the refrigerant. At high flow rates the suction pressure will rise and at low flow rates the suction pressure will fall. When the heat load in the air passing across the evaporator surface is high, the suction pressure will rise. When the heat load across the evaporator coil falls, the suction pressure will also fall.

Suction Pressure Charts

Some manufacturers provide charts that are used to plot the required suction pressure at combinations of outdoor air temperature and indoor heat load. When charged properly to the suction pressure requirement of the chart, the system will fluctuate it's pressure properly as outdoor air and indoor air temperatures change.

It is very important for the technician charging the air conditioning system to get the system operating at the suction pressure requirement indicated by these charts. When suction pressure charts are not available, the suction pressure should stabilize at the correct charge level when the metering piston is properly sized and indoor air volume is at the correct level.

Suction Pressure and Capacity

With R-22 systems, the capacity of the system will fluctuate 1% for every 1 pound of suction pressure change. For example, if a suction pressure chart indicates the system should have 85 PSIG suction pressure and it was actually operating at 82 PSIG, the system capacity will be reduced by 3%.

R-410A has better capacity performance than R-22. Every 1 PSIG of pressure loss will reduce the capacity of the system by .6%. Therefore, a 5 PSIG loss of suction pressure will result in a 3% drop in cooling capacity.

The capacity change that occurs with changes in suction pressure is due to the vapor density of the refrigerant vapor changing with changes in pressure. When the suction pressure is high, the vapor entering the compressor is heavy. When the suction pressure is low, the refrigerant vapor entering the compressor is light. In other words, the compressor pumps more pounds of vapor refrigerant at higher suction pressures.

If the suction line has excessive pressure drop due to a kink or undersizing, the suction pressure measured at the condensing unit will be lower than at the outlet of the evaporator coil. If this problem is suspected, place a pressure port in the suction line at the outlet of the evaporator coil

Suction Pressure Table

Indoor air temperature is plotted on 4 diagonal lines labeled with wet bulb temperature from a low of 59°F to a high of 71°F

Outdoor air temperature is plotted across the bottom of the chart from 60°F to 115°F.

and compare it to the pressure at the condensing unit pressure port. If excessive pressure drop is detected, confirm line size and check for a restriction in the line.

Fixed Metering Evaporator Coil Pressure at Proper Charge Level

Most R-22 and R-410A air conditioning systems are designed to operate at a Full Load evaporator coil temperature of 46°F-55°F. This temperature occurs when the suction pressure of the system is at proper level and the conditions at the home are 95°F Outdoor Air/80°F Indoor Air Dry Bulb/67°F Indoor Air Wet Bulb temperatures. At other combinations of outdoor air temperature and indoor air wet bulb temperature, the evaporator saturation temperature will vary from this range.

The evaporator saturation temperature range fluctuation is caused by changes in suction pressure. R-22 based systems will operate at suction pressures within a pressure range of 56 PSIG up to 93 PSIG. Below 56 PSIG the evaporator coil may freeze and above 93 PSIG most residential compressors are outside of their maximum operating pressure range.

R-410A systems will operate at equivalent temperatures as R-22 systems. The suction pressure range of the R-410A system will be higher than R-22 systems. For example, at 84 PSIG, R-22 systems will operate at a 50°F evaporator saturation temperature. At 50°F saturation temperature, an R-410A system will operate at a pressure of 143 PSIG. Although the pressures are different, the operating temperatures of the evaporator coils are equal.

The actual operating suction pressure and corresponding evaporator saturation temperature will depend upon the outdoor air temperature and indoor heat load. The pressure change will occur with no change in system charge level. For example, at low outdoor air temperature the suction pressure is lower than at high temps.

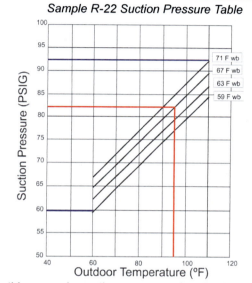

In this example suction pressure charging table, the lowest plotted suction pressure is under 60 PSIG and the maximum pressure is 93 PSIG.. Highlighted in blue.

Note operating suction pressure at 95°F outdoor air/67°F Indoor air wet bulb. Highlighted in red.

PRESSURES ARE R-22 REFRIGERANT. CONVERTING TO SATURATION TEMPERATURE SHOWS A RANGE OF TEMPERATURE FROM 32°F - 55°F.

THE SWING IN EVAPORATOR TEMPERATURE IS DUE TO CHANGES IN THE OUTDOOR AIR TEMPERATURE AND THE INDOOR AIR HEAT LOAD. (INDICATED BY WET BULB TEMPERATURE)

THE SWING IN PRESSURE OVER A WIDE RANGE OF OPERATING TEMPERATURES IS A GOOD CASE FOR NOT CHARGING A SYSTEM UNTIL IT "LOOKS RIGHT TO YOU." SINCE IN A <u>SHORT TIME, WHAT LOOKS RIGHT IS GOING TO CHANGE.</u>

Field Service Guide: Charging Procedures

Superheat and Suction Pressure Changes as the Charge is Increased

When adding refrigerant charge to the system, the suction pressure will rise and the suction vapor superheat level will fall. In this series of photos, we added charge to a piston equipped system and show the changes to suction line temperature and suction pressure.

Suction pressure and suction line temperature before charge is added

Suction pressure and suction line temperature after addition of 1/2 Pound of R-22

Suction pressure and suction line temperature after addition of 1 Pound of R-22

Field Service Guide: Charging Procedures

Liquid Pressure

The proper amount of liquid pressure must be present for the fixed metering device to flow the proper amount of refrigerant into the evaporator coil. The pressure level is affected by cleanliness of the condenser coil, outdoor air temperature, and charge level.

Some systems include liquid pressure charts that plot the required liquid pressure at a given outdoor air temperature and indoor heat load level. Other systems may not include these charts.

When the system comes with a liquid pressure chart, charge the system to the required superheat level and then compare the operating liquid pressure against the value indicated by the chart. If the chart value pressure and the actual pressure are not close, the metering piston may be the wrong bore size, or the air volume may be incorrect. Also, always ensure the suction line pressure loss is within acceptable range. *(See Refrigerant Line Chapter.)*

Typical Liquid Pressure Chart
Top Line = 71 Wet Bulb
Bottom Line = 59 Wet Bulb

Notice the outdoor air temperature range on the chart only goes down to 60°F. At temperatures below 60°F, liquid pressure is too low for proper charging of the system.

Some systems do not come with operating pressure charts. When these charts are not available, make certain that suction vapor superheat is operating at the proper level and that suction pressure falls within ranges that equal typical evaporator coil saturation temperatures as indicated in this chapter.

If the proper suction vapor superheat range cannot be reached, and the suction pressure appears to be off, check for proper piston size, air volume, and suction line size.

Liquid Pressure Versus Piston Bore Size

Make certain the piston is the proper size when charging a fixed metering system. Piston sizes are matched to the operating head pressure of the outdoor condensing unit. Low SEER units with high head pressure will have smaller bore requirements than high SEER units operating with lower head pressure.

Bore size is printed on pistons

Look for improper piston sizing to be predominantly found in high SEER equipment where the installer failed to replace the lower SEER piston shipped with the evaporator coil.

<u>Proper piston size can be found in the installation literature shipped with the condensing unit.</u>

11

Field Service Guide: Charging Procedures

Conditions With Improper Piston Size and Charging Attempt

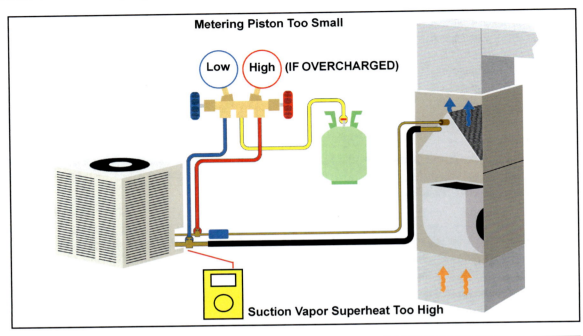

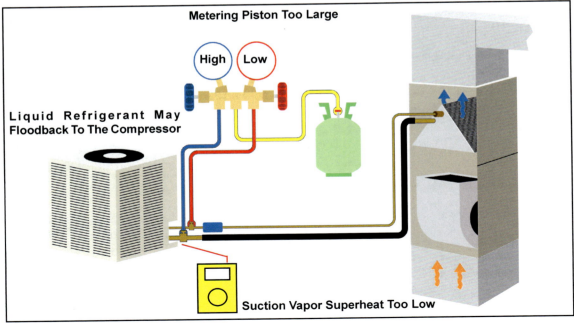

Liquid Subcooling at Proper Charge Levels (Fixed Metering Systems)

The liquid subcooling level in a fixed metering system will fluctuate with changes in outdoor air temperature and indoor heat load. Typical ranges of liquid subcooling under normal system operation for a piston metering system can be from about 8°F-20°F.

At proper charge levels where the system is operating at the correct discharge or liquid line pressure, the amount of subcooling produced in the condenser circuiting should be at a level that is matched to the liquid line pressure loss level required by the system manufacturer.

Compressor Operation at Proper Charge Levels

The compressor performance changes with fluctuations in suction pressure, discharge pressure, and suction vapor superheat levels. Peak performance is achieved when the system is operating at high suction pressure, low discharge pressure, and low superheat levels. Performance falls off when suction pressure drops, superheat rises, or discharge pressure rises. All of these changes occur naturally throughout normal operation of a fixed metering system.

Compressors will run cooler at lower superheat ranges and hotter as superheat rises. The temperature of the compressor oil will be kept at optimum temperatures when operating within proper charge limits.

Even when operating at lowest superheat levels, under proper charge, liquid will not floodback to the compressor during run operation.

Compressors should be protected from liquid migration occurring during off cycle periods. Charge level affects the amount of liquid that migrates during the off cycle period. As charge rises, the amount of liquid that migrates into the compressor oil rises. A good preventative measure is to always add a crankcase heater to systems where charge level is high. (Long line sets.)

Summary Of Important Information About Fixed Metering System Operation and Proper Charge Level

Fixed metering systems fluctuate suction vapor superheat based upon changes in outdoor air temperature and indoor heat load.

Superheat charts are used to plot the required suction vapor superheat level.

Suction pressure levels will vary from about 56 PSIG up to 93 PSIG.

Indoor air volume must be set to proper level before attempting charge adjustment.

The metering piston size must be proper before attempting charge adjustment.

Improper piston size can be detected with abnormal superheat and pressure readings.

System capacity will be reduced when systems operate at low suction pressure levels.

System capacity will be reduced when systems operate at high liquid/head pressure levels.

Do not charge at outdoor air temperatures below 60°F. (Liquid pressure is too low.)

Field Service Guide: Charging Procedures

Undercharged Systems

Suction Pressure

When systems do not have enough refrigerant charge, the suction pressure will be lower than specified. The low suction pressure will cause the compressor capacity to fall. The low suction pressure will also cause the evaporator coil temperature to be below the design level established by the system manufacturer. If the charge level is low enough, and the suction pressure low enough, the evaporator coil may develop a coating of ice due to freezing condensate on the surface of the coil.

Suction Vapor Superheat

The suction vapor superheat level will be higher than specified. The high superheat level is caused by the fact that there is not enough liquid refrigerant in the evaporator circuiting. The lack of liquid will cause the liquid to be boiled off to all vapor too early in the evaporator circuiting.

Compressor

The compressor will run hotter than design due to the high suction vapor superheat level. The compressor will also run hot due to a lack of enough vapor to properly cool the compressor motor. The hot temperatures may trip the internal overload protection embedded in the compressor motor windings. The temperature of the compressor oil will also be too high which can over time, cause bearing damage.

The Condenser and Liquid Line Pressure

The lack of charge level will cause the condenser

to starve for liquid refrigerant. The condensing pressure will be lower than design and the liquid subcooling will be low. The lack of condensing pressure will cause low liquid line pressure.

The low liquid pressure and inadequate subcooling may cause flash gas to form in the liquid line.

Overall, the performance and long term reliability of the system will be degraded.

Summary Of Important Information About Fixed Metering System Operation and undercharged Level

Suction pressure will be lower than required. The evaporator coil may freeze if the temperature of the evaporator is cold enough.

The suction vapor superheat level will be too high.

The compressor will overheat.

The condenser will lack adequate liquid line pressure and liquid subcooling.

System capacity will be low.

The compressor may overheat and go off on internal temperature overload protection.

Overcharged Systems

Suction Pressure

When systems have too much refrigerant charge, the suction pressure will be higher than specified. The high suction pressure will also cause the evaporator coil temperature to be above the design level established by the system manufacturer. The abnormally high evaporator temperature will reduce the evaporator coil's ability to remove moisture from the air. The home may experience abnormal humidity levels.

Suction Vapor Superheat

The suction vapor superheat level will be lower than specified. The low superheat level is caused by the fact that liquid refrigerant is circulating too far into the evaporator circuiting. The system may experience liquid floodback to the compressor during run operation.

Compressor

The compressor may experience liquid floodback during run operation. The floodback may cause the compressor to experience a running oil pump out. In extreme cases, the liquid refrigerant may cause internal damage to compressor components. In either case, the reliability of the compressor will be degraded.

The excess refrigerant charge will also cause an increase in the amount of liquid refrigerant migration to the compressor oil that occurs during periods where the compressor has been off. This liquid migration will cause oil foaming during compressor start up and oil pump out will occur.

The Condenser and Liquid Line Pressure

The condenser coil will be flooded with excess liquid refrigerant. The excess refrigerant will cause abnormally high condensing pressure and corresponding liquid line pressure. The liquid subcooling level will be above normal levels.

Summary Of Important Information About Fixed Metering System Operation and Overcharge Level

High suction pressure and abnormally high evaporator coil temperature

Superheat will be low compared to chart requirement

The compressor may have liquid flooding back during run operation. During off cycle periods liquid migration may cause starting problems.

The condensing/liquid line pressure will be higher than it should be. The high pressure will reduce efficiency and capacity.

Liquid subcooling will be high.

Field Service Guide: Charging Procedures

Tools: **Digital Temperature Probe / Sling Psychrometer / Refrigerant Gauges**

Fixed Metering Device Charging

STEP 1

Make certain the evaporator coil and condenser coil are clean. If the coils are not clean, the pressures will be adversely affected as effective coil surface has now been altered from design conditions.
Confirm proper metering piston size.
Confirm the suction line is properly sized and not kinked.
<u>It must be at least 60°F to charge the system.</u>

STEP 2

Measure the outdoor air temperature near the condenser coil. Make certain to measure the air temperature entering the coil, not the temperature of the air leaving the coil.

STEP 3

Use a sling psychrometer to measure the indoor air dry bulb and wet bulb temperatures. A mechanical type sling pyschrometer or a digital type meter may be used to take these temperatures.

STEP 4

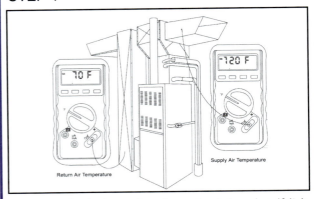

Measure the indoor air volume to determine if it is within specifications set by the charging chart. Make adjustment to air volume if necessary. Failure to get the air volume to proper levels will invalidate the superheat charge process.

Field Service Guide: Charging Procedures

STEP 5

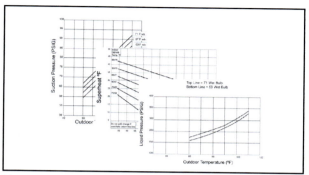

Using the charging charts, plot the required system pressures and superheat level. If one is not available at the jobsite, see the Generic chart in this chapter.

STEP 7

Next, open the blue suction side dial on the refrigerant gauge. The refrigerant will now enter the system via the suction service valve. Close the gauge valve and wait for pressures to stabilize. Repeat as needed.

STEP 6

Connect the center hose of the refrigerant gauge manifold to the valve on the refrigerant cylinder. The blue suction hose should be connected to the suction service valve. The red high pressure hose should be connected to either the liquid line service valve or the discharge line pressure port. The charging chart will indicate which port the hose should be connected to. Turn the system on.

NOTE:

If the refrigerant used is R-410A, make certain to charge the system with the refrigerant drum in the proper orientation as indicated on the refrigerant cylinder.

Add or recover refrigerant until pressures match the charging chart requirements.

17

Field Service Guide: Charging Procedures

STEP 8

Once system pressures are set to factory required levels, measure the temperature of the suction line near the service valve on the outdoor condensing unit. Calculate the superheat. (See Measuring Superheat.)

STEP 9

If the superheat is too low, recover refrigerant.

If the superheat is too high, add refrigerant.

Allow time for system temperatures and pressures to become stable and then re-measure.

Continue process until the pressures and superheat are within chart allowances.

Note:

It is good practice to check the temperature of the suction line at the outlet of the evaporator and at the inlet to the condensing unit. Compare the temperatures. The temperatures should be close to the same. If there is a significant drop in temperature from the evaporator outlet to the condensing unit, check for a kink or restriction in the suction line. If there is a significant rise in temperature, check for a lack of insulation on the suction line.

Field Service Guide: Charging Procedures

THIS CHART SHOULD ONLY BE USED WHEN THE ORIGINAL FACTORY CHART CANNOT BE FOUND

GENERIC SUPERHEAT CHARGING TABLE FOR FIXED PISTON METERING

OAT	INDOOR AIR DRY BULB / WET BULB TEMPERATURE			
	70/58	75/63	80/67	85/71
55°F	21°F	25°F	29°F	33°F
60°F	17°F	22°F	27°F	31°F
65°F	14°F	19°F	24°F	29°F
70°F	10°F	16°F	22°F	27°F
75°F	6°F	13°F	19°F	25°F
80°F	5°F	11°F	17°F	23°F
85°F	5°F	8°F	15°F	20°F
90°F	5°F	5°F	12°F	18°F
95°F	5°F	5°F	10°F	16°F
100°F	5°F	5°F	7°F	14°F
	SUPERHEAT LEVEL			

This table is provided as a general charging guide to use when the original chart cannot be found. In all cases, try to get a copy of the original chart. Use of this chart does not guarantee that the charge obtained by use of this chart will deliver certified rated capacities and efficiencies. This chart is only designed as a general guide to get the charge of the system close to factory requirements. Prokup Media inc. assumes no responsibility for the operation and reliability of systems charged using the data provided in this table. The data was gathered by comparing a wide range of superheat charging table data from various manufacturers and then compiling average values for various combinations of outdoor air and indoor air conditions.

Use of this chart requires that the indoor air volume be set to the manufacturer required level and that the metering piston be properly sized.

Field Service Guide: Charging Procedures

TXV Charging Procedure

Introduction to TXV Charging Procedure

Thermostatic expansion valves (TXV) maintain a constant level of suction vapor superheat over a wide range of liquid line pressure changes and indoor air heat loads. They stabilize the suction vapor superheat level by varying the size of their internal orifice in response to changes in the liquid line pressure and indoor air heat load. Suction vapor superheat may range from a low of about 8°F to a high of around 12°F at normal charge levels and proper system operation.

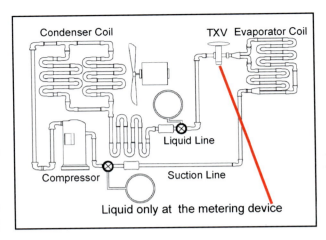

Liquid Condition at Entrance to TXV

To operate properly, the TXV must receive a solid column of liquid refrigerant from the liquid line. In liquid form, refrigerant is in a subcooled state, meaning its temperature is below the saturation temperature equal to the pressure of the liquid line right before the entrance to the TXV. The amount of subcooling needed will depend upon the design of the liquid line and the charge level requirement of the condensing unit.

Liquid Subcooling Charging Method

The method of charging used to charge a TXV equipped air conditioning system is the subcooling method. In this charging method, the liquid subcooling level is monitored as refrigerant is added or recovered from the system. When the subcooling level has been adjusted to the required level, the system will operate at proper efficiency and capacity.

Technician measures the liquid line temperature with a digital temperature probe.

TXV Metering Overview

Thermostatic expansion valves sense the leaving evaporator suction vapor temperature via a remote sensing bulb that is attached to the suction line at the outlet of the evaporator circuiting. The suction line temperature will change due to changes in the condition of the refrigerant entering the TXV and changes in the indoor air heat load.

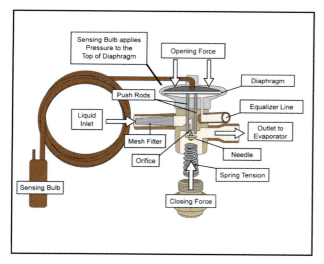

The TXV sensing bulb is filled with refrigerant. When the temperature of the suction line changes, the pressure inside the sensing bulb also changes. The sensing bulb capillary tube transmits pressure to the top of the TXV diaphragm assembly. The pressure in the sensing bulb is opposed by the pressure from the expansion valve equalizer line and the internal spring of the TXV. The pressure that is higher, either the sensing bulb, or combination spring/equalizer line, will move the internal orifice to either a smaller or larger size. The new orifice size will either allow more refrigerant into the evaporator circuiting or less depending upon which pressure is greater.

If the sensing bulb pressure is higher, the evaporator circuiting receives more refrigerant. If the equalizer line/spring pressure is higher, the refrigerant flow into the evaporator circuit is decreased. As pressure adjusts, the two opposing pressures eventually equalize and the orifice size remains stable.

If the expansion valve is operating properly, the suction vapor leaving the evaporator circuiting will be at a superheat level of about 10°F.

TXV Metering and Evaporator Heat Load

Expansion valve equipped systems that are operating within proper application ranges of outdoor air temperature and indoor air heat load can adjust refrigerant flow into the evaporator circuit to maintain a constant level of suction vapor superheat. The suction vapor superheat range of about 10°F that is maintained by the TXV, enhances the performance of the evaporator circuit which increases efficiency. As the heat load on the evaporator coil decreases, the expansion valve throttles back refrigerant flow into the evaporator circuit. When the heat load on the evaporator coil is high, the expansion valve will open to allow more refrigerant to enter the evaporator circuit.

If the heat load on the evaporator coil is too low, such as when there is a dirty return air filter and corresponding low air volume, the TXV will struggle to regulate refrigerant flow into the evaporator circuit. The valve will continually throttle open and then close in a failed attempt to balance the refrigerant level with the heat load. This struggle is called "hunting" and will show up as a fluctuating suction pressure gauge and corresponding changes in the temperature of the suction line.

Field Service Guide: Charging Procedures

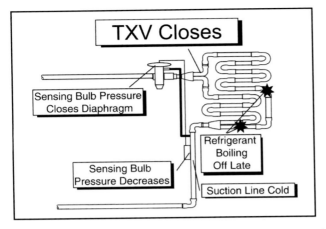

If the heat load on the evaporator coil is too high, such as when a leaking return air duct is allowing hot attic air to enter the evaporator circuit, the TXV will open wide but may not be able to get the superheat down. The resulting suction pressure will be high and the suction vapor superheat will be higher than it should be. This condition may also occur when the temperature in the conditioned space is very high such as when the system is first started. As the air temperature drops, the expansion valve will take better control of refrigerant flow and resulting superheat will fall.

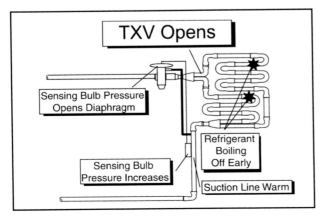

About High Heat Load on Evaporator Coils

When charging systems where the air temperature in the home is high, such as a new system start up on a hot day, run the air conditioning system and allow the air temperature in the home to reach comfort temperature ranges before making final charge adjustment. Comfort temperature range is close to 75°F-80°F dry bulb.

The indoor air volume must also be set to proper level before attempting charge adjustment. Typically air volume is set to 400 CFM per ton of cooling capacity. This range may deviate in some instances to a low of 350 CFM per ton of cooling to a high of 450 CFM per ton of cooling. Verify air volume requirement on system charging charts. If no reference to required air volume is found, adjust the air volume for 400 CFM per 1 ton of cooling capacity.

TXV Metering and Changes in Outdoor Air Temperature

Residential systems typically use a balanced port type expansion valve as a metering device. Balance port type expansion valves cancel out the affect of liquid line pressure on the pressure drop across the valve. By using this type of metering valve, system efficiency can be enhanced by lowering head pressure and corresponding liquid pressure without affecting the ability of the expansion valve to flow adequate refrigerant to the evaporator circuiting. The lower head pressure increases the volumetric efficiency of the compressor and overall system capacity.

There is a limit to how low condensing/liquid line pressure can be. At some level the lack of liquid line pressure will cause metering problems at the evaporator circuit. The expansion valve will not be able to flow enough refrigerant into the evaporator circuit to maintain proper suction pressure and suction vapor superheat. The amount of liquid pressure available under proper charge and clean coils will be determined by outdoor air temperature and indoor heat load.

The system charging chart will have a minimum outdoor air temperature at which charging using the subcooling method can be done. If the outdoor air temperature is below the minimum outdoor air temperature specified on the charging chart, the system should only be charged by weight method, not subcooling method. The minimum outdoor air temperature for charging using the subcooling method is typically around 60°F.

Condenser Coils and Subcooling

As previously stated, to operate properly, an expansion valve must receive pure liquid refrigerant from the liquid line. When vapor is present in the liquid line the expansion valve will not function correctly. The vapor portion of the liquid vapor mix is sometimes called flash gas. When flash gas is present, the expansion valve will not meter enough refrigerant into the evaporator circuiting to control superheat. In this condition the superheat will be too high which is an indication of a lack of refrigerant in the evaporator circuiting. To eliminate flash gas formation and the problems it causes, the system is charged to ensure the refrigerant that enters the expansion valve is always pure liquid.

The amount of liquid subcooling required to get pure liquid to the metering device will depend upon the pressure drop in the liquid line that occurs from the outlet of the condensing unit to the inlet of the expansion valve. The liquid subcooling amount decreases as the liquid travels down the liquid line. This is due to pressure drop that occurs naturally in liquid lines and to heat that gets into the liquid when the liquid travels in hot spaces such as attics. Under proper charge level there will be enough subcooling to ensure that subcooled liquid refrigerant is present at the end of the liquid line.

This illustration shows an example of how subcooling decreases as liquid travels down the liquid line. In the illustration there are two pressure port taps in the liquid line. The first tap is at the outlet of the condenser coil, the second in the liquid line at the entrance to the indoor metering device.

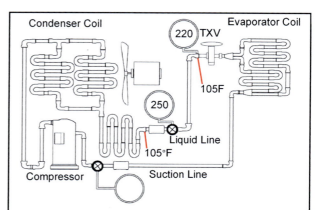

Liquid Subcooling at the outlet of the condenser is equal to 250 PSIG (R-22) = 117°F-105°F = 12°F

Liquid Subcooling at the gauge port located near the entrance to the metering device is equal to 220 PSIG(R-22) = 108°F-105°F = 3°F

In this example, the subcooling was reduced by 9°F due to a 30 PSIG pressure loss in the liquid line.

Field Service Guide: Charging Procedures

Most R-22 systems will have a maximum liquid line pressure drop allowance of 30 PSIG. R-410A liquid lines are typically designed for a maximum pressure drop of 50 PSIG. Both levels of pressure drop require 10 degrees of liquid subcooling for the liquid to make it from the condenser to the metering device without flash gas forming.

Charge Level and Subcooling

Adding or recovering refrigerant from an air conditioning system will change the amount of liquid subcooling that is done in the condenser coil. When refrigerant is added to the system, the amount of liquid that condenses in the condenser coil increases. The liquid backs up further into the condenser circuiting and a corresponding increase in condensing and liquid line pressure takes place. The increase in pressure raises the corresponding saturation temperature in the condenser coil and a wider difference between liquid line temperature and condensing temperature (saturation temperature). The condensed liquid also travels further in the condenser circuiting.

Backing up liquid into the condenser circuits raises liquid line pressure and increases liquid subcooling. The addition of charge increases pressure and the amount of coil circuiting used to subcool liquid.

The result is a higher level of subcooling with slightly higher condensing pressure.

If refrigerant is removed from the system, the condensing pressure falls and the amount of liquid refrigerant condensing in the condenser circuiting drops. The amount of coil circuiting used for subcooling decreases. The result is less difference between condensing temperature and liquid line temperature and lower liquid subcooling.

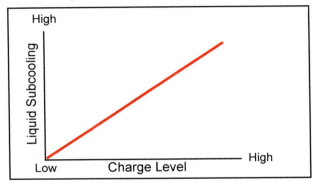

System Subcooling Level Requirements

Every system requires a different amount of liquid subcooling based upon the pressure drop in the liquid line and the design and size of the condenser coil. In some cases, the subcooling level required for proper operation of the system is printed on the nameplate of the condensing unit. As previously stated, 10 degrees of subcooling will overcome design pressure drop for most properly sized liquid lines. However, some systems may require more subcooling than 10 degrees. These systems are typically high efficiency models where the outdoor condenser coil is very large. The large coil may require significant refrigerant charge to develop the required condensing pressure. The high subcooling is a result of the large amount of refrigerant in the condenser coil.

Field Service Guide: Charging Procedures

Liquid Subcooling Levels as Charge is Added

In this series of photos, liquid line pressure and liquid line temperature are displayed in order as charge is added to an R-22 system. An interval of 15 minutes was allowed between each change in charge to allow for stabilization of liquid line temperature and pressure.

Liquid Line pressure and Liquid Line temperature before charge is added.

Liquid Line pressure and Liquid Line temperature after addition of 1/2 Pound of R-22.

Liquid Line pressure and Liquid Line temperature after addition of 1 Pound of R-22.

Subcooling Charts

Some air conditioners will come with a subcooling charging chart that plots the required subcooling based upon the length and vertical liquid lift of the liquid line.

Two charts are usually provided, one chart to determine the pressure drop range of the liquid line and the other to determine the liquid pressure and liquid line temperature requirements.

The first step when using these charts is to plot the length of the liquid line and any vertical lift of liquid to determine which range the liquid line application falls into. In this chart, these ranges are labeled lower, middle, and upper. Each range

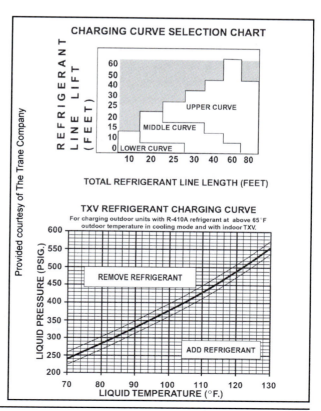

25

Field Service Guide: Charging Procedures

represents a different level of liquid subcooling requirement.

For example, let's plot the subcooling requirement for a 10 foot vertical lift of liquid and 20 feet length of liquid line onto the chart below.

Find the vertical lift on the left column and the length of the liquid line at the bottom of the chart. In this example, the line falls into the middle range.

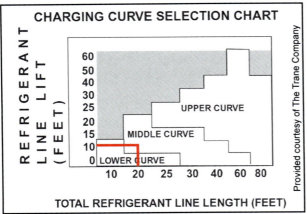

Next we go to a liquid pressure/liquid line temperature chart. We see there are three lines on this chart, a lower, middle, and upper line. These lines are used to plot the intersection of the pressure of the liquid line versus the required

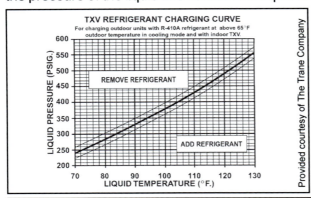

liquid line temperature. Notice the three intersecting lines represent different liquid line temperatures based upon the length and lift of the liquid line.

Let's plot an example on the chart shown below: If the liquid line pressure was 350 PSIG, and the lower line was the plot line, the required liquid line temperature would be 98°. If the upper line was the plot line, the liquid line would need to be 90°. The difference between the two examples equals a difference in required liquid subcooling levels based upon two different liquid line applications. The lower line example equals 9 degrees of subcooling while the upper line equals 17 degrees of subcooling.

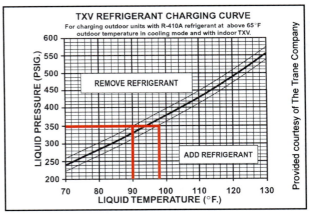

Notice on the chart that when the liquid line temperature is too warm compared to the required liquid line temperature, the chart directs to add refrigerant into the system. When the temperature of the liquid line is below the required liquid line temperature, the chart directs to recover refrigerant from the system. The addition of, or removal of refrigerant from the system will change the pressure and liquid line temperature. The change will not be instantaneous and may take up to 20 minutes to become stable.

Re-measure both liquid pressure and liquid line temperature and re-compare to the chart. Make charge adjustments as needed until the pressure and temperature are equal to the values indicated on the liquid subcooling charging chart.

Allow time for the liquid line temperature to reach desired temperature. Up to 20 minutes may be required.

When the System is Properly Charged

The Evaporator Coil

The evaporator coil will operate with stable suction pressure. The saturation temperature range of the evaporator coil will be slightly higher than a similar system equipped with a fixed piston type metering device. The suction vapor superheat level will be stable at close to 10°F.

During times where the system operates at cooler outdoor air temperatures, the TXV will increase the diameter of its internal metering orifice to maintain suction pressure at a higher level than a piston system. The higher suction pressure will result in better compressor performance.

The Compressor

With proper air volume heat load, the compressor will not experience any liquid floodback due to the careful metering action of the expansion valve. The constant suction vapor superheat level will also keep the compressor running cooler than a piston equipped system.

The Condenser Coil and Liquid Subcooling Levels

The condenser coil will have enough refrigerant to maintain proper liquid subcooling level for the liquid line application. If the liquid line is properly sized, no flash gas will form.

Summary Of Important Information About TXV Metering System Operation and Proper Charge Level

Normal and stable suction pressure.

Superheat will be steady at around 10°F.

Compressor will operate at best temperature and not experience liquid floodback during run operation.

Liquid subcooling will be adequate to prevent flash gas formation in the liquid line.

When the System is Undercharged

The Evaporator Coil

The evaporator coil may operate normally with proper suction pressure and suction vapor superheat. During periods of high liquid line pressure drop, the system may lack adequate subcooling and flash gas may form in the liquid line. The flash gas will cause fluctuations in suction pressure and suction vapor superheat.

The Compressor

If the charge level is low enough to cause high suction vapor superheat, the compressor will run hot and may overheat. The compressor internal motor temperature protector may open to shut down the compressor. High operating temperatures may cause oil breakdown and bearing wear or damage.

The Condenser Coil and Liquid Subcooling Levels

The condenser coil will operate at lower than required pressure. The lack of charge will result in lower than required liquid subcooling level. The low subcooling level may cause flash gas to form in the liquid line.

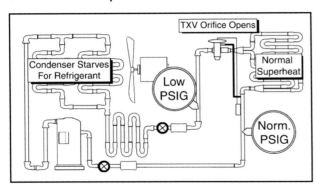

Summary Of Important Information About TXV Metering System Operation and Undercharge Level.

Normal and stable suction pressure if charge is slightly low. Suction pressure will fall to low levels if charge is excessively low.

Superheat may be normal or high.

Compressor will be hot.

Condensing pressure will be low. Liquid subcooling will be low.

When the System is Overcharged

The Evaporator Coil

The evaporator coil may operate normally with proper suction pressure and suction vapor superheat. The expansion valve will throttle back flow of refrigerant in an attempt to maintain proper suction vapor superheat levels.

The Compressor

The compressor will lose capacity due to elevated condensing pressure caused by an overcharge condition in the condenser. The expansion valve will prevent excessive flooding of the evaporator coil.

The Condenser Coil and Liquid Subcooling Levels

The condenser coil will operate at higher than required pressure. The excess charge will cause high condensing pressure and low compressor capacity. The liquid subcooling level will be abnormally high.

Field Service Guide: Charging Procedures

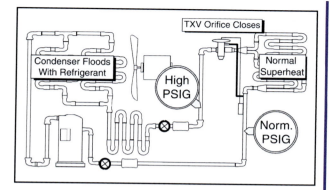

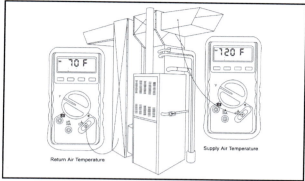

STEP 1

Make sure that indoor air volume has been adjusted to the proper level. See the charging chart for CFM specification. If it is not present, adjust the indoor air volume for 400 CFM per 1 ton of cooling capacity.

The outdoor air temperature should be above 60°F. If it is colder, weigh the charge in using a charging scale. Return when outdoor air temperature is above 60°F to make final charge adjustment.

STEP 2

Make certain the evaporator coil and condenser coil are clean. Confirm proper suction and liquid line sizing.

Summary Of Important Information About TXV Metering System Operation and Overcharge level.

Suction pressure will be in normal or slightly elevated range.

Superheat will be normal.

Compressor capacity will be low.

Condensing pressure will be high. Liquid subcooling will be high.

TXV Metering Device Charging Procedure

Tools — Digital Temperature Probe
Sling Psychrometer
Refrigerant Gauges

Field Service Guide: Charging Procedures

STEP 3

Attach refrigerant gauges to the system.

Attach a digital temperature probe to the liquid line at the outlet of the condensing unit.

STEP 4

Run the system and add refrigerant. Allow system pressures to stabilize. Then find the liquid pressure and convert to saturation temperature. Find the liquid line temperature. Subtract liquid line temperature from the saturation temperature to determine liquid subcooling level.

STEP 5

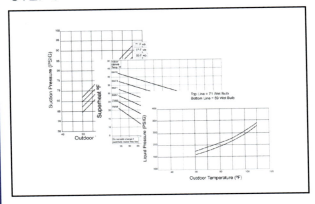

If subcooling charging chart is present, calculate the required liquid subcooling level for the liquid line application. If the chart is not available, check the condensing unit nameplate for possible liquid subcooling charge data. If this is not present, charge the system for a subcooling level of 10°~12°F.

STEP 6

If the liquid subcooling level is below the required value, add some refrigerant to the system. If the liquid subcooling level is too high, recover refrigerant from the system. Re-check subcooling level to confirm proper charge. (Allow up to 20 minutes for the system conditions to stabilize.)

STEP 7

Confirm proper operation of the expansion valve by measuring suction pressure and suction line temperature. Calculate suction vapor superheat. The measured superheat should be in a range of 8°F~15°F. (Some systems where large evaporator coils are matched to smaller condensing units may show higher levels of superheat. 2 stage capacity air conditioning systems operating at first stage may also show high suction vapor superheat levels.)

NOTE:

R-410A SYSTEM CHARGING INFORMATION

When adding refrigerant charge to an R-410A system, add the refrigerant in a liquid state. See the refrigerant cylinder information for details. (Use a Charge Faster cylinder on your gauge manifold to speed up the charging process.)

**Refrigeration Ckt
Diagnostics**

**Refrigeration Ckt
Diagnostics**

Field Service Guide: Diagnosing Problems In Your Refrigeration Circuit

Chapter

Diagnosing Problems in the Refrigeration Circuit

Table of Contents

How to Test Refrigeration Circuits 3
    Introduction 3
    Superheat and Use in Diagnostics 3
    Condensing Pressure and Liquid Subcooling Measurement use in Diagnostics 4
    Pressure Loss and Temperature Drop 4
Diagnosing Problems with Systems that have Fixed Metering Orifices 5
    Causes of Lower than required Suction Pressure 5
Step-by-Step Procedures for Determining Cause of Low Suction Pressure:
    FIXED METERING EQUIPPED SYSTEMS 5
Determining if the Problem is caused by Suction Line Pressure Loss:
    Step By Step 5
Determining if the Problem is caused by Low Head Load: Step By Step 6
Determining if the Problem is caused by a Lack of Refrigerant in the
    Evaporator Coil: Step By Step 7
    Causes of Higher than Required Suction Pressure 10
Step-by-Step Procedure for Determining Cause of High Suction Pressure:
    FIXED METERING EQUIPPED SYSTEMS 10
Determining if Problem is caused by too much Refrigerant in the
    Evaporator Coil: Step by Step 10
Determining if Problem is caused by too much Heat entering the
    Evaporator Coil: Step by Step 12
Determining if Problem is caused by a Bad Compressor: Step By Step 13
Determining if Problem is caused by Non-condensable Gasses in the
    System: Step by Step 13
Diagnosing Problems with Systems that have TXV Metering 15
    Causes 15
Diagnosing Normal Operation: Step By Step 15
Overcharge in Condenser if Condensing Pressure and Subcooling are too High;
    Suction Pressure and Superheat are Normal: Step By Step 16
Undercharge if Condensing Pressure is too Low and Subcooling is too Low;
    Suction Pressure and Suction Vapor Superheat Normal: Step By Step 17
Pressure Hunting back and forth with fluctuating Superheat: Step By Step 17
Lower than Normal Pressure with High Superheat: Step By Step 18
Higher than Normal Pressure with Low Superheat: Step By Step 20
Higher than Normal Pressure with High Superheat: Step By Step 21
QUICK CHARTS
    Low Evaporator Heat Load: Fixed & TXV Metering Device 22
    High Evaporator Heat Load: Fixed & TXV Metering Device 23
    Low System Charge: Fixed & TXV Metering Device 24

Field Service Guide: Diagnosing Problems In Your Refrigeration Circuit

High System Charge: Fixed & TXV Metering Device 25
Non-Condensable Gasses: Fixed & TXV Metering Device 26
   Solution Cont. 27
Suction Line Restriction: Fixed & TXV Metering Device 28
Liquid Line Restriction: Fixed & TXV Metering Device 29
   Solution Cont. 30
Restricted Metering Device: Fixed & TXV Metering 31
   Solution Cont. 32
Condenser Parallel Circuit Restriction: Fixed Metering 33
   Solution Cont. 34
Condenser Parallel Circuit Restriction: TXV Metering 35
Condenser Subcooling Circuit Restriction: Fixed & TXV Metering 36
Over-Feeding Metering Device: Fixed & TXV Metering Types 37

Evaporator Conditions
   Fixed Metering Device **38**
   TXV Metering Device **40**

Field Service Guide: Diagnosing Problems In Your Refrigeration Circuit

How to Test Refrigeration Circuits

Introduction

Troubleshooting refrigeration cycle problems starts by determining what the system should be doing when it is operating normally. This includes using charging charts to determine what the pressures should be. If the system is using a fixed metering device, the suction vapor superheat requirement needs to be determined. Liquid subcooling levels on average should be around 10-15 degrees depending upon manufacturer brand. Once operating requirements are known, the low side of the system and then high side of the system can be analyzed.

Troubleshooting refrigeration circuit problems requires an understanding of why refrigerant pressures go up and down. Troubleshooting also requires an understanding of how suction vapor superheat and liquid subcooling fluctuate. All of these topics are covered in their respective chapters in this book.

Superheat and Use in Diagnostics

These illustrations of evaporator conditions can help aid in diagnostic choices. Larger images can be found on pages 38-42.

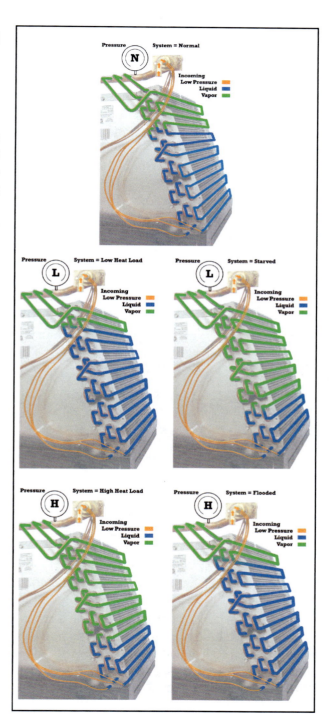

Field Service Guide: Diagnosing Problems In Your Refrigeration Circuit

Condensing Pressure and Liquid Subcooling Measurement use in Diagnostics

Condenser coils should operate at the pressures indicated on system charging charts. When abnormal pressure is present, the temperature of the liquid leaving the condenser coil should be measured. At no time should the liquid be colder than the temperature of the air that passes across the condenser coil. If there is refrigerant leaving the condenser coil at a low temperature, there is a pressure drop in the coil. To find the pressure drop use a digital thermometer to measure the inlet and outlet circuits of the coil. The temperature of these circuits will not always be uniform but will have some deviation. If a cold circuit is found, there is a pressure drop in that circuit.

If the liquid checks out warmer than the air entering the condenser coil, the liquid subcooling level should be calculated. If the pressure is high and the liquid hot, with low subcooling, there is a lack of heat transfer at the condenser coil. Check for a dirty condenser coil or air that is recirculating and somehow bypassing the condenser coil (Panel off). Next, perform a non-condensable gas check.

If the coil is clean and the liquid is warm with normal subcooling, there is likely a high load on the evaporator coil.

If the condensing pressure is high and the subcooling also high, the condenser has too much refrigerant in it.

Pressure Loss and Temperature Drop

Filter driers drop pressure right out of the box. Typically, filter driers are sized to drop 1 PSIG of pressure when new. As they load up with moisture and debris, the pressure drop will increase. A digital temperature probe placed at the inlet and then outlet of the drier can detect some levels of pressure loss. If the temperature drop exceeds 3°F, change the drier.

Line kinks can also be detected with a digital thermometer. A temperature drop in excess of 3°F indicates a pressure drop above 3 PSIG. Fix the kink.

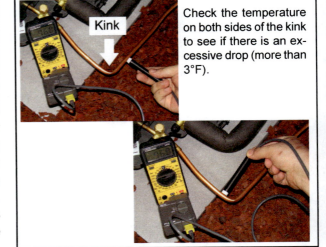

Check the temperature on both sides of the kink to see if there is an excessive drop (more than 3°F).

Diagnosing Problems with Systems that have Fixed Metering Orifices

There are three states the suction pressure can be in, they include:

- Normal pressure as required by the charging chart.
- Lower than normal pressure, which will cause a cold evaporator coil that may form ice or frost on the surface.
- Higher than normal suction pressure.

How do you know if the suction pressure is normal? By using a charging chart to find the required suction pressure as published by the manufacturer of the system. If this chart is not available, realize that for every pound of pressure your gauge is off what the required pressure is, the capacity will deviate by 1% if R-22 and by .6% if R-410A.

Causes of Lower Than Required Suction Pressure

If the system suction pressure is too low, there are three potential causes:

- The suction line may be undersized or kinked.

- The heat load on the evaporator coil is not high enough. This could be a dirty evaporator coil or a lack of indoor air volume, or simply a cold return air temperature.

- The evaporator coil may be starving for refrigerant due to restrictions or charge problems.

Step-by-Step Procedures for Determining Cause of Low Suction Pressure: FIXED METERING EQUIPPED SYSTEMS

Determining if the Problem is Caused by Suction Line Pressure Loss

Tools: **Refrigeration Gauges Thermometer**

STEP 1

Inspect the suction line size. Determine if the line size may be too small. (Read the Line Sets chapter.) If the line size may be the problem, install a pressure tap on the suction line at the outlet of the evaporator circuit.

Field Service Guide: Diagnosing Problems In Your Refrigeration Circuit

STEP 2

Run the system and compare the pressure at the outlet of the evaporator circuit versus the suction pressure at the outdoor condensing unit. If there is a pressure drop in excess of 3 PSIG for R-22 or 5 PSIG for R-410A, the line is either undersized or it may be kinked.

STEP 3

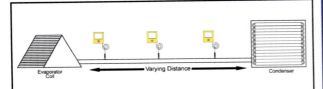

Check the temperature at different points along the suction line in order to find an excessive drop in temperature, which will indicate a pressure loss.

Check for a kink in the suction line. Measure the temperature of the suction line at various points on the line. If a temperature drop in excess of 3°F is detected across two points, there is a pressure drop. Find the cause of the pressure loss.

Determining if the Problem is Caused by Low Heat Load

Tools: **Refrigeration Gauges / Sling Psychrometer**

STEP 1

Measure the return air wet bulb and dry bulb temperature at the filter rack of the air handler/furnace. Plot the required suction vapor superheat on the factory-charging chart. If a chart is not available, use the generic chart located in the charging chapter.

STEP 2

With the system operating in cooling mode, measure the suction pressure and suction vapor superheat. If the suction pressure is low, and the superheat is lower than required, the system lacks air volume or heat.

6

Field Service Guide: Diagnosing Problems In Your Refrigeration Circuit

STEP 3

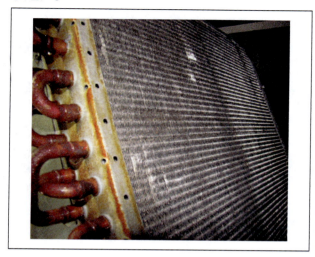

Check to ensure evaporator coil and indoor blower wheel are clean. Clean if necessary.

STEP 4

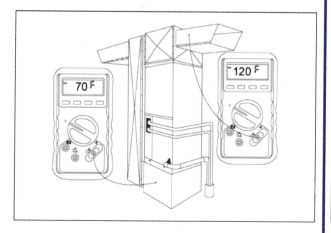

Perform an air volume calculation and correct the air volume problem.

Determining if Problem is Caused by a Lack of Refrigerant in the Evaporator Coil

STEP 1   Tools: Refrigeration Gauges / Sling Psychrometer

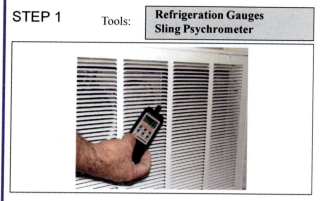

Measure the return air wet bulb and dry bulb temperature at the filter rack of the air handler/furnace. Plot the required suction vapor superheat on the factory-charging chart. If a chart is not available, use the generic chart located in the charging chapter.

STEP 2

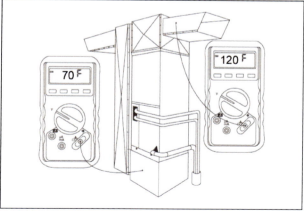

Measure air volume and adjust to proper level. 350-450 CFM per 1 ton of cooling.

7

Field Service Guide: Diagnosing Problems In Your Refrigeration Circuit

STEP 3

With the system operating in cooling mode, measure the suction pressure and suction vapor superheat. If the suction pressure is low and the superheat is higher than required, the evaporator coil circuits are not getting enough refrigerant.

If the pressures both come up and superheat comes down, the system is low on charge. If both pressures stay low despite the addition of refrigerant and the compressor amp draw goes up, there is a restriction in the refrigeration system. If the addition of the refrigerant charge causes the high pressure to rise rapidly yet the suction pressure stays low, there is now an overcharge in the condenser and a liquid circuit restriction.

STEP 4

Check high pressure to ensure it is at factory required level. If it is lower than required, add refrigerant to the system.

STEP 5

If a restriction is present it can be in the condenser coil, the liquid line drier, liquid line, or metering device. Check the temperature of the liquid line at the outdoor unit service valve. The liquid temperature should be above or at the temperature of the outdoor air. If the liquid line is colder than the outdoor air, the restriction is in the condenser circuits or a drier inside the condenser cabinet.

Field Service Guide: Diagnosing Problems In Your Refrigeration Circuit

STEP 6

Make sure to check the temperature from both exits of the parallel circuits

Measure the temperature of the refrigerant leaving the condenser circuits. They should all be close in temperature and not below the temperature of the outdoor air. (Unit is running) If one of these points is cold, there is a restriction in that circuit of the condenser coil.

STEP 7

Check the temperature of the liquid entering and leaving the liquid line service valve and drier. There should be very little temperature change through the service valve. The drier may have up to a 2°F difference in temperature between the inlet and outlet of the drier. If there is an excessive temperature drop, the drier is plugged and must be replaced.

STEP 8

Check the temperature of the liquid line at the outlet of the liquid line drier and about 1 foot in front of the metering device. There should be no noticeable difference in temperature. If there is a large temperature drop, there is a kink or restriction in the liquid line. Locate the point where the line becomes cold. At that point in the line there is a pressure loss causing the temperature drop.

STEP 9

The restriction must be in the metering device or metering device distributor tubes as all other components in the liquid line have checked out OK. Recover the charge and inspect the metering piston for proper size and debris plugging the bore of the piston. Check screen assembly protecting distributor tubes for debris. Re-install orifice and re-charge the system.

9

Finding the causes of low suction pressure were performed in a specific order. They were:

1. Inspect the suction line because this is a field installed component that is sized by someone other than the equipment manufacturer. Likely point of error is high.

2. Check for kinks in the suction line because many installers do not use tubing benders. Likely point of error is high.

3. Determine if low heat load is present. Fans work against static pressure in ducting. Humans size ducting. Likely point of error is high.

4. If those two are OK, then the system needs refrigerant in the evaporator coil. Superheat confirms it. Add refrigerant. If pressures do not come up, follow the step by step to find restriction.

Causes of Higher than Required Suction Pressure

- Too much refrigerant entering the evaporator coil. Metering device too big, charge too high, metering device not seating properly/bypassing liquid into the evaporator circuits.

- Too much heat load on the evaporator coil. Infiltration of hot air into the return ducting. New system startup with high temperature in the home.

- Dirty condenser raising condensing pressure. (Non-condensable gasses in system.)

- Failure of the compressor valves. (Reciprocating compressors.)

Step-by-Step Procedure for Determining Cause of High Suction Pressure: FIXED METERING EQUIPPED SYSTEMS

Determining if Problem is Caused by too much Refrigerant in the Evaporator Coil

STEP 1   Tools: Refrigeration Gauges / Sling Psychrometer

Measure the return air wet bulb and dry bulb temperature at the filter rack of the air handler/furnace. Plot the required suction vapor superheat on the factory charging chart. If a chart is not available, use the generic chart located in the charging chapter.

Field Service Guide: Diagnosing Problems In Your Refrigeration Circuit

STEP 2

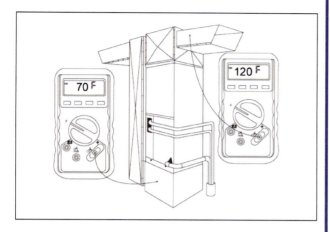

Measure air volume and adjust to proper level. 350-450 CFM per 1 ton of cooling.

STEP 3

With the system operating in cooling mode, measure the suction pressure and suction vapor superheat. If the suction pressure is high, and the superheat is lower than required, the evaporator coil circuits are getting too much refrigerant.

STEP 4

If the condensing pressure is lower than it should be, go to step 5.

If the condensing pressure is high, check the temperature of the liquid line. If the line is hot, clean the condenser coil and repeat step 3. If the liquid line is warm, recover charge until both pressures are within normal ranges.

STEP 5

Shut off the system and recover the refrigerant charge. Access the metering piston. Check it for proper size and make sure it is firmly seated. If there is no metering piston in the coil, install one of the right size.

Re-charge the system. Start the system. If the pressures are still not correct test the compressor for proper pumping and replace if necessary.

Field Service Guide: Diagnosing Problems In Your Refrigeration Circuit

Determining if Problem is caused by too much Heat entering the Evaporator Coil

Tools: **Refrigeration Gauges**
Sling Psychrometer

STEP 1

Measure the return air wet bulb and dry bulb temperature at the filter rack of the air handler/furnace. Plot the required suction vapor superheat on the factory-charging chart. If a chart is not available, use the generic chart located in the charging chapter.

STEP 2

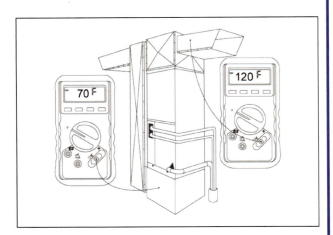

Measure air volume and adjust to proper level. 350-450 CFM per 1 ton of cooling.

STEP 3

With the system operating in cooling mode, measure the suction pressure and suction vapor superheat. If the suction pressure is high, and the superheat is higher than required, the evaporator coil circuits may be getting too much heat. Confirm by checking the condensing pressure. If the condensing pressure is also high,

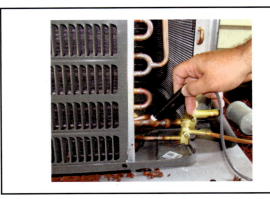

check the liquid subcooling level. If it is normal, the system is under a heavy load. If the subcooling is low, the liquid line will be hot. Check for a dirty condenser and potential non condensable gas in the system.

If the system checks out as a high evaporator load problem, go to the next step.

Field Service Guide: Diagnosing Problems In Your Refrigeration Circuit

STEP 4

Measure the room air temperature near the thermostat. The temperature at the thermostat should be the same as at the filter rack. If the room air is cooler than the air at the filter rack, air is infiltrating into the return air ducting. Find the air leak source.

STEP 5

As the system runs the suction pressure and suction vapor superheat should fall.

Allow the system to run. As the return air temperature falls, the suction pressure and suction vapor superheat will drop. If the room air temperature does not come down, the system may not have enough capacity to cool the structure.

Determining if Problem is caused by a Bad Compressor

STEP 1

Go to the Compressor chapter and check for proper pumping of reciprocating and scroll models.

Determining if Problem is Caused by Non-condensable Gasses in the System

STEP 1   Tools:

| Refrigeration Gauges |
| Recovery Cylinder |
| Thermometer |

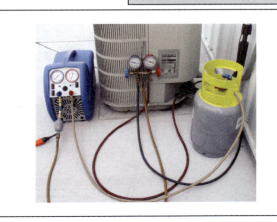

Recover the refrigerant from the system into an empty evacuated refrigerant recovery cylinder.

13

Field Service Guide: Diagnosing Problems In Your Refrigeration Circuit

STEP 2

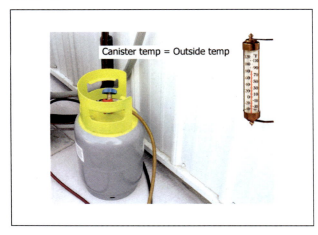

Allow the temperature of the recovery cylinder to reach the same temperature as the outdoor air and then measure the pressure in the recovery cylinder.

STEP 3

R-410A PSIG	Saturation Temp. (F)	R-22 PSIG
318	100	195
322	101	200
346	106	215
356	108	220
364	110	225
370	111	230

Refer to a temperature pressure table for the refrigerant that was recovered. The pressure in the cylinder should be equal to the corresponding saturation temperature of the refrigerant drum. For example: R-22 @ 101°F = 200 PSIG in the cylinder.

STEP 4

If the pressure is higher than chart value, non-condensable gas is mixed with the refrigerant. Pull evacuation on air conditioning system and re-charge with new refrigerant.

Finding the causes of high suction pressure were performed in a specific order. They were:

1. Check for overcharge and oversized/bypassing piston.

2. Check for infiltration air or non-condensable gas.

3. Perform compressor test.

Diagnosing Problems With Systems that have TXV Metering

There are five states the evaporator coil can be in, they include:

- Normal pressure and normal superheat.
- Pressure hunting back and forth with fluctuating superheat.
- Lower than normal pressure with high superheat.
- Higher than normal suction pressure with low superheat.
- Higher than normal pressure with high superheat.

Causes

Normal pressure with normal superheat
- Normal operation.
- Overcharge in condenser if condensing pressure and subcooling are too high.
- Undercharge if condensing pressure is too low and subcooling is too low.

Pressure hunting back and forth with fluctuating superheat
- Low air volume/low heat load on evaporator coil.
- TXV wrong size for coil. (Too large.)
- Flash gas entering TXV from liquid line.

Lower than normal pressure with high superheat
- Low charge.
- Restriction in the refrigeration system.

Higher than normal pressure with low superheat
- Liquid bypassing TXV.

Higher than normal pressure with high superheat
- High heat load on evaporator coil.

Diagnosing Normal Operation

Tools: Refrigeration Gauges

STEP 1

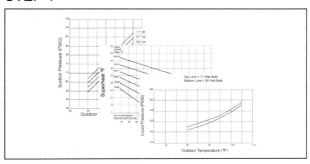

From factory-charging chart confirm required suction pressure. The suction vapor superheat level should be close to 10°F for both R-22 and R-410A systems. Confirm required condensing pressure. Use factory-charging charts to find subcooling requirement. Typical systems are 10°F but newer systems may be higher. In many cases, the subcooling design is printed onto the nameplate of the outdoor condensing unit.

Field Service Guide: Diagnosing Problems In Your Refrigeration Circuit

STEP 2

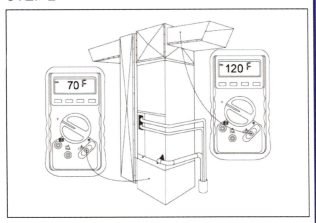

Adjust air volume to 350-450 CFM per 1 ton of cooling.

STEP 3

Condensing pressure will be at factory-required level. Measure the liquid subcooling level. It should be close to 10°F or slightly higher. If subcooling is not correct and condensing pressure is not correct, continue on to the next procedure

STEP 4

Measure the suction pressure and suction vapor superheat at the condensing unit. Pressure should be close to chart requirements. If it is low, check condition of suction line.

Overcharge in Condenser if Condensing Pressure and Subcooling are too High; Suction Pressure and Superheat are Normal

STEP 1   Tools: **Refrigeration Gauges
Recovery Tank**

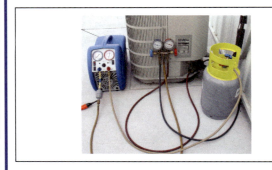

Recover refrigerant until condensing pressure and liquid subcooling levels are reduced to normal range. Allow up to 20 minutes for liquid line temperature to become stable.

Field Service Guide: Diagnosing Problems In Your Refrigeration Circuit

Undercharge if Condensing Pressure is too Low and Subcooling is too Low. Suction Pressure and Superheat Normal.

STEP 1   Tools: **Refrigeration Gauges**

Add refrigerant to the system until condensing pressure and liquid subcooling level are at factory-required levels. Allow up to 20 minutes for liquid line temperature to become stable.

Pressure Hunting back and forth with fluctuating Superheat

STEP 1   Tools: **Refrigeration Gauges
Thermometer**

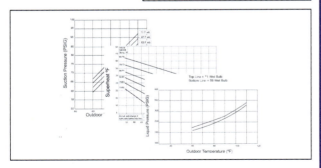

From factory-charging chart confirm required suction pressure. The suction vapor superheat level should be close to 10°F for both R-22 and R-410A systems. Confirm required condensing pressure. Use factory-charging charts to find

Check the outdoor condensing unit for factory suggested sub-cooling temps.

subcooling requirement. Typical systems are 10°F but newer systems may be higher. In many cases the subcooling design is printed onto the nameplate of the outdoor condensing unit.

STEP 2

Measure liquid subcooling level at the condenser. If it is within factory specifications and the liquid line is properly sized, there should be no flash gas at entrance to the metering device. Use piping charts to determine pressure loss in liquid line if necessary.

If subcooling is too low, add refrigerant. If subcooling is OK, go to STEP 3.

Field Service Guide: Diagnosing Problems In Your Refrigeration Circuit

STEP 3

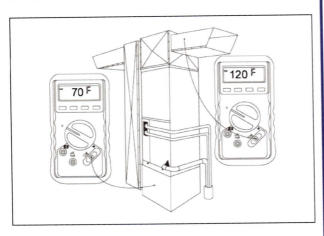

Inspect evaporator coil for dirty surface and clean if needed. Adjust air volume to 350-450 CFM per 1 ton of cooling.

STEP 4

If TXV continues to hunt after air volume is at proper level, evaporator coil is clean, and liquid line is sized right with no flash gas present, check for improper metering device sizing. Contact manufacturer of system.

Lower than Normal Pressure with High Superheat

Tools: **Refrigeration Gauges / Thermometer**

STEP 1

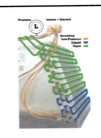

See page 39 for a larger image of the starved evaporator state

Systems operating in this condition lack refrigerant in the evaporator circuits. Confirm the system is properly charged. If the addition of charge does not significantly change system pressures, or if the condensing pressure rapidly rises, there is a restriction in the system. If a restriction is present, go to the STEP 2.

STEP 2

Run the system and check the temperature of the liquid leaving the condensing unit. The liquid should be warm, not hot, and not cold. If the liquid line is hot, check for a dirty condenser. If the line is warmer than the outdoor air or at outdoor air temperature, continue to the next step.

18

Field Service Guide: Diagnosing Problems In Your Refrigeration Circuit

This factory installed drier may or may not be present in the system. If it does not exist, move to step 3.

If the liquid line is colder than the air entering the outdoor condenser coil, check for a drier in the outdoor unit. Measure the temperature drop across the drier. If it is in excess of 3°F, change the drier.

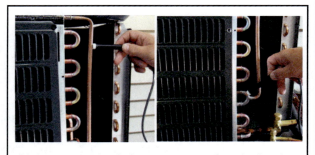

Make sure to check the temperature from both exits of the parallel circuits

If the drier is OK, check the temperature of the refrigerant at the outlets of the condenser coil circuits. If the refrigerant leaving a circuit is cold, there is a pressure drop in the circuit. Repair as needed.

STEP 3

If a factory installed drier is not present, make sure to check any that may have been installed in the field.

Check for a temperature drop across the liquid line drier. If the temperature drop is in excess of 3°F, change the drier (If a drier is present).

STEP 4

Check the temperature of the liquid line at the entrance to the metering device. If there is a significant difference between the liquid line temperature outside versus inside, install a pressure port on the liquid line and compare the two pressures. (Use a pressure port that can be installed on a pre-charged system.)

If a large pressure drop is present, repair the cause of the pressure drop. (Kink.)

Field Service Guide: Diagnosing Problems In Your Refrigeration Circuit

STEP 5

With the system operating, remove the TXV sensing bulb from the suction line. Hold the bulb in your hand. The heat from your hand should momentarily cause a noticeable increase in the flow of refrigerant into the evaporator coil. If nothing changes, change the TXV.

Higher than Normal Pressure with Low Superheat

Tools: **Refrigeration Gauges / Thermometer**

STEP 1

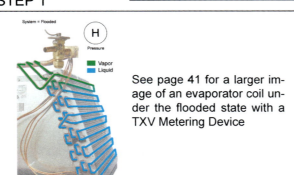

See page 41 for a larger image of an evaporator coil under the flooded state with a TXV Metering Device

If the suction pressure is too high and the suction vapor superheat is too low, the evaporator circuits are operating in a flooded condition. The sensing bulb may not be insulated properly.

The TXV sensing bulb should be covered with insulation. The insulation has been removed in this image to show proper placement of the bulb.

Check to ensure it is well insulated and positioned at 2 or 10 o'clock on the suction line. If it is not positioned properly, or if the insulation is not present, correct the problem.

STEP 2

The equalizer line is a closing pressure. In this problem the TXV is allowing too much refrigerant into the circuits. Confirm the equalizer line is not plugged. If it is not plugged, change the TXV.

Field Service Guide: Diagnosing Problems In Your Refrigeration Circuit

Higher than Normal Pressure with High Superheat

STEP 1

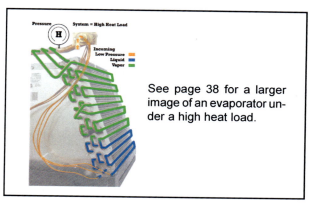

See page 38 for a larger image of an evaporator under a high heat load.

If the suction pressure is too high and the suction vapor superheat is too high, the evaporator circuits are operating with a large amount of heat entering the refrigerant in the evaporator circuits.

The expansion valve is wide open and cannot get enough refrigerant into the refrigerant circuits. Measure the dry bulb temperature of the air at the filter rack with the system running.

STEP 2

Measure the temperature of the air at the thermostat. The two temperatures should be equal. If the air at the filter rack is hotter than the air at the thermostat, heat is entering the return air ducting. This heat is coming from an unconditioned source. (Such as attic air.) Correct the infiltration problem.

STEP 3

If the air temperatures are equal and the system cannot cool the space, the system may be too small for the heat load. Make sure all windows are closed. Replace the system if necessary.

21

Field Service Guide: Diagnosing Problems In Your Refrigeration Circuit

QUICK CHARTS

Low Evaporator Heat Load: Fixed & TXV Metering Device

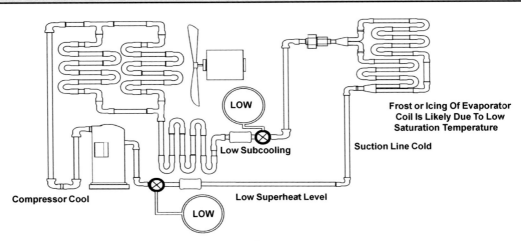

Problem Overview

Low evaporator heat loading occurs when there is not enough heat entering the refrigerant at the evaporator coil. This condition can cause the evaporator coil to form a coating of frost or ice on its' surface. In extreme cases, superheat could fall to zero degrees and liquid can flood back to the compressor.

Symptoms (Fixed Metering)

Systems running with low evaporator loading will run at pressures below factory required levels. Abnormally low superheat and subcooling levels will be present when the evaporator coil lacks heat load.

The low heat load condition could cause the evaporator coil temperature to be very cold. Ice or frost may form on the evaporator surface and suction line surface. The compressor shell may sweat and the hot gas temperature will be cool.

Symptoms (TXV Metering)

Same as above but TXV may hunt in an attempt to maintain adequate superheat.

Causes

- Dirty Return Air Filter
- Dirty Indoor Fan Blower Assembly
- Indoor Fan Motor Not On High Speed
- Undersized Ductwork
- Dirty Evaporator Coil
-
Thermostat Setpoint Too Low

Solution

- Thaw out the evaporator coil if it ice or frost is present.
- Inspect the return air filter to determine if it is dirty.
- Inspect the evaporator coil to ensure it is clean.
- Inspect the indoor blower assembly to ensure it is clean.
- Make sure the indoor blower motor is operating at high speed.
- Make sure the supply and return air ducting are sized properly
- Perform an indoor airflow measurement to ensure you have adequate CFM present. Airflow should be between 350-450 CFM per ton of cooling capacity.

Field Service Guide: Diagnosing Problems In Your Refrigeration Circuit

QUICK CHARTS

High Evaporator Heat Load: Fixed & TXV Metering Device

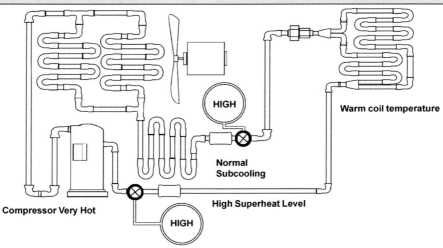

Problem Overview

High evaporator heat loading occurs when there is excessive heat entering the refrigerant at the evaporator coil. This condition can cause the compressor to shut off on its' internal overload, or trip the electrical circuit breaker.

(Fixed Type)

Systems running with high evaporator loading will run at pressures above factory required levels. Abnormally high superheat and normal subcooling levels will be present when the evaporator coil is exposed to higher than allowed heat load.

The high heat load condition could cause the evaporator coil temperature to be very warm. The warm evaporator temperature will inhibit the amount of moisture being removed from the air.

The compressor shell and hot gas temperature will be extremely high.

(TXV Metering)

Same as above but the TXV may keep superheat level close to the required range of 10-15°F. *In extreme cases of high load the superheat may go much higher.*

Causes

- Infiltration of unconditioned air into the return duct
- New systems started on a very hot day
- Temporary high people loads (occupancy high)
- System undersized for structure heat gain

Solution

The following steps will help you find the problem:

- Measure the temperature of the conditioned space and then check the temperature of the air entering the evaporator coil at the filter rack. If the air entering the evaporator is warmer than the conditioned space, infiltration of unconditioned air is present.

- If the system is a new start up on a hot day, allow time for the indoor temperature to fall within charging chart range.

- If the system is still overloaded and the outdoor air temperature is within design range for your area, run a heat load to determine if the system is properly sized.

23

Field Service Guide: Diagnosing Problems In Your Refrigeration Circuit

QUICK CHARTS

Low System Charge: Fixed & TXV Metering Device

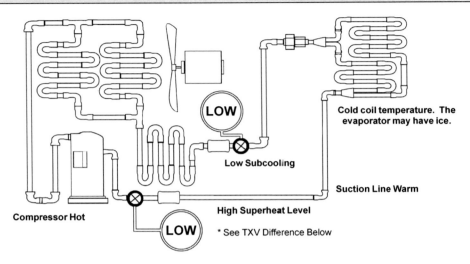

Problem Overview

Low system charge can be caused by a leak or poor installation skills. A system running with a low charge will have low capacity, low efficiency, and a hot compressor motor.

Symptoms (Fixed Metering)

Systems running with low charge will run at pressures below factory required levels. Abnormally high superheat and low subcooling levels will be present. The compressor motor will run hot due to a lack of refrigerant vapor to cool the motor windings. The low suction pressure will create a cold evaporator coil which may form a coating of ice.

Symptoms (TXV Metering)

When a system is undercharged with a TXV metering device, the TXV may open enough to maintain adequate suction pressure and suction vapor superheat.

The condensing pressure will be low along with low subcooling. If the system charge is very low, the system will appear with the same symptoms as a fixed metering type.

Causes

- Poor Installation Skills
- Refrigerant Leaks

Solution

The following steps will help you find the problem:

- Leak test the system.
- Charge to Charging Chart requirements.

Field Service Guide: Diagnosing Problems In Your Refrigeration Circuit

QUICK CHARTS

High System Charge: Fixed & TXV Type Metering Device

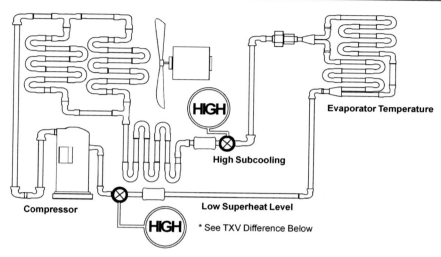

Problem Overview

High system charge is caused by poor installation skills. A system running with a high charge will experience excessive energy consumption, possible starting problems, internal overload tripping, indoor air humidity complaints, compressor failure due to liquid flood back.

Symptoms (Fixed Metering)

Systems running with high charge will run at pressures above factory required levels. Abnormally low superheat and high subcooling levels will be present. The compressor motor may experience liquid flood back problems.

Symptoms (TXV Metering)

When a system is overcharged with a TXV metering device, the suction pressure and superheat may appear normal.

The normal conditions are caused by the TXV as it throttles back the excess refrigerant flow into the evaporator coil. The excess charge is then stored in the condenser coil which elevates the head pressure and liquid subcooling levels.

If the charge is high enough, the suction pressure may be too high with slightly low superheat present.

Causes

- Poor Installation Skills

Solution

The following steps will help you find the problem:

- Charge to factory requirements.

25

Field Service Guide: Diagnosing Problems In Your Refrigeration Circuit

QUICK CHARTS

Non-Condensable Gasses: Fixed & TXV Metering Device

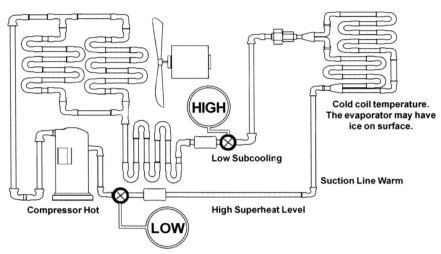

Problem Overview

Air, Nitrogen, Hydrogen and other foreign gasses present in a refrigerant system are referred to as non-condensables since they will not condense into a liquid at pressures encountered in a refrigeration system. Theses gasses will accumulate in the condenser coil and take up valuable condenser coil circuiting.

Symptoms

Systems running with non-condensables present will experience higher than required head pressure. The suction pressure will be low if there is no subcooling present. If subcooling is present, the suction pressure may be slightly high with fixed metering systems and may be normal with TXV systems.

The subcooling level with non-condensables will be lower than required. If no subcooling is present, there will be flash gas in the liquid line before the metering device.

The superheat level will be high when flash gas is present. If there is subcooled liquid entering the metering device and the suction pressure is high with a fixed metering system, the superheat may be low. If the system is using a TXV, the superheat may be normal

Causes

- Poor Installation Skills.

- Failure to properly evacuate the system after the system has been opened.

Solution

The following steps will help you find the problem if a discharge line pressure tap is present:

Field Service Guide: Diagnosing Problems In Your Refrigeration Circuit

QUICK CHARTS

Non-Condensable Gasses: Fixed & TXV Metering Device

Solution Cont.

• Connect your refrigeration gauges to the system. Call for cooling. With the system running shut the liquid line service valve and pump the system down.

• When the system has pumped down, shut off power to the condensing unit.

• Disconnect the wires that feed power to the compressor at the compressor contactor terminals.

• Connect power back to the condensing unit and call for cooling.

• The condenser fan motor will run but the compressor will not.

• Measure the temperature of the outdoor air and the temperature of the air leaving the condenser coil via the condenser fan. When both outdoor air temperature and condenser fan air temperature are equal, read the discharge line pressure.

• Compare the pressure reading to the corresponding saturation temperature for the refrigerant being used. The corresponding saturation temperature should equal the temperature of the outdoor air.

• If the pressure conversion is indicating a temperature higher than outdoor air temperature, non-condensables are present.

If the system has no discharge line pressure port, recover the refrigerant, evacuate the system and charge.

Field Service Guide: Diagnosing Problems In Your Refrigeration Circuit

QUICK CHARTS

Suction Line Restriction: Fixed & TXV Metering Device

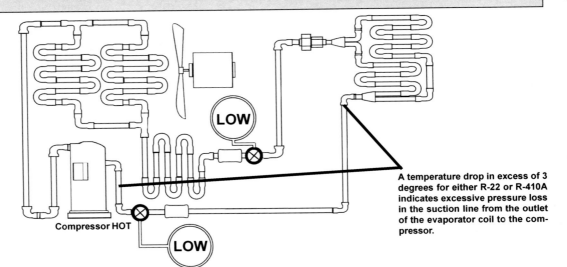

A temperature drop in excess of 3 degrees for either R-22 or R-410A indicates excessive pressure loss in the suction line from the outlet of the evaporator coil to the compressor.

Problem Overview

Excessive pressure loss in the suction line will cause low cooling capacity along with potential evaporator coil freezing.

Symptoms

Systems running with a large pressure loss in the suction line will run at pressures below factory required levels. Because the pressure is being read downstream from the restriction, the actual calculated superheat will be inaccurate. Find the problem by checking the temperature of the suction line at the outlet of the evaporator coil and then comparing it to the temperature of the suction line at the inlet to the compressor. You should have a maximum temperature drop of 3 degrees. If the actual temperature drop is higher, find the cause of the pressure drop.

Causes

- Undersized suction lines
- Kinks in the suction line tubing
- Restricted suction line driers
- Excessive use of suction line pipe fittings

Solution

The following steps will help you find the problem:

- Run the system and allow temperatures and pressures to stabilize.
- Measure suction line temperature at the outlet of the evaporator coil.
- Measure suction line at the inlet to the compressor.
- If temperature drop is in excess of 3°F, check for kinks in line.
- If no kinks present, check suction line sizing chart to ensure proper size tubing is being used.
- If tubing size is too small, replace line set with proper size.

Field Service Guide: Diagnosing Problems In Your Refrigeration Circuit

QUICK CHARTS

Liquid Line Restriction: Fixed & TXV Metering Device

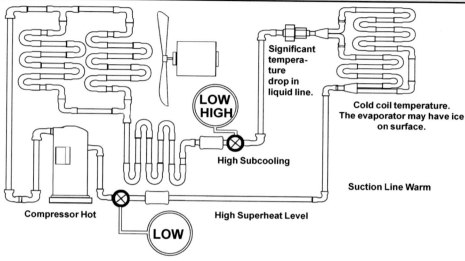

Problem Overview

Restrictions in the liquid line will prevent the evaporator coil from receiving the proper amount of refrigerant. The restriction will cause a large pressure drop between the condenser coil and the metering device. This large pressure drop can be detected by checking the temperature of the liquid line at the outlet of the condenser coil and at the inlet to the metering device.

Symptoms

Systems running with a liquid line restriction will have low suction pressure along with high superheat. The liquid pressure will initially be low which will make the system appear undercharged. When refrigerant is added to the system, the liquid pressure will rise but the suction pressure will remain low. At this point, you should be able to identify there is a problem in the liquid circuit. If subcooling is measured, at this time, it will be high. The high subcooling level is an indication that excess refrigerant is being stored in the condenser coil. Look for frosting or sweating of the liquid line or liquid line drier.

Causes

- Restricted Liquid Line Drier
- Undersized Liquid Line
- Excessive Liquid Line Pipe Fittings
- Kinked Liquid Line

Solution

The following steps will help you find the problem:

- If the liquid and suction pressure are low, and no obvious sweating of frosting of the liquid line is present, begin to add refrigerant.

Field Service Guide: Diagnosing Problems In Your Refrigeration Circuit

QUICK CHARTS

Liquid Line Restriction w/Fixed & TXV Metering

Solution Cont.

- If the system is undercharged, both pressures will begin to rise. If the liquid pressure rises significantly, but the suction pressure remains low, the liquid circuit has a restriction.

- Check the temperature of the liquid line at the outlet of the condenser coil and at the inlet to the metering device. No significant drop in temperature should be detected. If you detect a large temperature drop, there is a pressure drop between the two test points. Isolate the restriction and make the repair.

- If there is no temperature drop between the outlet of the condenser and inlet of the metering device, yet the liquid pressure is elevated, suction pressure low, superheat and subcooling high, advance to a RESTRICTED METERING DEVICE.

Field Service Guide: Diagnosing Problems In Your Refrigeration Circuit

QUICK CHARTS

Restricted Metering Device: Fixed & TXV Metering

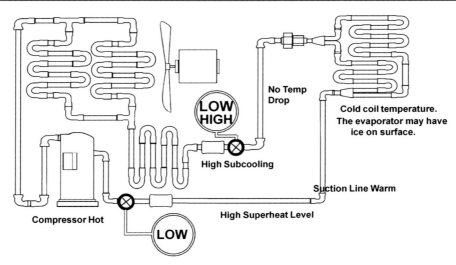

Problem Overview

Restrictions in the metering device will prevent the evaporator coil from receiving the proper amount of refrigerant. The restriction will cause the suction pressure to be too low. With low suction pressure present, the saturation temperature of the refrigerant in the evaporator is very low. Because of the low saturation temperature, freezing of the evaporator surface is likely.

Symptoms

Systems running with a metering restriction will have low suction pressure along with high superheat. The liquid pressure will initially be low which will make the system appear undercharged. When refrigerant is added to the system, the liquid pressure will rise but the suction pressure will remain low. At this point, you should be able to identify there is a problem in the liquid circuit. If subcooling is measured, at this time, it will be high.

The high subcooling level is an indication that excess refrigerant is being stored in the condenser coil. There will be no obvious sign of frosting between the condenser coil and the metering device.

Causes

- Undersized Fixed Metering Device (Piston)
- Failed Expansion Valve Sensing Bulb
- Debris in Metering Device (Poor Installation Skills)
- Moisture Freezing At Metering Device (Not Evacuated Properly)

Solution

The following steps will help you find the problem:

31

Field Service Guide: Diagnosing Problems In Your Refrigeration Circuit

QUICK CHARTS

Restricted Metering Device: Fixed & TXV Metering

Solution Cont.

- If the liquid and suction pressure are low, and no obvious sweating of frosting of the liquid line is present, begin to add refrigerant.

- If the system is undercharged, both pressures will begin to rise. If the liquid pressure rises significantly, but the suction pressure remains low, the liquid circuit has a restriction.

- Check the temperature of the liquid line at the outlet of the condenser coil and at the inlet to the metering device. No significant drop in temperature should be detected. If you detect a large temperature drop, there is a pressure drop between the two test points. Isolate the restriction and make the repair.

- If there is no temperature drop between the outlet of the condenser and inlet of the metering device, yet the liquid pressure is elevated, suction pressure low, superheat and subcooling high, the problem is in the metering device assembly.

- Pump the system down or recover the refrigerant.

- Open the system and inspect the metering device assembly for proper size, operation, or debris.

Field Service Guide: Diagnosing Problems In Your Refrigeration Circuit

QUICK CHARTS

Condenser Parallel Circuit Restriction: Fixed Metering

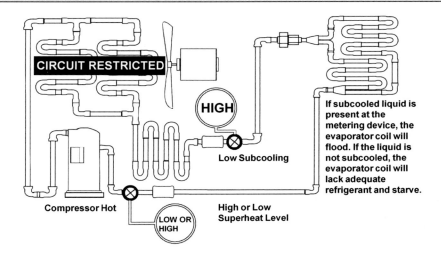

Problem Overview

When a parallel circuit is 100% or partially restricted, condenser surface area is decreased.

Symptoms

Systems running with partially, or fully restricted parallel circuit will run at liquid pressures above factory required levels. The suction pressure could be high or low depending upon if there is enough condenser coil surface area to provide adequate subcooling function for the amount of liquid line present. If there is adequate subcooling, the high liquid pressure will flood the evaporator coil. In a flooded state the evaporator suction pressure will be high and the superheat level low. If there is not enough subcooling to overcome the pressure loss in the liquid line, flash gas will be present before the metering device. This condition will starve the evaporator coil and low suction pressure along with high superheat will be present. The restriction in the circuit will cause a corresponding drop in refrigerant temperature.

Therefore, the circuit with the restriction will have refrigerant leaving the circuit at a temperature much colder than the other circuits.

Causes

- Debris
- Handling Damage

Solution

The following steps will help you find the problem:

- Call for cooling and run the system
- Measure the temperature of the refrigerant leaving the parallel circuits. (Fig. 1)

33

Field Service Guide: Diagnosing Problems In Your Refrigeration Circuit

QUICK CHARTS

Condenser Parallel Circuit Restriction: Fixed Metering

Solution Cont.

- Measure the temperature of the refrigerant leaving the parallel circuits.

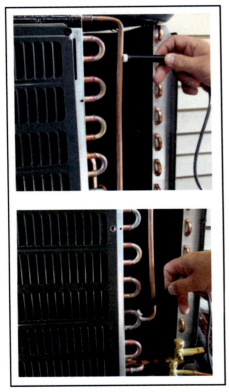

- If the conditions indicate a restriction in the coil and one of the circuits has a considerable (greater than 20 degree temperature difference) temperature difference at its outlet, the circuit has a restriction.

- Replace or repair the condenser coil.

Field Service Guide: Diagnosing Problems In Your Refrigeration Circuit

QUICK CHARTS

Condenser Parallel Circuit Restriction: TXV Metering

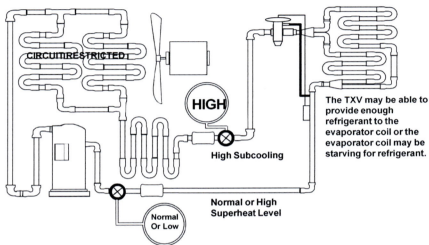

Problem Overview

When a parallel circuit is 100% or partially restricted, condenser surface area is decreased.

Symptoms

Systems running with partially, or fully restricted parallel circuit will run at liquid pressures above factory required levels. The system may have adequate subcooling for the liquid line pressure loss or it may not. If there is enough subcooling to maintain a subcooled liquid at the metering device, the evaporator will perform normally with the TXV. If flash gas forms in the liquid line due to inadequate liquid subcooling, the TXV will try to open and provide more refrigerant to the evaporator coil. If the TXV cannot feed enough refrigerant into the evaporator coil it will starve.

The restriction in the circuit will cause a corresponding drop in refrigerant temperature. Therefore, the circuit with the restriction will have refrigerant leaving the circuit at a temperature much colder than the other circuits.

Causes

- Debris
- Handling Damage

Solution

The following steps will help you find the problem:

- Call for cooling and run the system
- Measure the temperature of the refrigerant leaving the parallel circuits.

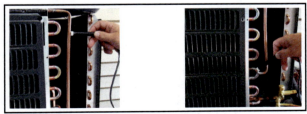

- If the conditions indicate a restriction in the coil and one of the circuits has a considerable (greater than 20 degree temperature difference) temperature difference at its outlet, the circuit has a restriction.
- Replace or repair the condenser coil.

35

Field Service Guide: Diagnosing Problems In Your Refrigeration Circuit

QUICK CHARTS

Condenser Subcooling Circuit Restriction: Fixed & TXV Metering

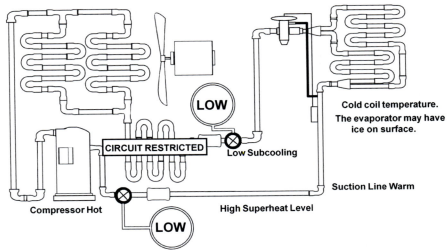

Problem Overview

When a subcooling circuit is 100% or partially restricted, metering of the refrigerant will take place in the condenser coil instead of the metering device.

Symptoms

When the subcooling circuit is restricted, the refrigerant will be metered to a low pressure. Since the liquid pressure gauge is downstream from this restriction, the liquid pressure gauge will be low. The actual temperature of the liquid line will correspond to the saturation temperature equal to the pressure being read on the liquid gauge.

The refrigerant leaving the condensing coil will be below the temperature of the outdoor air circulating through the condenser surface. It is likely there will be frosting or sweating of the liquid line present.

Causes

- Debris
- Handling Damage

Solution

The following steps will help you find the problem:

- Call for cooling and run the system
- Measure the temperature of the refrigerant leaving the condenser coil subcooling circuit.

- If the temperature of the refrigerant is below outdoor air temperature along with other symptoms, a restriction is present.
- Replace or repair the condenser coil.

Field Service Guide: Diagnosing Problems In Your Refrigeration Circuit

QUICK CHARTS

Over-Feeding Metering Device: Fixed & TXV Metering Types

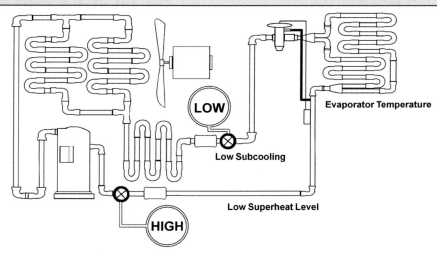

Problem Overview

An evaporator coil that is receiving a higher than normal flow of refrigerant through the metering device will operate in a flooded condition. The system may experience high humidity complaints, compressor starting problems, or compressor failure.

Symptoms

The metering device isolates the high side pressure from the low side pressure. When an overfeeding condition is present, the suction side of the system operates in a flooded state while the high side of the system operates in a starved state. The suction pressure will be high and the superheat low. The liquid pressure will be low and the subcooling will be low.

If the system is using a reciprocating type of compressor, it may appear that the compressor valve plate is bad.

Causes

- Too large of a piston (Fixed Metering)
- Dirty piston seat not allowing metering device to seat properly.
- TXV Sensing Bulb not insulated or in good contact with suction line.

Solution

The following steps will help you find the problem:

- Call for cooling.
- Close the liquid service valve and pump the system down. If the system does not hold a pump down and the liquid line service valve is properly closed. Replace the compressor. (Reciprocating Only)
- If the system holds a pump down cycle, inspect the metering device to determine if it is seated properly or too large. (Fixed Type)
- If the system is using a TXV, make sure the sensing bulb is properly insulated and in good contact with the suction line. If it is not, correct the problem. If it is, replace the TXV.

Field Service Guide: Diagnosing Problems In Your Refrigeration Circuit

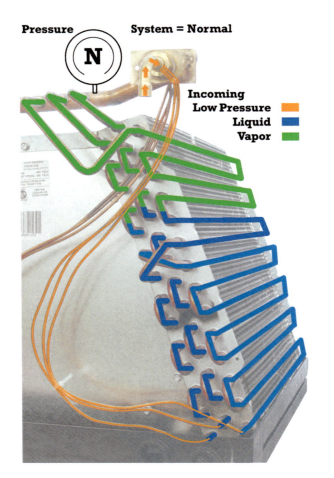

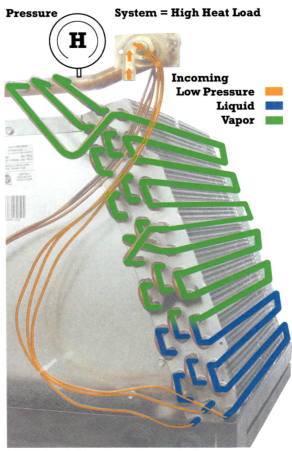

The coil is performing to factory specifications. The refrigerant liquid is boiling off at various points based upon the temperature of the outdoor air and indoor heat load.

The coil is running out of liquid refrigerant earlier in the circuit than it should. The coil is not undercharged because the suction pressure is high. The suction vapor superheat level will be higher than charging chart requirement.

This condition is caused by excess air volume or heat.

Field Service Guide: Diagnosing Problems In Your Refrigeration Circuit

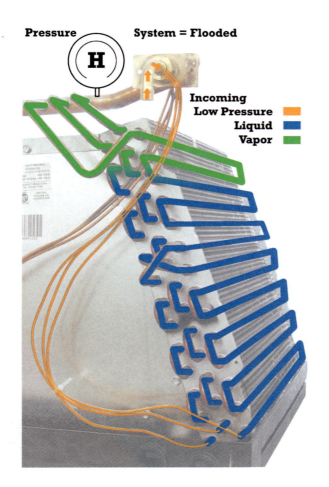

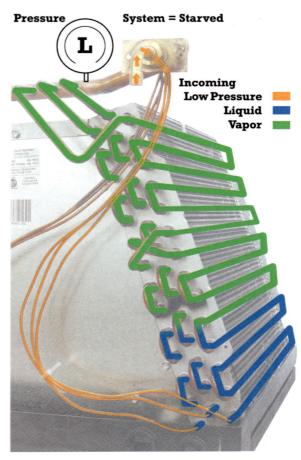

The coil is flooded with liquid refrigerant. The coil pressure is high and the liquid is present very late in the circuiting. If the system were operating at full load conditions, this may appear as a normal coil except for the fact that suction pressure is higher than it should be.

Causes include overcharging and oversizing of the metering piston.

The coil is lacking refrigerant. The saturated liquid is running out early in the circuit and the suction pressure is too low. Superheat is above the required chart value.

Causes include undercharging and liquid restrictions.

Field Service Guide: Diagnosing Problems In Your Refrigeration Circuit

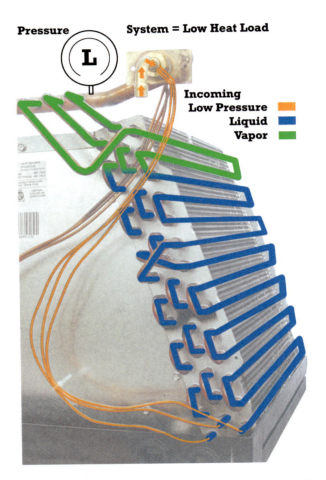

The coil is flooded with liquid refrigerant. The coil pressure is low. This can be due to low air volume or a lack of heat in the air.

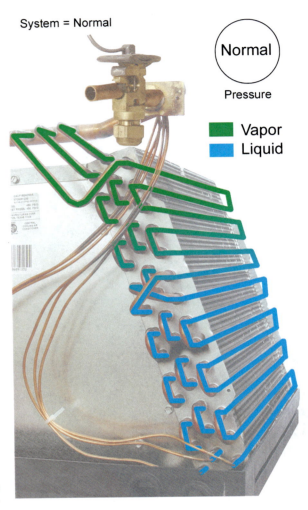

Coils with TXV metering operate at 10°F of suction vapor superheat over a wide range of operating heat load and outdoor air temperatures.

Be aware that a TXV can mask undercharged conditions by maintaining normal evaporator conditions under certain combinations of indoor heat load and outdoor air temperature. The problem will appear intermittently.

Field Service Guide: Diagnosing Problems In Your Refrigeration Circuit

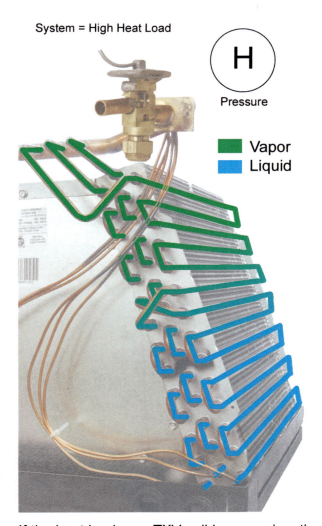

System = High Heat Load

H Pressure

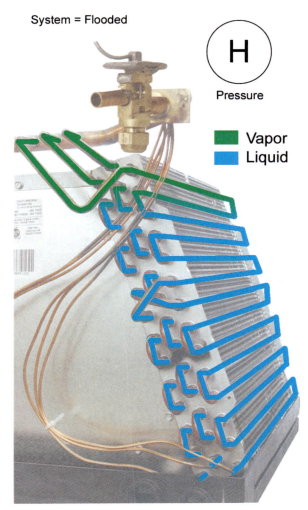

System = Flooded

H Pressure

If the heat load on a TXV coil is excessive, the valve will open to try and maintain proper superheat. The suction pressure will be high. If the heat load is high enough, the TXV may not be able to maintain adequate superheat and the superheat will rise to a level above normal.

If the TXV over-feeds refrigerant into the circuiting, the suction pressure will be too high and the suction vapor superheat too low.

Causes include sensing bulbs that are not insulated, and improperly functioning TXV.

41

Field Service Guide: Diagnosing Problems In Your Refrigeration Circuit

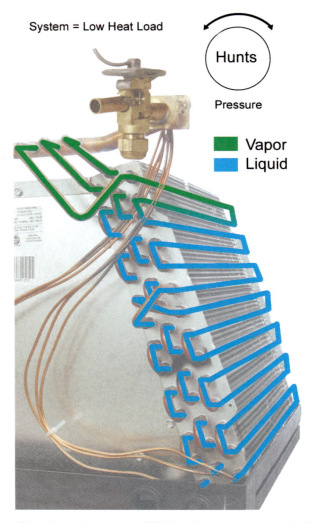

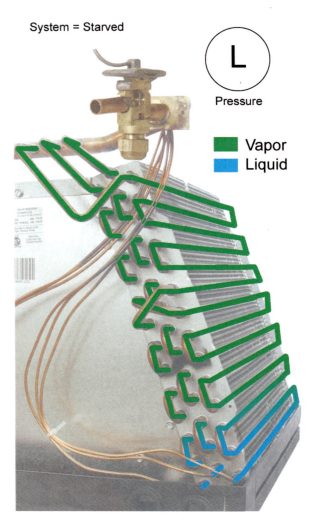

If the heat load on a TXV coil is too low, the TXV will struggle to maintain adequate superheat. The TXV will open and close as it tries to find a balance of refrigerant.

Causes are low air volume and low heat content in the air.

If the coil lacks refrigerant, the suction pressure will be low and the suction vapor superheat high.

Causes include low charge, refrigerant circuit restrictions, and failed TXV.

High Voltage
Circuits

High Voltage Circuits

Field Service Guide: High Voltage Circuit

Chapter
High Voltage Circuit

Table of Contents

Sequence of Operation: Single Phase (Single Speed Condenser Fan) 2
    Single Speed Fan Circuit: Call for Cooling 2
Schematic Diagram Reference: Single-Phase Condensing units Call for Cooling
        (Single Speed Condenser Fan) 3
Confirming a Call for Cooling: Step By Step 4
Sump Heater Circuit 5
    Introduction 5
    Circuit Operation 5
Single Phase Compressor Circuit 6
    Introduction 6
    Circuit Operation 7
Single Phase Compressor with Hard Start Kit 9
    Introduction 9
    Circuit Operation 9
Single Speed Condenser Fan Circuit 10
    Introduction 10
    Circuit Operation 10
Single Speed Condenser Fan Motor Testing 11
    Introduction 11
Checking the Line Voltage Supply and Contactor 24 Volt Solenoid Coil: Step By Step 11
Checking the Contactor Load Terminals for Proper Line Voltage: Step By Step 12
Checking the Condenser Fan Motor Windings: Step By Step 13
Checking the Motor Winding For Grounding: Step By Step 13
Testing the Run Capacitor: Step By Step 14

Field Service Guide: High Voltage Circuit

Sequence of Operation: Single Phase (Single Speed Condenser Fan)

Single Speed Fan Circuit: Call for Cooling

When the system **calls for cooling**, the thermostat makes a circuit from the thermostat's **subbase terminal R** to **Y**. The field installed low voltage "Y" wire carries this potential to the indoor unit's **low voltage terminal strip** which tells the indoor unit to run the indoor fan at **cooling speed**. At the same instant, the thermostat also makes a circuit between the **subbase terminal R** and **G**. This signal is carried back by the field installed thermostat wire to the indoor unit to the G terminal on the **low voltage terminal strip** to energize the **fan relay** system.

The Y signal is then conducted out to the condensing unit and 24-volt potential is placed on the condensing unit's 24 volt contactor. The 24 volts will energize the contactor's **24-volt low voltage solenoid coil**. When the solenoid coil is energized, it creates a magnetic field, which attracts the contactor's contacts, and they close.

When the contactor closes it's CC-1 contact, the condensing unit's high voltage circuit is energized. The contactor directs both the L1 and L2 potential to the condenser fan motor circuit and the compressor motor circuit.

When the CC-1 contact closes, 120 volt potential from the L1 leg is conducted to the compressor circuit to begin operation of the compressor motor and momentary operation of the compressor starting circuit. The L2 120 volt potential, which is already present at the compressor's common terminal, places a total potential of 240 volts across the compressor motor circuit.

The CC-1 contacts also place the L1 potential at the outdoor fan motor. The motor will then start. The system will continue to energize the **outdoor fan motor** and compressor motor as long as there is line voltage to the condensing unit and the compressor contactor CC remains energized by the low voltage potential on the 24 volt solenoid coil.

The sequence of operation just described can be followed on the schematic diagram shown on the next page. The low voltage circuit is shown in dashed lines on the lower portion of the diagram labeled "A".

Schematic Diagram Reference: Single-Phase Condensing Units Call For Cooling (Single Speed Condenser Fan)

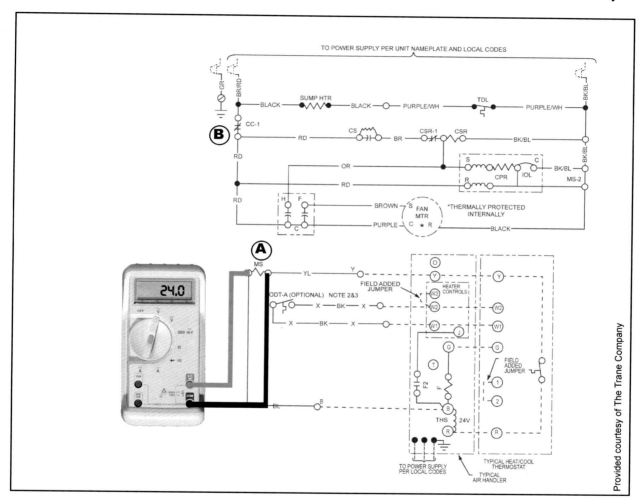

Place one voltmeter lead to the CC contactor terminal with the yellow wire connection. Place your other voltmeter lead to the CC contactor terminal with the blue wire.

Notes:

(A) 24 volts placed on CC solenoid from thermostat circuit.

(B) CC-1 contact closes and switches L1 to the compressor circuit and the condenser fan circuit.

Field Service Guide: High Voltage Circuit

Confirming A Call for Cooling

If the system is not running, and you would like to confirm that your system is receiving a CALL FOR COOLING at the condensing unit's CC contactor, perform the following test:

STEP 1   Tools: **Multimeter**

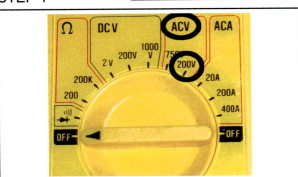

Set your voltmeter to measure low voltage.

STEP 2

Place voltmeter leads across the 24 volt contactor solenoid terminals.

STEP 3

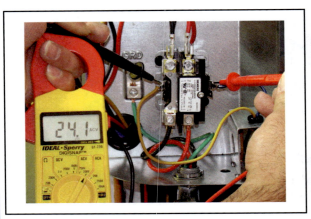

If the voltmeter reads 24 volts, the system is receiving a call for cooling.

STEP 4

If the voltmeter reads 24 volts, yet the system does not run, check for line voltage to the contactor.
DO NOT RESET THE CIRCUIT BREAKER WITHOUT FIRST CHECKING FOR A SHORT TO GROUND IN THE COMPRESSOR MOTOR. SEE COMPRESSOR SECTION.

STEP 5

If the voltage is significantly less than 24 volts, and the system is experiencing control chattering or no has operation, check for a short in the low voltage wiring between the thermostat, indoor unit and outdoor condensing unit.

Sump Heater Circuit

Introduction

The sump heater circuit prevents liquid refrigerant from migrating to the compressor shell during the off cycle. The circuit protects the compressor by energizing a high voltage heater that heats up the compressor shell during periods when the compressor is not running.

The circuit is needed because refrigerant will move to the point of lowest temperature in a refrigeration system when the system is not calling for compressor operation. If the system is off and the outdoor air temperature is cooler than the temperature of the air at the evaporator coil located in the conditioned space, the refrigerant moves to the cold compressor. This liquid must be boiled out of the compressor shell prior to the compressor starting. If the liquid refrigerant is present during compressor start-up, damage to the compressor could occur.

Circuit Operation

This schematic diagram of a typical single phase condensing unit shows a highlighted area that is the sump heater circuit.

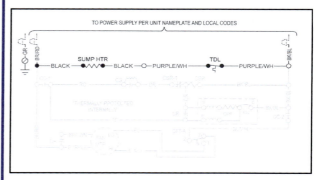

The circuit consists of two components, a heater labeled SUMP HTR, and a normally closed heat activated switch labeled TDL. Electrically, the heater and temperature-activated switch are wired in series with each other.

The circuit operates the heater by applying both L1 and L2 power to each side of the heater when switch TDL closes. This makes the heater a 240 volts heater since the potential between L1 and L2 is 240 volts. If switch TDL is open, the electrical circuit to the heater is broken and the heater remains off.

The wires that connect the heater and switch are identified by color. The heater has two black wires at either side connected to a wire labeled Purple/Wh. This means the wire is purple with a white stripe. The other side of the switch also has a purple wire with white stripe. This wire is connected to a black wire with a blue stripe. On the L1 side of the circuit the sump heater's black wire is connected to a wire labeled BR/RD. or brown wire with a red stripe. Notice that L1 is supplied to the circuit via the brown wire with red stripe. By following the wire color code and schematic diagram shown here we can easily find our way around this electrical circuit.

L1 power is applied directly to the left side black heater lead via the brown wire with red stripe. L2 is supplied to the right hand side of switch TDL via the purple wire with white stripe. With power present at both L1 and L2, the heater is ready to operate when switch TDL closes.

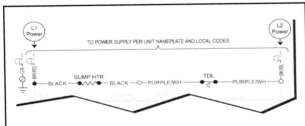

In this diagram the brown wire with red strip can be found supplying L1 power on the left side.

The switch TDL is used to shut the heater off when the discharge line gets hot during compressor operation. When the compressor cools down after shutdown, the switch re-closes to energize the heater.

The TDL shown here is used to shut the heater off when the discharge line reaches a specific temperature during compressor operation.

If this switch were to stick and remain in the closed position, the heater would remain on during compressor operation. The compressor would then overheat and could open it's motor winding temperature protector.

Single Phase Compressor Circuit

Introduction

A single-phase compressor electrical circuit provides power to the compressor's motor whenever a call for mechanical cooling operation is received from the thermostat circuit.

The PSC motor of the compressor is hermetically sealed and is inaccessible to service technicians.

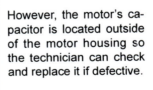

However, the motor's capacitor is located outside of the motor housing so the technician can check and replace it if defective.

The motors used in single-phase compressors are Permanent Split Capacitor Type Motors or more commonly referred to as PSC Type motors. The PSC Motor is hermetically sealed in the compressor shell. The motor's capacitor is located on the condensing unit's electrical box. The other component used in the circuit is the electrical contactor, which is also located in the unit's electrical control box.

Field Service Guide: High Voltage Circuit

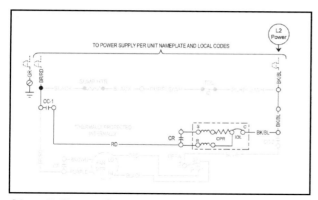 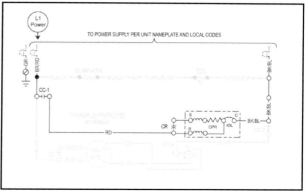

Circuit Operation

This wiring diagram (above) illustrates a typical single-phase 240-volt compressor circuit. At the right side of the circuit L2 power is connected to the common terminal of the compressor motor via a connection point at the compressor contactor. Because this point is tied directly to the L2 line voltage. We have a potential of 120 volts to ground anytime there is power supplied to the unit. The color of the wire carrying the L2 potential is black with a blue stripe. In this circuit, you can see that there is no switching the L2 line.

In order for the compressor motor to run, L1 potential must be switched to the compressor run and start terminals. The L1 power leg is connected to the contactor's normally open contacts labeled CC-1 via the brown wire with red stripe (shown above right). The CC-1 contacts are normally open therefore they will only close when power is delivered to the contactor's 24 volt electrical solenoid.

The load side of the contacts CC-1 has a red wire connected to it, which carries the L1 signal down to one of the capacitor's electrical terminals. From that terminal, another red wire leads to the run winding terminal on the compressor shell. The other side of the capacitor has an orange wire that connects to the start winding of the compressor.

The compressor remains off until the contactor's 24-volt solenoid coil is energized during a call for cooling.

The potential to ground at the load side of the CC-1 contact will be 120 volts even when the contactor is not energized. This is due to feed of the L2 line through the compressor motor windings and capacitor. When checking for voltage at the load terminals of the contactor, always check the potential from both L1 and L2 to confirm you have 240-volt power to the circuit.

When a call for cooling takes place (next page), the thermostat's cooling switch makes a circuit between the 24-volt "R" terminal to the low voltage terminal designated "Y." 24 volts is then fed via the low voltage thermostat wire out to the condensing unit.

At the condensing unit, the 24 volt signal on the Y wire is received by the condensing unit's Yellow wire via a wire nut connection between the low voltage thermostat wiring and the condensing unit's internal wiring. The yellow wire carries the 24-volt signal to the contactor's 24-volt solenoid coil, which causes the contactor to close its nor-

Field Service Guide: High Voltage Circuit

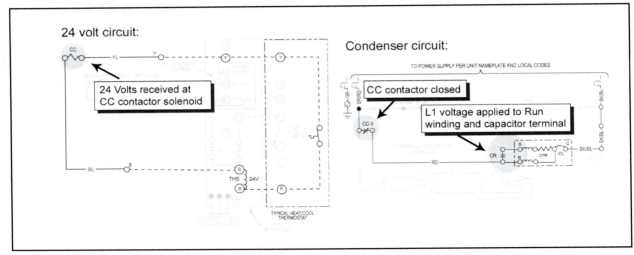

mally open CC contacts.

The CC-1 contact makes a circuit from L1 to the run winding terminal and one of the capacitor terminals. At the first one-half cycle of the AC sine wave, the capacitor is charged, and power is applied to the run winding. The other side of the capacitor completes the start winding circuit to L2. The motor now has 240 volt potential between it's common terminal and the run winding.

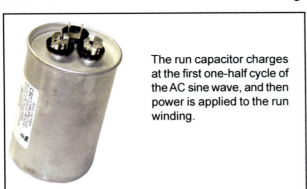

The run capacitor charges at the first one-half cycle of the AC sine wave, and then power is applied to the run winding.

When the AC sine wave changes polarity in the other half cycle, the potential difference between the plates of the capacitor causes the capacitor to discharge through the start winding and a voltage lag results in the start winding.

The out of phase condition between current and voltage in the start winding helps the motor start. Once the motor is running, the run capacitor continues to create a phase displacement that aids in power factor correction during running operation.

A voltage is also generated in the start winding at about 75% of full RPM. This voltage is higher than the line voltage. It is called back EMF, which means back electromotive force. This voltage will be present at the start terminal of the compressor motor whenever the motor is running.

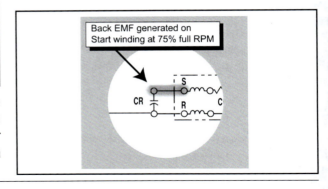

Back EMF generated on Start winding at 75% full RPM

Field Service Guide: High Voltage Circuit

Single Phase Compressor with Hard Start Kit

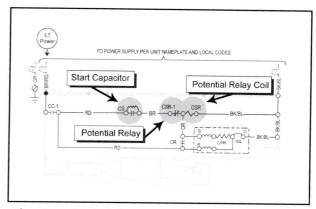

Introduction

Hard start kits help single phase compressors start against potential heavy working loads by generating an out of phase current condition between the motor's start and run windings. The circuit operates by temporarily placing a starting capacitor in the compressor circuit during the initial start sequence. The circuit removes this capacitor when the motor reaches about 75% of full running RPM. The circuit consists of a high microfarad capacitor with bleed resistor and a potential relay with a normally closed set of contacts. Both components are located in the condensing unit's electrical control box.

Circuit Operation

Pictured here are two different start kits. The one on the left combines the potential relay and start capacitor. The kit on the right has separate units.

This wiring diagram (above right) highlights a typical single-phase compressor circuit with a hard start kit. The wiring diagram shows that a red wire feeds the L1 signal from the CC-1 contacts to one terminal of a start capacitor. The other terminal of the start capacitor has a brown wire connected to a normally closed set of contacts labeled CSR-1. An orange wire on the load side of these contacts carries the voltage down to the start winding terminal on the compressor. A bleed resistor discharges the capacitor during off cycle time.

The potential relay coil that opens the CSR-1 contact is wired in series with the start capacitor, and CC-1 contacts. The pick up or voltage at which the relay's coil energizes is higher than 240 volt line voltage therefore the relay will not energize when the CC-1 contacts close.

When the CC-1 contacts close, the motor is energized. The normally closed CSR-1 contact allows the start capacitor to help create a significant out of phase current condition within the motor's internal windings (below). This

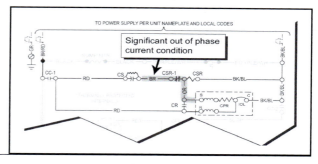

9

Field Service Guide: High Voltage Circuit

out of phase condition allows the windings to generate an incredibly strong hold on the motor's rotor. This strong hold on the rotor allows the compressor to overcome the initial starting loads.

Once the compressor motor begins to reach it's full RPM, very high counter voltage is generated by the motor's start winding. This voltage travels out on the start winding terminal and places a large potential at the potential relay's CSR coil via the orange wire. The CSR coil energizes and

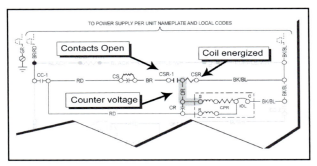

opens the CSR-1 contacts to remove the start capacitor from the electrical circuit. The relay will remain energized as long as the compressor is running at full RPM. When the compressor shuts off at the end of a call for cooling operation, the CSR-1 contacts close to again place the start capacitor in a position to be active on the next call for cooling.

Single Speed Condenser Fan Circuit

Introduction

The condenser fan circuit energizes the condenser fan motor on a call for mechanical cooling operation. The circuit is comprised of a 240 volt PSC single speed motor with run capacitor. The speed of this motor will remain constant regardless of the outdoor air temperature; therefore head pressure problems can be encountered when outdoor air temperature falls below the minimum allowable level. In the case of residential condensing units, the minimum allowable run operation for this type of circuit is 55° F.

The single speed condenser fan circuit consists of a 240 volt PSC single speed motor and a run capacitor. The diagram below shows the actual wiring schematic of the circuit.

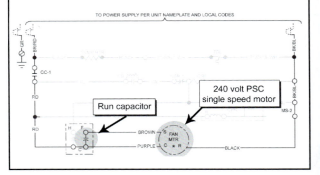

Circuit Operation

The L2 leg of the supply voltage is wired directly to the condenser fan motor's run winding terminal via a connection on the load side terminal of contact L2.

Since the L2 signal is not switched, there will be 120 volts potential to ground from the run terminal of the condenser fan motor whenever line voltage is applied to the condensing unit.

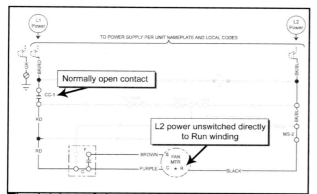

The L1 leg of the supply voltage is brought to the line terminal of the CC contactor by the brown and the red wire. A normally open set of contacts called CC-1 prevents the L1 voltage from reaching the condenser fan motor when no call for cooling is present.

A red wire is connected to the load side terminal of the CC-1 contacts. The wire delivers the L1 power to the condenser fan motor's common winding when a call for cooling occurs. When de-energized, you will have some voltage potential from the start and common windings to ground when there is 120 volt potential applied to the run terminal of the condenser fan motor by the L2 leg.

When a call for cooling occurs, the 24 volts is applied to the CC contractor's 24 volt solenoid coil which causes the contractor to close it's normally open set of contracts. The contactor's CC-1 contact closes and allows the L1 120 volt potential to be placed on the load terminal.

The red wire carries this voltage to the common winding terminal on the condenser fan motor. With L1 and L2 potential voltage now at the motor's common and run terminals, the motor starts.

When the call for cooling ends, 24 volts is removed from the CC contactor's 24-volt electrical solenoid, which causes the contractor to de-energize. The L1 120 volt potential is removed from the common winding terminal causing the motor to de-energize.

Single Speed Condenser Fan Motor Testing

Introduction

In this section troubleshooting of the single-speed condenser fan circuit will be covered. When there is a problem with the single-speed condenser fan circuit, the problem will be in four areas: line voltage supply, the contactor, the capacitor, or internal motor problems.

Checking The Line Voltage Supply And Contactor 24 Volt Solenoid Coil

If there is a call for cooling and both the condenser fan motor and compressor are off, there may be a problem with either the line voltage or the contactor.

> Note:
>
> The compressor may have shut off on its IOL due to high pressure conditions caused by a lack of condenser fan motor operation.

Field Service Guide: High Voltage Circuit

STEP 1   Tools: **Multimeter**

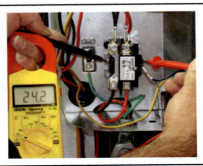

Check to make sure the CONTACTOR is energized (Pulled in). If it is not, measure for 24-volts across the contactor 24-volt solenoid coil by placing one meter lead to each of the two solenoid coil terminals. If 24 volts is not present, troubleshoot the low voltage circuit to determine the problem. **If 24-volts is present at the 24-volt solenoid coil, yet the contactor is not pulled in, replace the contactor.**

STEP 2

If the contactor is pulled in, place one voltmeter lead to the L1 LINE TERMINAL of contactor. Place the other lead to the L2 LINE TERMINAL of contactor. You should measure around 240 volts. If you do not have the proper voltage, there is a problem with the LINE VOLTAGE SUPPLY. **Check for open fuse or circuit breaker.** If you do measure 240 volts, the problem is not with the LINE VOLTAGE SUPPLY.

Checking the Contactor Load Terminals for Proper Line Voltage

If the line voltage to the contactor is at the proper level, the contactor points may be obstructed or pitted. This would prevent the L2 line voltage from reaching the condenser fan motor circuit. The compressor would run because the L2 line is not switched to the compressor circuit. (Single-Phase units only.)

STEP 1   Tools: **Multimeter**

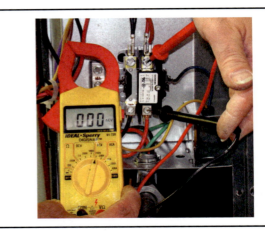

To check the condition of the contacts, place one voltmeter lead to the contactor line terminal and the other voltmeter lead to the contactor load terminal. (Fig. 3) With power applied to the unit and the contactor energized, the meter should read 0 volts. If you read voltage across these two terminals, there is resistance present between the two electrical sets of contacts. When working properly, these contacts should not drop any voltage.

If you read voltage, disconnect power to the unit and inspect the contacts for pitting or an obstruction. **If you find either, repair or replace the CONTACTOR.**

Field Service Guide: High Voltage Circuit

Checking the Condenser Fan Motor Windings

If the contactor is OK, the problem is either an open IOL or an open motor winding, or bad run capacitor. To determine the problem, disconnect power to the unit and disconnect the wires leading to the condenser fan motor at both the contactor and the condenser fan motor run capacitor. Discharge the condenser fan motor run capacitor.

Resistance should be slightly higher than previous reading. A reading of infinite resistance means that the internal overload is open.

Tools: **Multimeter**

STEP 1

Using an ohmmeter, check the resistance between the **black wire** and the **purple wire**. (Run to common) (Fig. 4). You should measure a very small resistance If you have infinite resistance, there is an open circuit between the run to common terminal. Next, measure the resistance between the **brown wire** and the **purple wire**. This is the start winding. You should measure a resistance that is slightly higher than the run winding. If you measure infinite resistance, both of the motor's internal windings have an open circuit to common. This indicates the motor's internal overload is open. (IOL) Allow time for the IOL to cool down and reset. **If the IOL does not re-close, replace the motor.**

If only one winding has infinite resistance to common, that winding is open. If this is the case, the motor must be replaced.

If the motor windings check out OK, proceed to checking the motor for internal grounding.

Checking the Motor Winding For Grounding

To check for internal grounding of the motor windings, set your multimeter to the OHM function.

Tools: **Multimeter**

13

Field Service Guide: High Voltage Circuit

STEP 1

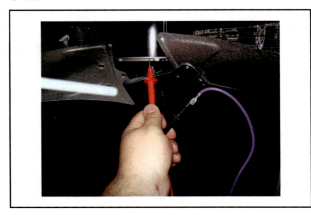

Place one meter lead to the **purple wire** and the other meter lead to the motor housing.

You should read infinite OHMS. If you read resistance, the motor is grounded from the common terminal. **Replace the motor**. If it is OK, move on to testing the other windings.

STEP 2

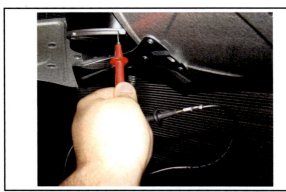

Place one meter lead to the **black wire** connected to the run winding terminal and the other motor lead to the motor housing (Fig. 2). Again, you should read infinite OHMS.

If you read resistance , the motor is grounded from the run terminal. **Replace the motor**. If it is OK, move on to testing the other winding.

STEP 3

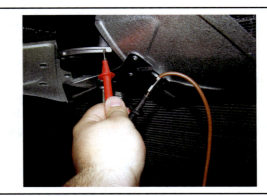

Place one meter lead to the **brown wire** connected to the start winding terminal and the other motor lead to the motor housing (Fig. 3). Again, you should read infinite OHMS. If you read resistance, the motor is grounded from the start terminal. **Replace the motor**.

If all of the motor windings check out OK, test the run capacitor.

Testing The Run Capacitor

Use your OHMMETER to perform this test. Make sure the capacitor is discharged.

STEP 1

Place multimeter to OHMMETER function.

14

STEP 2

The bar indicated will ramp up and down as the multi-meter charges and discharges the capacitor.

Place one meter lead to each capacitor terminal. The meter should slowly register resistance and then return to infinite ohms reading as the ohmmeter battery charges and discharges the capacitor. If the meter fails to respond, switch your ohmmeter leads and try again. If the meter still does not show charging and discharging of the capacitor, or if the meter reads a steady resistance, **replace the run capacitor**. If the meter does respond properly, the capacitor is good.

Compressors

Compressors

Chapter
Compressors

Table of Contents

Compressors **4**
    Introduction to "How Maximum Capacity is Achieved." 4
    Suction Pressure and Compressor Capacity 4
    Suction Vapor Density of Refrigerants 4
    BTU's in a Pound of Suction Vapor 5
    Compressor Displacement in CFM 6
    Capacity Loss Relationship to Suction Pressure: R-22 and R-410A 6
        Causes of Low Suction Pressure 6
    Discharge Pressure and its Affect upon the Compressor Capacity 6
        Causes of High Discharge Pressure 7
    A Note about Evaporator Saturation Temperature 10
    A Worst Case Example that Takes Place Due to Contractor Error 10
    Summary 11
Why Compressors Fail Mechanically **11**
    Liquid Migration into the Compressor Oil during Shut Down Periods 11
    Liquid Floodback during Run Operation 12
    Oil Breakdown 13
    Moisture 13
    Summary 14
Unique Features of Scroll and Reciprocating Compressors **14**
    Reciprocating Compressor Process 14
    Scroll Compressor Process 15
    Separation of Scrolls 15
    Discharge Check Valve 15
    Low Vacuum Protection 15
    Pressure Test Limits 16
    Starting Characteristics of Scrolls Compressors 16
    Starting Characteristics of Reciprocating Compressors 16
    Crankcase Heat Requirements 16
    High Temperature Limit 17
    Internal Motor Overload 17
    Open Internal Pressure Relief Valve (IPR) 17
    Scroll Compressors - Noise 17
    Broken Scroll Assembly 17
    Seized Scroll Assembly 17
    Internal Bearing Damage 17
    Reciprocating Compressors - Broken Valve Plate 18
2-Step Unloading Scroll Compressors **19**

Field Service Guide: Compressors

Summary 21
Introduction to Compressors Electrical Operating Characteristics:
   208/230 1 Phase Reciprocating and Scroll Models 21
Residential Compressors use Permanent Split Capacitor (PSC) Motors 21
How PSC Motors Work 21
PSC Motors use a Run Capacitor (Continuous Duty) 22
Start Assist Devices can be added to the compressor circuit 22
   Potential Relay and Start Capacitor 22
   PTC Start Assist Device 23
Fusite Plugs: Safety 24
Checking Motor Winding Resistances and Winding Condition 25
Checking Internal Motor Winding Overload Protector Switch 26
   Checking for a Grounded Motor Winding:
      Resistance from the Motor Winding Pins to the Compressor Shell 26
Diagnostic Tests 27
Finding the Cause of Compressor Starting Problems 27
Testing to Find the Cause of Compressor Starting Problems: Step By Step 27
When a Compressor Trips the Circuit Breaker or Opens a Line Fuse 30
Testing for a Grounded Compressor: Step By Step 30
Troubleshooting a Compressor Start Circuit 32
Testing the Compressor Start Circuit: Step By Step 32
Testing a Start Capacitor for Proper Operation 34
Testing a Start Capacitor for Proper Operation: Step By Step 34
Testing a Run Capacitor for Proper Microfarad Rating: Step By Step 34
Testing a Run Capacitor with a "Power On" Test 35
Troubleshooting 2 Step Compressor to Determine if it is Loading and Unloading 36
Testing the Unloading Solenoid of a 2 Step Compressor: Step By Step 36
Checking a Compressor for a Damaged Valve Plate 38
Testing for a Damaged Valve Plate (Reciprocating Compressors Only): Step By Step ...39
Checking a Single or Three Phase Scroll Compressor for Mechanical Failure 40
Testing a Scroll Compressor for the Proper Pumping Capability: Step By Step 40
Detecting Compressor Bearing Damage 42
Testing for Damaged Bearings: Step By Step 42
Diagnosing a Seized Compressor - Single Phase 43
   Symptoms 43
Seized Compressor - Single Phase: Step By Step 43
Performing a Single Phase Motor Winding Test 45
   Symptoms 45
Single Phase Motor Winding Test: Step By Step 45
Performing a Three Phase Motor Winding Test 47

Symptoms...47
Three Phase Motor Winding Test: Step By Step **47**
Detecting a Three Phase Voltage Imbalance **48**
Calculating Voltage Imbalance: Step By Step **48**

Compressors

Introduction to "How Maximum Capacity is Achieved"

A compressor is used to compress low pressure cold refrigerant vapor into a high pressure hot discharge gas. By compressing the refrigerant and making it hot, the refrigerant can reject heat it absorbed at the evaporator to either the outside air or in some cases water (Hot goes to cold).

To service the compressor, technicians need to know how the performance of the compressor is lost and also how it is optimized. Both topics will be discussed in this chapter.

Suction Pressure and Compressor Capacity

A compressor is nothing more than a pump that compresses refrigerant vapor.

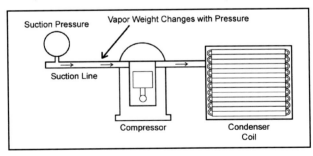

The refrigerant suction vapor that enters the compressor varies in weight based upon suction pressure. When the suction pressure is low, the refrigerant suction vapor is light. When the suction pressure is high, the refrigerant suction vapor is heavy. The amount of refrigerant the compressor pumps changes with the suction pressure and corresponding refrigerant weight, therefore, the capacity of the compressor is constantly changing.

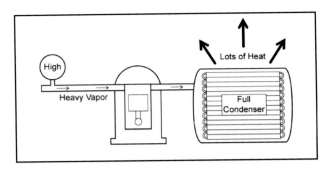

When suction pressure is high, a large amount of refrigerant is pumped into the condenser. The heat transfer of the system will increase because each pound of refrigerant being moved to the condenser contains a large amount of heat that was gathered into the refrigerant at the evaporator coil.

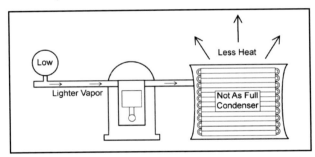

If for some reason, the suction pressure at the compressor inlet were to fall, such as when the indoor air filter is dirty, the resulting low pressure will cause a light vapor to enter the compressor. Each stroke of the piston in the compressor will result in a reduced amount of refrigerant being pumped to the condenser and consequently, less heat.

Suction Vapor Density of Refrigerants

The weight property of refrigerants is called SUCTION VAPOR DENSITY. Suction vapor density is measured in pounds (#) per cubic foot of vapor. Refrigerant manufacturers publish

Field Service Guide: Compressors

Saturation Properties of R-22

Saturation Temp	Gauge Pressure PSIG	Suction Vapor Density (lbs. cu ft)	Enthalpy Liquid (btu lbs)	Vapor
26	49.95	1.191	17.5	106.93
28	52.39	1.234	18.05	107.11
30	54.9	1.279	18.61	107.28
32	57.47	1.324	19.17	107.46
34	60.12	1.372	19.73	107.63
36	62.84	1.42	20.29	107.8
38	65.64	1.47	20.86	107.97
40	68.51	1.521	21.42	108.14
42	71.46	1.573	21.99	108.31
44	74.48	1.627	22.56	108.47
46	77.58	1.683	23.13	108.63
48	80.77	1.74	23.7	108.8
50	84.03	1.798	24.28	108.95
52	87.38	1.859	24.85	109.11
54	90.81	1.92	25.43	109.26
56	94.32	1.984	26.01	109.42
58	97.93	2.049	26.59	109.56
60	101.62	2.115	27.17	109.71

charts that list the refrigerant suction vapor density at given suction pressures. These charts are available for both saturated refrigerants and superheated suction vapors. For easy understanding, we will only discuss saturated refrigerant properties in this chapter.

In this example of a saturated properties table for refrigerant R-22, 40°F saturated temperature is highlighted in yellow. This temperature occurs at a gauge pressure of about 69 PSIG. From the table, it is determined that vapor entering the compressor at a suction pressure of 69 PSIG will have a weight of about 1.521 pounds per cubic foot.

From the same table, 50°F saturated temperature is now highlighted in blue. The corresponding suction pressure at this temperature is about 84 PSIG. From the chart, you can see the weight of R-22 is now much greater at almost 1.8 pounds per cubic foot.

BTU's in a Pound of Suction Vapor

Go to the last column of the table. This column, highlighted in red, is called suction vapor enthalpy. It is the rating of how many BTU's are contained in each pound of vapor refrigerant. At 40°F, there is about 108 BTU in each pound of vapor and at 50°F, there is about 109 BTU in each pound of vapor.

5

Field Service Guide: Compressors

Compressor Displacement in CFM

The compressor displacement is rated in how many cubic feet of vapor it can pump per minute (CFM). If a 10 CFM compressor were pumping R-22 saturated refrigerant where the suction pressure is 85 PSIG, the refrigerant being compressed would weigh about 1.8 pounds per cubic foot. (Fig 1) The 10 CFM compressor would therefore pump about 18 pounds of refrigerant per minute. The same compressor operating at a suction pressure of 68 PSIG would have vapor entering the cylinder at a weight of about 1.5 pounds per cubic foot. (Fig 2) Therefore, the compressor would only pump 15 pounds of refrigerant per minute. This lower pump flow would cause a reduction in system capacity.

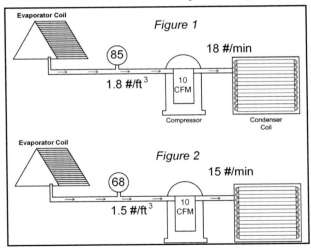

Capacity Loss Relationship to Suction Pressure: R-22 and R-410A

The amount of capacity lost by a drop in suction pressure is a 1% drop for every 1 pound of suction pressure loss for units using R-22. Units using R-410A refrigerant lose .6% of their capacity for every pound of suction pressure loss.

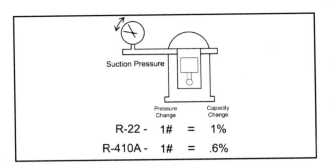

Important Note about our Example

Although our example uses saturated property values of R-22, compressors should not operate with a saturated refrigerant mix entering the suction inlet to the compressor, this theory needs to be learned. That theory is the relationship between the compressor capacity and the suction pressure. At higher suction pressures, the weight of the refrigerant goes up and therefore the compressor capacity goes up with it. To summarize the theory: Avoid conditions that cause the suction pressure to drop.

Causes of Low Suction Pressure

There are three main causes of low suction pressure; low heat load at the evaporator coil, suction piping pressure drop, and lack of refrigerant entering the evaporator circuit.

Discharge Pressure and its Affect upon Compressor Capacity

Discharge gas pressure also affects the capacity of the compressor. High discharge gas pressure reduces the capacity of the compressor. This capacity loss is due to the fact that all compressors have clearance area that allows liquid oil drops to clear the compression process without causing abnormal stresses to the compressor. This clearance area is called clearance volume. At the end of the compression stroke, some hot gas will be trapped in this clearance volume area. This gas is called clearance volume gas. On the suction stroke, this gas will expand and fill up a portion of the compressor cylinder thereby reducing the amount of refrigerant that can be drawn in from the suction line.

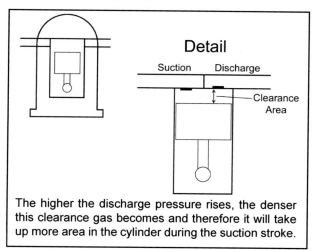

The higher the discharge pressure rises, the denser this clearance gas becomes and therefore it will take up more area in the cylinder during the suction stroke.

When the discharge pressure is high, the condensing temperature in the condenser goes up. The higher condensing temperature will cause an increase in the temperature of the liquid that is leaving the condenser coil. The extra heat in the liquid is heat the system did not get rid of. This heat is sent back to the evaporator coil. This additional heat in the liquid also reduces the capacity of the system.

Causes of High Discharge Pressure

Causes of high discharge gas pressure include high outdoor air temperature, overcharging, dirty outdoor condenser coil, non condensable gasses, and low indoor air volume during heat mode operation (Heat pumps).

This is a performance data table that lists the cooling capacity of a compressor based upon the saturation temperature of the evaporator coil and the condensing temperature of the condenser.

Performance Information

Evap Temp		\multicolumn{6}{c}{Condensing Temperature}
		80	90	95	100	110	120	130
35	BTUH	19194	17715	16965	16211	14700	13195	11712
	WATTS	1046	1146	1191	1233	1307	1369	1418
	AMPS	3.62	3.81	3.9	3.98	4.14	4.28	4.4
	LB/HR	232.6	222.6	217.2	211.7	200	187.6	174.5
40	BTUH	21708	20095	19278	18456	16807	15161	13535
	WATTS	1047	1164	1217	1267	1355	1430	1492
	AMPS	3.62	3.84	3.95	4.04	4.23	4.4	4.55
	LB/HR	261.6	251	245.4	239.5	227.2	214.1	200.2
45	BTUH	24381	22632	21745	20854	19062	17273	15500
	WATTS	1037	1172	1234	1292	1395	1485	1560
	AMPS	3.61	3.86	3.98	4.09	4.31	4.51	4.7
	LB/HR	292.1	28.1	275.2	269.1	256.1	242.3	227.7
50	BTUH	27210	25321	24363	23400	21463	19525	17602
	WATTS	1015	1169	1239	1305	1426	1530	1620
	AMPS	3.59	3.87	4	4.13	4.38	4.62	4.84
	LB/HR	324.2	312.7	306.6	300.2	286.6	272.2	256.9
55	BTUH	30192	28158	27128	26091	24005	21916	19838
	WATTS	979	1152	1232	1308	1445	1566	1671
	AMPS	3.55	3.86	4.01	4.16	4.44	4.72	4.98
	LB/HR	357.7	345.8	339.5	332.8	318.7	303.6	287.7

Published compressor performance information confirms what you have just learned. Table courtesy of Tecumseh Cool Products

Field Service Guide: Compressors

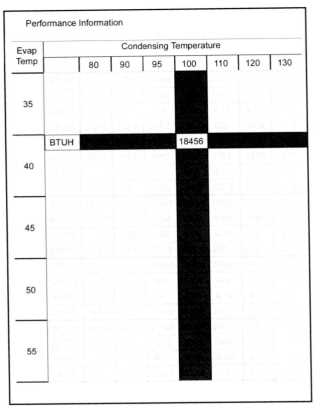

Table 1

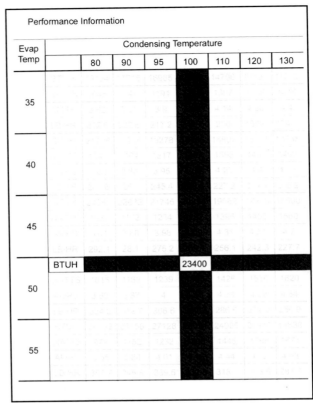

Table 2

Start by referring to a 40°F evaporator coil on the far left column. (Table 1) This temperature equals a suction pressure of 69 PSIG. Now go to the 100°F condensing temperature column at the top of the table. This equals a discharge pressure of about 200 PSIG. Move down the table until you intersect the capacity in BTUH at 40°F. This compressor has a capacity of 18,456 BTUH at these pressure combinations.

Now we are going to raise the suction pressure by placing a larger evaporator coil on the compressor. For this example we will not change the condensing temperature. Now go to the 50°F column on the left which equals a suction pressure of about 85 PSIG. (Table 2) Go down the 100°F condensing temperature column and note the capacity has gone up to 23,400 BTUH. This increase in capacity is due to the increase in vapor weight entering the compressor cylinder.

Field Service Guide: Compressors

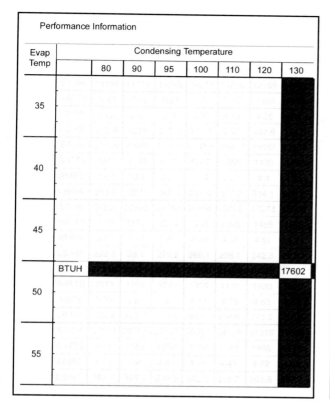

Table 3

Table 4

Next, let's take a look at the discharge pressure affect upon the compressor. Keep the suction pressure at 85 PSIG with a saturated temperature of 50°F at the evaporator coil. (Table 3) Raise the head pressure by simply overcharging the outdoor unit up to 300 PSIG. This will cause the condensing temperature to rise to 130°F. Follow the 130°F column down to the 50°F saturated temperature and note the cooling capacity has been reduced to 17,602 BTUH. This reduction had nothing to do with the weight of the suction vapor. It was due to clearance volume and liquid line heat causing an adverse affect upon the performance of the system.

Beware of what your buddy may have taught you!

A friend or instructor may have taught you that high suction pressure and low head pressure are an indication of an inefficient compressor. In fact, in almost all cases the truth is opposite of this. The performance data table will show you the truth.

On this table (Table 4) go down to a 55°F saturation temperature at the evaporator coil. This saturation temperature is equal to an evaporator coil operating with 93 PSIG of suction pressure. Next, find the 80°F condensing

9

Field Service Guide: Compressors

temperature column. This condensing temperature equals a system operating with a very low discharge pressure of around 147 PSIG. At these combinations of pressure, the capacity is all the way up to 30,192 BTUH and the Watts used is the lowest on the chart. This makes the EER of the compressor at maximum rating. Do not condemn a compressor as inefficient when operating at these pressures, as it is actually at maximum rated performance.

A Note about Evaporator Saturation Temperature

Comfort cooling systems that condition homes operate at saturated suction temperatures that average between 35°F and 55°F. The colder coil temperatures can better dehumidify air in the home. Even though a 55°F evaporator temperature equals super high efficiency, it might not produce comfort. The lack of comfort will be due to the coil's relatively high temperature and its inability to remove moisture from the home's air.

High saturated operating temperatures at the evaporator coil are due to high suction pressures. Causes of high suction pressure include: very large evaporator coils that absorb large amounts of heat; oversized metering pistons; high levels of indoor heat or air volume; new system start up with large levels of heat in the air, and overcharging piston equipped systems.

A Worst Case Example that takes place due to Contractor Error

A perfect example of the worst compressor capacity can be explained with a mismatch between the indoor evaporator coil and outdoor condensing unit.

Older evaporator coils were smaller than today's higher efficiency evaporator coils. To gain efficiency, modern high efficiency air conditioning systems use larger evaporator coils to raise the weight of the refrigerant suction vapor by running higher suction pressures than older, less efficient models. By raising the weight of the refrigerant entering the compressor cylinder, the size of the compressor could be reduced to increase the efficiency of the system. Yes, today's 3 ton condensing units do not have 3 ton compressors in them. Take a look inside the cabinet at the compressor, it is likely you will find a 2 ½ ton model.

A contractor not realizing that the compressor is matched to a larger evaporator today, may make the mistake of selling a consumer a replacement outdoor unit and leaving the older evaporator in place. The old evaporator will not generate a high enough suction pressure to get the compressor pump capacity up to its rated limit. Remember, for every pound it loses, the system capacity is reduced by 1% with R-22 units.

When the system is installed, there is another problem. The older coil has a metering device that was sized for the higher head pressure of the older inefficient model. New systems run lower discharge pressures than older inefficient models. When the charge is released into the system, the new system will have to be overcharged to get the discharge pressure high enough to meter refrigerant through the older unit's small metering device. The result is abnormally high discharge pressure that will reduce the capacity of the system, and lower suction pressure which further reduces the capacity of the system.

The consumer will complain that on hot days the new system does not cool as well as the old one did. The consumer is not crazy, they are in fact absolutely correct.

Summary

Higher suction pressure raises system capacity due to a greater amount of refrigerant being moved by the compressor.

Low suction pressure reduces the density of the suction vapor and therefore reduces system capacity.

There are three primary causes of low suction pressure which include, low heat load at the evaporator, suction line piping pressure loss, and a lack of refrigerant entering the evaporator circuit.

All compressors have clearance area for liquid to clear during the compression stroke.

Hot gas is trapped in the clearance area. This gas reduces the size of the compressor cylinder.

Avoid all system conditions that can cause low suction pressure and high discharge pressure.

The best system capacity occurs when the suction pressure is high and the discharge pressure is low.

Why Compressors Fail Mechanically

Whether the compressor is a scroll model or a reciprocating model, causes of mechanical failure are pretty much the same for both types of compressors. Mechanical failure can be typically isolated to damage from liquid refrigerant entering the compressor during both off and run cycles, moisture, and high discharge gas temperatures due to abnormal refrigeration circuit operation. The potential for each problem to cause damage can be minimized by proper installation and service practices.

Liquid Migration into the Compressor Oil during Shut Down Periods

Liquid refrigerant entering the compressor will cause oil lubrication problems. Liquid refrigerant enters the compressor during off cycle periods, as the refrigerant will migrate to the point of lowest pressure and temperature, which is the compressor oil. When the compressor is started, the refrigerant that has migrated into the compressor oil flashes, which foams the refrigerant oil and carries it out of the

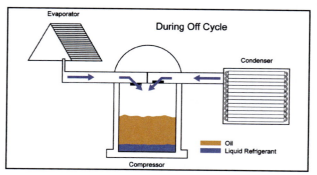

During off cycles, the liquid refrigerant will move from areas of higher pressure, the Evaporator and Condenser, to areas of lower pressure, namely the compressor.

Field Service Guide: Compressors

compressor. The oil enters the refrigeration circuit coils and tubing. The compressor now operates with a lack of oil reaching internal weight bearing surfaces. Bearings are scored and the compressor motor must work harder. The additional work on the motor increases the electrical amps being drawn by the compressor. Additionally, the bearing damage may cause compressor starting problems.

This migration of refrigerant increases in volume as the charge level of the system increases. With new high efficiency systems having very large condenser coils, the factory charge levels are getting quite high. The high charge level will increase the amount of liquid migration potential. Long line set applications will also result in large charge levels.

To minimize liquid migration, a crankcase heater should be added to the compressor. Crankcase heaters will keep the compressor oil warm and prevent excessive liquid migration from occurring during periods where the system is off. Most manufacturers of air conditioning systems will install a crankcase heater at the factory during production when the charge level in the system has exceeded the maximum level of charge before the addition of a crankcase heater.

The recommended limit of charge where a crankcase heater should be applied is surprisingly low. In some cases, scroll compressors, due to their small shell, need a crankcase heater when as little as about 7# of refrigerant charge is in the system. To determine the limit for maximum charge before the addition of a crankcase heater, consult with the manufacturer of the system, or when in doubt put a crankcase heater on the system.

Liquid Flood Back during Run Operation

Liquid refrigerant may leave the evaporator circuit when the system is lacking heat load on the evaporator, when the system is overcharged, or when the metering device is overfeeding the evaporator circuit. When the liquid refrigerant leaves the evaporator coil, the suction line carries it back to the compressor. If liquid is present in the suction vapor, the liquid refrigerant will be vaporized by the compressor motor windings. The flashing of refrigerant into vapor will also foam the refrigerant oil. The compressor will then carry the refrigerant oil with the discharge gas and direct it to the condenser coil and send it for a ride through the refrigeration circuit.

This well type heater should be installed in the heater well under the compressor.

Image Courtesy of Trane

If there is liquid refrigerant present in the suction vapor, it will be vaporized by the compressor motor windings and will foam the refrigerant oil.

Field Service Guide: Compressors

During the time the oil is moving through the system, the compressor is operating without proper lubrication. The result is potential bearing damage inside of the compressor.

Oil Breakdown

Compressor discharge temperature will rise when the indoor heat load is high, when refrigerant circuit restrictions are present, or when the evaporator circuit is lacking refrigerant. As temperature rises, the refrigerant oil in the compressor may begin to break down and form varnish and sludge in the refrigeration system. In extreme cases, sludge can circulate in the system and cause mechanical failure of internal compressor components such as suction valves.

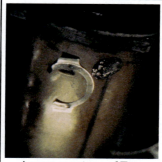

The sludge produced from oil break down can cause damage to internal compressor components such as the broken suction valve shown here.

Image courtesy of Trane

Older scroll compressor models have external temperature limit switches that monitor the discharge temperature of the compressor. If the temperature reaches close to 300°F, these limits will open and shut off low voltage to the condensing unit contactor. Later scroll models feature an internal temperature activated hot gas bypass limit that will open the compressor motor winding protector in the event of high discharge temperature. It is best to keep compressor discharge temperatures below 250°F to avoid sludge formation.

Moisture

Moisture in the refrigeration system will react with the refrigerant and oil and can form acids. The amount of moisture where acid will begin to form is quite low. For example, with R-410A systems using POE oil, acid may form when there are over 75 Parts Per Million PPM moisture in the system. This level of moisture is where some moisture indicator glasses begin to show caution color warnings.

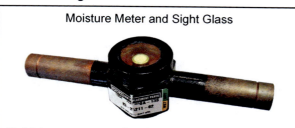

Moisture Meter and Sight Glass

Sightglasses are used to keep track of the moisture level in refrigerants.

If acid does form in the refrigeration circuit, driers can remove some of it, but if the system is acidic enough, corrosion will occur. The acid will attack copper surfaces. This copper will find its way to weight bearing surfaces in the compressor such as bearing areas. The bearing areas can be hot and cause the copper to attach to the surface of the bearing area. This is called copper plating. The copper plating reduces the

Image Courtesy of Trane
Copper plating can occur on weight bearing surfaces if the acidity of the refrigerant oil is too high.

13

area for lubricants and increases friction. The result is increased work on the compressor motor. Compressor amp draw and starting load will increase.

> *Summary*
>
> To prevent or reduce the potential for mechanical damage to internal compressor components, the following practices should be followed:
>
> Install crankcase heaters on units where the factory does not include one. This is especially true for long line set applications and high efficiency systems.
>
> Measure and adjust air volume to match factory charging chart requirements. Make sure evaporator surfaces are clean.
>
> Charge for proper superheat levels to prevent liquid floodback. Superheat should also be kept to a minimum to prevent oil breakdown due to excessive compressor discharge temperature.
>
> Make sure metering piston sizes are correct to prevent abnormally high discharge temperatures.
>
> Evacuate all systems to 500 microns when opened for installation or service. This prevents excess moisture upon start-up.
>
> Install and replace driers when installing new equipment or opening existing equipment for service.

The Unique Features of Scroll Compressors and Reciprocating Compressors

First of all, when I teach a compressor troubleshooting class for residential service technicians, I like to point out to the class that we cannot access the internal compressor components. All diagnostic information must be gathered from the motor winding terminals and from the refrigerant gauge ports. From the gauge ports the system pressures can be monitored and the oil can be tested. Beyond that, the compressor components are beyond our reach. Therefore diagnostic decisions must be made based upon the information gathered at the electrical terminals and pressure ports.

Reciprocating Compressor Process

Reciprocating compressors have a cylinder and piston that moves up and down within the cylinder. At the top of the cylinder are tensioned valves that open and close based upon whether the piston is moving up or down. These valves

Reciprocating Compressor Cutaway Courtesy of Trane

Field Service Guide: Compressors

are called the suction and discharge valves. When the piston goes down, the suction valve is drawn open to allow refrigerant to enter the cylinder. When the piston goes up, the suction valve is forced closed and eventually the discharge valve opens to allow the refrigerant to escape into the discharge line of the compressor.

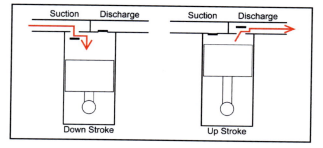

The piston does not travel all the way to close the space between the valves and top of the piston. There is an area of clearance left that allows droplets of liquid to clear without causing damage due to the fact liquid cannot be compressed. This liquid may be refrigerant or oil. The area of clearance is called clearance volume.

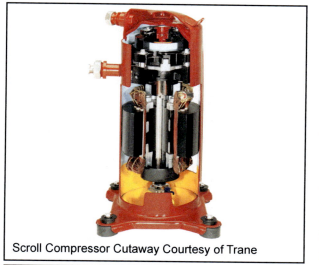
Scroll Compressor Cutaway Courtesy of Trane

Scroll Compressor Process

Scroll compressors rotate two helix type assemblies that compress refrigerant gas. The compressor motor energizes and rotates the rotor assembly which is attached to the scroll. Refrigerant is drawn into the rotating scrolls and discharged into the discharge line.

Separation of Scrolls

Popular brand scroll models have an internal safety that will allow the scrolls to separate if excessive liquid refrigerant or slugs of oil enter the scrolls. The scrolls will not compress the liquid and the liquid will pass without breaking the scroll compression assembly. This is called separating.

Discharge Check Valve

A discharge line check valve is inside the compressor shell. This check valve will help prevent hot gas from circulating back through the scrolls during shut down. The check valve will keep the discharge pressure gauge high yet internally the compressor is in an unloaded state. This means the suction and discharge sections of the compressor are at equal pressure.

Low Vacuum Protection

Pumping a compressor into a vacuum can damage the compressor. Starting a compressor in a vacuum can cause the motor to fail electrically and could cause injury if one of the motor terminal pins vent from the compressor motor terminals. To prevent low vacuum operation, modern scrolls have an internal safety feature that will cause the scrolls to equalize pressure if the discharge gas pressure is 10

Field Service Guide: Compressors

times higher than the suction pressure. The equalizing of discharge gas to the suction side of the system will open the compressor internal temperature protector and shut the compressor off.

Pressure Test Limits

When leak testing systems with nitrogen, the maximum pressure used should not exceed 150 PSI. If exposed to excessive nitrogen pressure, a compressor shell can and has exploded. UL ratings require the compressor shell to be able to withstand a specific amount of pressure based upon the type of refrigerant in the system. This pressure can be pretty low considering many nitrogen regulators can supply 500 PSI. In fact, R-12 compressors by UL rating had to withstand 350 PSI of pressure on the low side of the shell. This pressure is well below what can be delivered by some nitrogen regulators. Best practice is to install a pressure relief in the nitrogen line between the regulator and air conditioner being serviced. This relief should relieve at 175 PSIG.

Starting Characteristics of Scrolls Compressors

When scroll compressors shut off, their internal compression components separate. The compressor's high and low side components are at equal pressure during the next call for operation. Therefore, the compressor always starts in an unloaded state.

The minimum voltage at start should not drop below 187 volts as the compressor tries to start as the contactor pulls in. The maximum voltage should not exceed 10% of the nameplate maximum voltage.

Starting Characteristics of Reciprocating Compressors

Reciprocating compressors must be started with refrigerant circuit pressures equalized. If the system is started with differential pressures present, the compressor will likely cycle off on internal overload as it will have a difficult time overcoming the pressure differential during start operation.

The minimum voltage at start should not drop below 187 volts as the compressor tries to start as the contactor pulls in. The maximum voltage should not exceed 10% of the nameplate maximum voltage.

Crankcase Heat Requirements

Crankcase heaters are required when the charge level is high in the system. The compressor may actually fill up with liquid refrigerant that reaches up into the scrolls if the amount of liquid migration is high enough. Most modern scroll compressors are made by Copeland. Go to their website and download technical information on maximum charge levels allowed by scroll model before the addition of a heater must be made.

In general, liquid migration can cause starting problems such as the compressor going off on overload, and lights dimming during starting attempts. The liquid will eventually clear out of the compressor shell from the heat generated during the starting attempt. Primary times of the day where this occurs is early morning when the system is started after a long shutdown period. Watch for long line sets and overcharge conditions as an aggravation to this problem.

Field Service Guide: Compressors

High Temperature Limit

There is a bi-metal temperature limit located at the top of the discharge area of the compressor. This limit will trip and dump hot gas onto the motor overload if the temperature gets too hot in the discharge line area. This limit will open at around 300°F. Earlier models had an external temperature limit located at the top of the compressor that opened the low voltage circuit to the compressor contactor when abnormally high temperature was sensed.

High discharge gas temperatures are due to high suction vapor superheat levels and excessive compression ratio, dirty outdoor condenser coils, and non condensable gasses in the system.

Internal Motor Overload

All motors used in air conditioning systems have a temperature overload that shuts off the motor when motor winding temperature is too high. These limits are automatic reset limits that will close when the temperature in the compressor cools. If the limit does not reset, the compressor must be replaced.

In most cases, these limits will open when the system lacks charge or when the motor is overloaded due to the same problems that cause a high temperature limit trip.

Open Internal Pressure Relief Valve (IPR)

The IPR valve is a spring loaded device that protects the compressor from excessively high pressure difference between the suction pressure and the discharge pressure. Trying to pump down refrigerant into the outdoor condenser coil during repairs can cause the IPR

valve to open. When the IPR valve opens, the compressor will make a loud internal clearing noise and gauge pressures will equalize. The internal motor overload protection will shut the compressor motor off. The valve is an auto reset device. At times, it may not reset. If this problem occurs, the compressor will need to be replaced.

Scroll Compressors - Noise

Single phase scroll compressors may run backwards if short cycled for a brief moment. The compressor will eventually shut off on internal overload. When the motor cools, the compressor will start in the correct direction. No damage to the compressor should occur.

Broken Scroll Assembly

If oil, sludge, or debris were to be compressed by the scrolls, modern scroll assemblies will separate and protect the compressor. In extreme examples, it may be possible to break the scroll assembly. If this occurred, the compressor may attempt to run but suction and discharge pressures may remain equal or far out of normal range.

Seized Scroll Assembly

When compressor bearings have been damaged to the point the compressor is seized, the compressor will trip overload protection and shut down during attempted starts. The compressor should be replaced.

Internal Bearing Damage

It is very common for compressors to experience bearing damage. Compressors operating with damaged bearings will operate at amperage

Field Service Guide: Compressors

levels higher than specified by the compressor manufacturer. The compressor may also have excessive vibration and a metallic sound to it as it runs.

Detecting bearing damage internal to a compressor is very difficult because the running amperage of the compressor must be compared to published charts from the compressor manufacturer. These charts publish the amp draw of the compressor at combinations of suction and discharge pressure. If the measured amps is around 15% higher than it should be, the compressor bearings may be damaged. Be aware that without the published data charts from the compressor manufacturer, this test cannot be performed.

Reciprocating Compressors - Broken Valve Plate

If a reciprocating compressor were to get liquid into the compression cylinder and the liquid volume was large enough, the liquid when compressed would potentially break the valve plate as the pressure generated is enormous. There is clearance area between the compressor valve plate/compression head and the top of the piston. If the liquid trapped in this area is great enough to fill the area, it will be compressed. The most likely component to break is the suction valve. When this valve breaks, the condensing pressure will bleed into the suction side of the system. The suction pressure will be high and the condensing pressure too low.

Many technicians are taught to perform a pump down test where the system is run and the liquid line service valve closed. The system suction pressure falls as refrigerant is pumped into the condenser coil. When the suction pressure reaches 0 PSIG, the system is shut off and the refrigerant gauges monitored. If the suction pressure rises slightly and then holds, the compressor valves are determined to be OK.

Image courtesy of Trane
A broken valve plate caused by liquid slugging.

This test is not approved by all compressor manufacturers as an approved method of detecting valve damage in a reciprocating compressor.

So what is the proper method for detecting valve plate failure? If the suction pressure is too high and the condensing pressure too low, the metering device may be overfeeding the evaporator circuit. Check for a properly sized piston. Make sure the indoor coil is properly sized for the outdoor condensing unit. A large evaporator will elevate suction pressure. Pump

If the suction pressure is too high and the condensing pressure is too low, the metering piston may be overfeeding the evaporator circuit. Check to make sure that it is properly sized for the system.

the system down and see if the compressor can hold some of the refrigerant in the condenser. If it quickly equalizes the suction and discharge pressure, it may have a broken valve. Contact the manufacturer to obtain proper confirmation of valve damage.

2-Step Unloading Scroll Compressors

Two stage capacity systems now feature scroll compressors that can reduce capacity from 100% to 67% in order to achieve higher efficiency ratings. This new scroll compressor is manufactured by Copeland. The compressor uses a standard single speed PSC motor. Many manufacturers are using the new 2 step compressors in high efficiency systems due to excellent reliability and performance.

The compressor features an unloading ring that is moved by a solenoid coil located inside the compressor. The ring opens or closes two internal unloading ports inside the compressor.

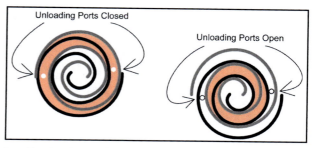

In first stage low capacity operation, the unloading ports inside the compressor are open. The system will operate at 67% capacity in this mode. When the thermostat inside the home closes the Y2 or second stage cooling circuit, 24 volts is directed to a bridge rectifier circuit that converts the 24 volts to DC voltage. The voltage output of the bridge rectifier circuit is typically between 15-27VDC.

The bridge rectifier circuit is usually found in two configurations, one as an external chip located in the control panel of the air conditioning system, and the other where the bridge rectifier is molded into the plug located on the side of the compressor.

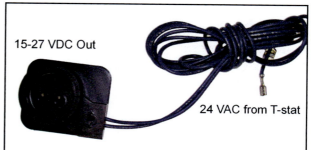

The bridge rectifier circuit can be found in a molded plug such as shown above.

When 24 VAC is applied to the rectifier circuit, the circuit in the molded plug applies DC volts to the compressor solenoid pins. The unloading ring then moves to close off the unloading ports and the compressor goes to 100% cooling capacity.

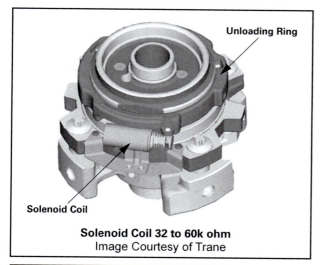

Solenoid Coil 32 to 60k ohm
Image Courtesy of Trane

Field Service Guide: Compressors

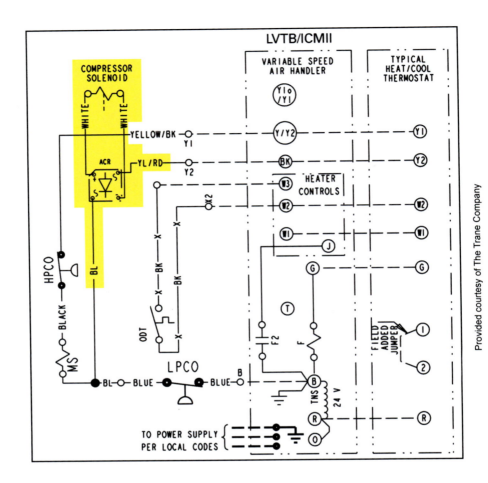

As the compressor loads to 100% capacity, a noticeable increase in compressor amps will be observed.

To ensure reliability and prevent possible failure of the compressor internal solenoid, voltage should never be applied to the unloading solenoid when the system is out of charge or when the refrigerant circuit low pressure switch has opened. If voltage is applied to the solenoid circuit and the system is out of refrigerant, the solenoid will likely overheat and burn out. With the solenoid burned out, the compressor can only operate at 67% of rated capacity.

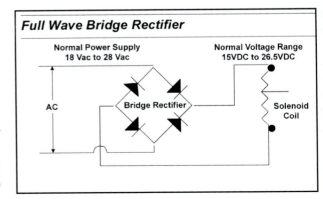

Field Service Guide: Compressors

Summary

Both reciprocating and scroll compressors have some capability of dealing with potential liquid in the compression process.

Compressors in residential systems should not be operated in a vacuum.

Do not leak test compressors above 150 PSIG nitrogen pressure.

Compressors may not start at voltages below 187V. (Measured as compressor tries to start at load side of the contactor. All major electrical appliances in the home should be turned on during the test.)

Crankcase heaters are required when system charge is above specified limits by manufacturers.

Internal bearing damage can be diagnosed if compressor manufacturer performance data is available. Contact compressor manufacturers for information on obtaining performance data tables.

Some reciprocating compressors were not designed to hold a pump down of refrigerant in the condenser.

2-step scroll compressors should never have the unloading solenoid energized if the low pressure switch is opened.

Introduction to Compressor Electrical Operating Characteristics: 208/230 Single Phase Reciprocating and Scroll Models

Residential Compressors use Permanent Split Capacitor (PSC) Motors

Other than super high efficiency variable speed air conditioning systems, all residential air conditioning systems use PSC motors inside the compressor shell. Compressor motors used in residential systems are single speed type. The motor uses an external run capacitor and may also have a start assist device in the electrical circuit.

In this picture of a cutaway reciprocating compressor you can see the rotor and copper windings of the PSC motor, the Run Capacitor is located outside of the compressor shell.

How PSC Motors work

PSC motors have two motor windings, one winding is called a START winding and the other winding is called a RUN winding. The windings are located around the compressor motor ROTOR. When electrical power is applied to the motor, a circular rotating magnetic field pulls

21

and pushes the rotor in a rotating circle to turn the rotor. The rotor will continually move as it is attracted to and repelled by the magnetized coils of wire. This motion will continue until power is disconnected.

PSC Motors use a Run Capacitor (Continuous Duty)

A run capacitor is a storage device that will charge and discharge with changes in the electrical polarity of the applied voltage. When these capacitors are applied to a motor winding circuit, they can create a time delay where the applied voltage to the winding must first charge and then discharge through the capacitor. PSC motors use run capacitors to create the best magnetic hold possible on the motor rotor by changing the timing of the magnetic field generated by the start winding.

This continuous duty run capacitor is wired in series with the Start Winding in order to create the best magnetic hold possible on the motor rotor.

A continuous duty run capacitor is wired in series with the START WINDING. The capacitor stores and discharges power and will change the timing of the start winding's magnetic field. This is done to position the electrical field at the optimum place in relationship to the run winding magnetic field. With both magnetic fields in proper place, the motor operates at its most efficient power performance level.

Capacitors are rated in microfarad range (storage capacity) and voltage range. Each PSC motor will have its own unique run capacitor rating to provide maximum performance. If a capacitor is replaced with one of incorrect microfarad range, the position of the magnetic field will be affected and motor performance will decrease. Voltage rating of the capacitor should always be equal to or greater than what is specified for the motor.

Start Assist Devices can be added to the Compressor Circuit

Potential Relay and Start Capacitor

Hard start kits help single phase compressors start against potential heavy working loads. A potential relay and a start capacitor are the two components that make up the kit. Start kit potential relay specifications and the start capacitor microfarad requirements are specified by the compressor manufacturer.

Shown here is a potential relay and start capacitor of a start kit, as well as a combo start kit that has both in one unit.

The hard start kit places an intermittent duty start capacitor in the compressor motor winding circuit for a very brief moment. The additional capacitor generates a stronger magnetic field hold on the motor rotor. This strong field helps get the compressor motor turning quicker. It is important to realize that it is a device that gets the motor started quicker, it does not limit the

Field Service Guide: Compressors

locked rotor amps at the initial moment when the power is applied to the motor.

The start capacitor must be removed very quickly from the motor circuit or it will fail electrically. To get the capacitor out of the circuit quickly, a special relay called a potential relay is used. A potential relay has a normally closed set of contacts that place the capacitor into the circuit when the compressor is not running. The relay has a coil that is energized by the back voltage generated when the compressor motor begins to turn. This voltage will energize the potential relay when the motor gets up to about 75% of compressor motor RPM. When the relay is energized, the normally closed contacts open to disconnect the start capacitor from the motor circuit.

The voltage that is generated by the motor to energize the relay is called a pick up voltage. The potential relay has a rating that indicates it's pick up voltage where the compressor voltage will energize the relay. If the wrong relay is used and the motor is not capable of generating enough pick up voltage quickly, the capacitor will remain in the circuit too long and will be destroyed.

Start capacitors can be used to reduce dimming light complaints in homes. Be aware that in many cases the start kit will not eliminate dimming lights but will reduce the amount of time it occurs and potentially the level of light dimming in a home.

Start kits should not be the first thing done to a compressor that is having problems starting. The first thing to determine is whether the run capacitor microfarad level is within 10% of the rating on the capacitor case. (See Motor section for details.) Make sure the system is not trying to start against unequalized refrigerant pressures. Next, the line voltage at the condensing unit should be measured as the compressor tries to start. All major electrical appliances in the home should be on and the voltage measured at the load side of the contactor as the contactor pulls in. The voltage should be above 187 VAC and no higher than 253 VAC. If the voltage is not within specified limits, perform the checks specified in the diagnostic section of the Line Voltage section of this book.

If the voltage and run capacitor check out good, the compressor may have bearing damage. Obtain the compressor manufacturer performance data for the compressor to determine if bearing damage is present. If there is no bearing damage, add a start kit to the system.

If the compressor still has problems starting, the compressor may need to be replaced.

PTC Start Assist Device

A PTC start assist device uses a special element that will allow current flow for a brief moment, and then quickly heats up and stops current flow.

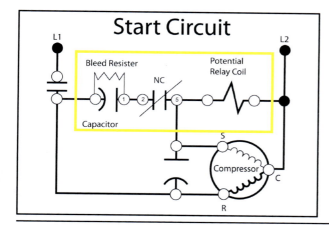

23

Field Service Guide: Compressors

The electrical resistance of the PTC device will rapidly rise as current flows through it. It is sometimes wired directly across the compressor run capacitor. In this configuration, there is a direct path to the compressor start winding during initial power up of the compressor. This direct current flow in the start winding increases motor torque. The device quickly opens and shuts off the path to the start winding. The run capacitor is then placed back into the compressor motor winding circuit.

Sometimes these devices are used in conjunction with a start capacitor to briefly place the start capacitor into the circuit. It replaces the potential relay as the switching device.

A PTC device shown before installation.

A disadvantage of this type of start device compared to a potential relay device is that if the system is short cycled, and starting is attempted against non-equalized system pressures, the PTC device will still be hot and will not be an active start component when it is needed.

Fusite Plugs: Safety

The motor windings are connected to a plug that is called a fusite plug. The fusite plug separates the internal electrical components of the compressor from the world outside the compressor shell.

There are three terminal pins located on a fusite plug. The pins are the connection between the motor windings and the wiring that is external to the compressor shell. <u>The pins are the common connection between the motor start and run windings, the run winding, and the start winding.</u> The resistance of the motor windings can be checked at the end of the wires that are connected to these pins. It is not recommended that motor winding resistance checks be made directly at these pins.

To reduce the potential for terminal venting, <u>never reset a condensing unit circuit breaker, or</u>

Fusite plug

The terminal pins on the fusite plug could potentially blow out of the fusite plug if an internal short circuit were to occur. When a pin blows out of the fusite plug, it is called terminal venting. If power is present, and an electrical short blows out a pin, the refrigerant oil and refrigerant will leave the system through the hole and may catch fire which will create a stream of flaming oil moving at high speed. This is called terminal venting with ignition. The force of a pin ejecting from the compressor shell is capable of potential physical harm or death. If there is any indication of electrical charring or burning on one of the fusite plug pins, be very careful to ensure the pin is not loose and about to eject the refrigerant charge and pin.

Field Service Guide: Compressors

Terminal venting can cause serious injury and/or death.

The leads have been removed from the compressor for clarity. Always perform this check on the wire leads.

replace an open/blown line voltage fuse, without first performing a motor grounding check. Also, never start or pump a residential compressor into a vacuum as internal arcing may occur inside the compressor shell which can lead to terminal venting.

At no time, should the protective cover be removed from the compressor motor terminal area when power is present to the condensing unit.

If a compressor is energized and sizzling or popping noise is heard coming from the compressor, get away from the compressor immediately as water may be in the compressor which may generate steam that may cause an explosion and release of scalding steam.

Checking Motor Winding Resistances and Winding Condition

First, when measuring compressor motor winding resistance, power to the condensing unit must be turned off. **DISCONNECT POWER TO THE OUTDOOR UNIT. FAILURE TO FOLLOW THIS INSTRUCTION CAN RESULT IN PERSONAL INJURY OR DEATH.**
The resistance of the compressor motor windings will typically be quite low. The start winding has greater resistance than the run winding. In the picture above, the resistance of the motor windings is being read between the common and the run winding. The run winding has a resistance of about 2 OHMS. In the bottom picture, the resistance of the start winding is read from between the common and the start winding. This reading has a resistance of about 3 OHMS. All compressors will have different

The leads have been removed from the compressor for clarity. Always perform this check on the wire leads.

motor winding resistance readings. In all cases, the start winding resistance will be higher than the run winding resistance.

25

Field Service Guide: Compressors

Checking Internal Motor Winding Overload Protector Switch

First, when measuring compressor motor winding resistance, power to the condensing unit must be turned off. **DISCONNECT POWER TO THE OUTDOOR UNIT. FAILURE TO FOLLOW THIS INSTRUCTION CAN RESULT IN PERSONAL INJURY OR DEATH.**

Inside the compressor, an internal motor overload protection switch will open when excessive temperature occurs in the motor windings. This switch is wired in series between the connection point for the run and start windings and the common pin on the fusite plug.

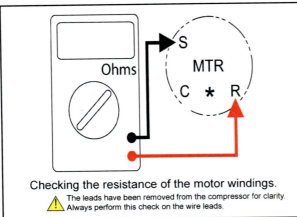

Checking the resistance of the motor windings.
⚠ The leads have been removed from the compressor for clarity. Always perform this check on the wire leads.

If the overload switch were to be in an open position, the motor would not try to start when power is applied to the compressor. When checking the resistance of the motor windings where the internal overload switch has opened, infinite resistance would be measured between the run winding and common and the start winding and common.

If the overload switch has opened, allow time for the compressor to cool off. The switch is an automatic reset type that should re-close after the motor has cooled. If the switch fails to reset, the compressor must be replaced.

To be sure the motor windings have not burned out (opened), measure the resistance between the run winding and the start winding. There should be measured resistance if the windings have continuity. If either winding is open, there will be infinite resistance read. An open winding cannot be repaired. The compressor would need to be replaced.

Checking for a Grounded Motor Winding: Resistance from the Motor Winding Pins to the Compressor Shell

First, when measuring for a grounded motor winding, power to the condensing unit must be turned off. **DISCONNECT POWER TO THE OUTDOOR UNIT. FAILURE TO FOLLOW THIS INSTRUCTION CAN RESULT IN PERSONAL INJURY OR DEATH.**

The motor windings can develop a short circuit to ground. This is a condition where there is an electrical short circuit inside the compressor where a wire is directly touching a metal portion of the compressor that is connected to ground. If this condition occurs, the excessive current flow will occur and either the circuit breaker or fuse should open to shut power off to the condensing unit.

To test for a grounded compressor motor, measure the resistance from each end of the wires connected to the fusite pins to the discharge line of the compressor. (Remember, measure the resistance at the end of the wire connected to the fusite pins, not directly at the pins.) Check the resistance to ground from the common pin, the run pin, and the start pin. There

Field Service Guide: Compressors

Testing for a grounded compressor
⚠ The leads have been removed from the compressor for clarity. Always perform this check on the wire leads.

should be measurable resistance above about 1,000,000 OHMS. If the resistance is below this level, contact the manufacturer of the condensing unit to determine if resistances below 1,000,000 OHMS is acceptable. In most cases it is not, but in some older systems, manufacturers have published acceptable OHMS to ground at 500,000 OHMS. If a compressor motor is shorted to ground, the compressor must be replaced.

Diagnostic Tests

Follow all proper electrical safety practices when performing these tests.

Finding the Cause Of Compressor Starting Problems

When a compressor has trouble starting, the problem may be as simple as a bad run capacitor, or as complicated as internal bearing damage to the compressor. The first step is to determine if anything in the refrigeration system is contributing to the compressor's inability or difficulty in starting. Refrigeration conditions that can cause starting problems include:

- Long line sets where system charge is high.
- Overcharge
- Buried suction lines that are full of liquid Refrigerant that is going to head right into the compressor at start operation.
- Restrictions causing unequalized refrigerant pressures during start operation.
- (Most new scroll compressors start unloaded internally even when gauges appear unequalized.)

If it appears there are no refrigerant circuit problems present, electrical tests must be done on the compressor and associated components.

Testing to Find the Cause of Compressor Starting Problems

Tools: Refrigeration Gauges
Multimeter
Ammeter

STEP 1

Make sure the compressor is not trying to start against unequalized refrigerant pressures. Also, make sure the compressor does not need a crankcase heater. If the charge level of the

27

Field Service Guide: Compressors

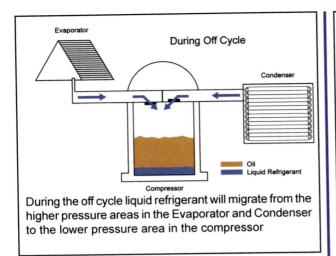

During Off Cycle

During the off cycle liquid refrigerant will migrate from the higher pressure areas in the Evaporator and Condenser to the lower pressure area in the compressor

system is high due to long refrigerant lines, the compressor may require a crankcase heater. The compressor may be full of liquid refrigerant that migrated to the compressor shell during off cycle. Call the manufacturer to confirm.

STEP 2

Disconnect power to the outdoor unit and discharge the run capacitor. Remove the wires from the run capacitor. Perform a run capacitor test to confirm proper microfarad rating is within 10% of nameplate rating. If the run capacitor is defective replace it with one of equal microfarad

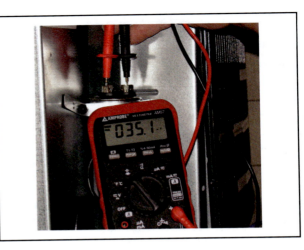

range. The voltage rating of the replacement capacitor should be equal to or greater than the one being replaced.

If the capacitor is OK, continue on.

STEP 3

Figure 1   Figure 2

Measure the line voltage at the load side of the compressor contactor as the compressor tries to start. (Fig 1) It should not fall below 187VAC. (Make sure all major electrical appliances in the home are on when you perform this measurement.) If voltage is below 187V, check

28

Field Service Guide: Compressors

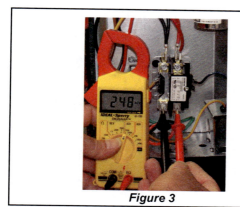

Figure 3

for voltage drop from the home's electrical panel to the disconnect outdoors at the condensing unit. (Fig 2) If there is a voltage drop, confirm proper wire sizing and make corrections. If the voltage is OK, check the voltage drop from the outdoor unit disconnect switch to the line side of the compressor contactor. (Fig 3) If there

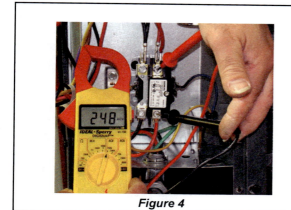

Figure 4

is excessive voltage drop, fix the problem. If it is OK, check for a voltage drop across the compressor contactor. (Fig 4) If voltage drop is present across the contacts of the contactor, replace the contactor.

STEP 4

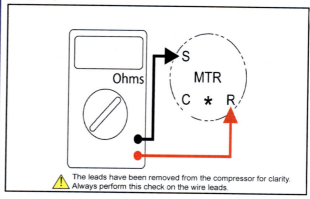

⚠ The leads have been removed from the compressor for clarity. Always perform this check on the wire leads.

If the first 3 steps check out OK, disconnect power to the condensing unit and make sure all capacitors are discharged. Find the wires that lead to the compressor motor fusite plug terminals: run, start, and common. Perform an ohm reading of the motor windings at the end of these wires. If a winding is open, replace the compressor. If they are OK, continue.

STEP 5

Install a hard start kit on the compressor. If the compressor runs, measure the amperage of the compressor motor on the common wire to the compressor motor and note the refrigerant pressures. Contact the system manufacturer to confirm what the amperage should be. If it is 15% higher than it should be, bearing damage may be present and the compressor may need to be replaced.

29

STEP 6

Amperage should read within normal parameters

If the system starts and runs with normal amperage, compressor is OK.

When a Compressor Trips the Circuit Breaker or Opens a Line Fuse

If a condensing unit is tripping the circuit breaker or opening a line fuse, there is excessive current in the outdoor unit or the fuse/breaker size is incorrect. If the outdoor unit is under a heavy heat load such as when it is very hot out, air temperature in the home is hot and the condensing unit is running, the compressor may overload and operate with excessive amperage. A dirty condenser coil will also cause excessive condensing pressure and higher than normal amperage draw. If there is no evident reason for the circuit breaker or fuse to open, the high current may be caused by a direct short to ground in the outdoor condensing unit. This short can come from any component in the high voltage circuit including crankcase heaters, wiring, contactors, capacitors, condenser fan motors, and compressors.

In all cases where the circuit breaker or line voltage fuses have opened, the compressor must be checked for a short to ground before the circuit breaker or fuse are reset/replaced. Failure to follow this instruction may result in injury or death.

Testing for a Grounded Compressor

Tools:
Refrigeration Gauges
Multimeter
Ammeter

STEP 1

Disconnect power to the outdoor condensing unit and discharge all capacitors.

Field Service Guide: Compressors

STEP 2

Set electrical multimeter to read OHMS at the highest resistance scale.

STEP 3

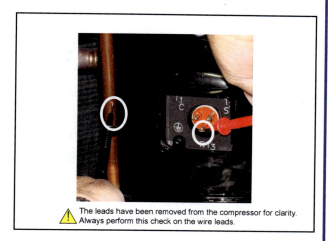

⚠ The leads have been removed from the compressor for clarity. Always perform this check on the wire leads.

Measure the resistance between the compressor discharge line and each wire leading to the motor fusite plug terminals: run, start, and common.

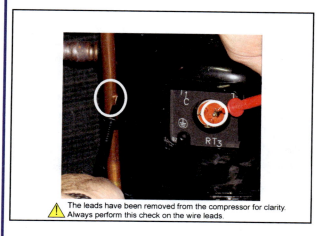

⚠ The leads have been removed from the compressor for clarity. Always perform this check on the wire leads.

Infinite resistance should be measured if the compressor has no conductive path between the motor and the discharge line. Resistance below

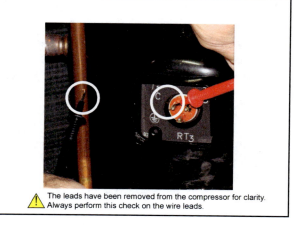

⚠ The leads have been removed from the compressor for clarity. Always perform this check on the wire leads.

1,000,000 OHMS is considered shorted by most compressor manufacturers. If low resistance is measured, the compressor is shorted to ground and must be replaced.

Field Service Guide: Compressors

STEP 4

If the compressor checks out OK, check other components for a short circuit to ground.

For three-phase motors, follow the same procedure as above, but check resistance from motor terminals 1, 2, and 3 to ground.

Troubleshooting a Compressor Start Circuit

Compressor start circuits consist of a potential relay with normally closed contacts and a start capacitor. When there is a malfunction of the start circuit, the start capacitor is usually destroyed. (Relief plug opens on top of capacitor.) The capacitor fails because it is an intermittent duty capacitor that should only be in the electrical circuit for a very brief moment.

Causes of start circuit failure include low line voltage where the compressor pick up voltage is too low to energize the potential relay so the capacitor remains in the circuit for too long of a period of time.

Testing the Compressor Start Circuit

When a compressor start circuit has failed, check to ensure that starting voltage at the compressor contactor does not fall below the minimum 187VAC requirement. Make sure all major electrical appliances in the home are on to simulate the lowest voltage possible at the condensing unit. If voltage is low, find the cause.

Potential relay failure where the relay contacts do not open. Capacitor mechanical failure.

Tools: | Screwdriver w/ Insulated Grip
       | Multimeter
       | Ammeter

STEP 1

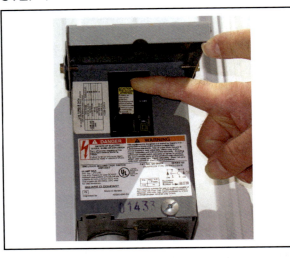

Disconnect power to the unit. Discharge the start capacitor using a screwdriver with an insulated handle. Remove the potential relay from the electrical circuit.

STEP 2

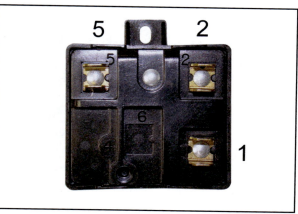

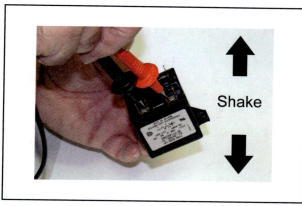

Testing the potential relay for problems is simple as there are three terminals on the relay. The terminals are labeled 1, 2, and 5. Terminals 1 and 2 are the normally closed contacts. Terminal 2 to 5 is the internal solenoid coil of the relay.

tone. Holding the meter leads against the relay terminals, shake the relay, the internal contacts should snap open and the tone will break. This indicates the relay contacts are not welded shut. If the relay contacts do not open, replace the relay. If the relay contacts do open, proceed to the next step.

STEP 3

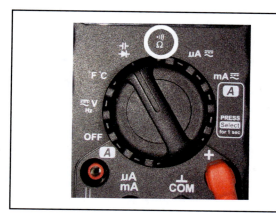

Measure the resistance between terminal 1 and 2. The resistance should be 0 OHMS. Normally closed. Next, turn the ohmmeter to the diode function test where a short circuit beeps a tone. Place ohmmeter leads against relay terminals 1 and 2. The ohmmeter should make a steady

Measure the resistance between relay terminals 2 and 5. There should be resistance measured. If there is no resistance or infinite ohms measured, replace the relay as the solenoid coil inside the relay has opened. If the relay coil checks out OK, the relay is not defective.

Field Service Guide: Compressors

Testing a Start Capacitor for Proper Operation

Disconnect power to the condensing unit. Before removing capacitor from the electrical circuit it must be discharged. Start capacitors should be discharged before handling. There is a bleed resistor soldered across most start capacitor terminals. This resistance slowly discharges the capacitor. Do not assume the capacitor is discharged by the bleed resistor. Discharge it using a screwdriver with an insulated handle.

Testing a Start Capacitor for Proper Operation

Tools: Screwdriver w/ Insulated Grip
Multimeter
Ammeter

STEP 1

Inspect the capacitor case for a vented top or cracks in the case. If the capacitor is vented or cracked, replace it with one of equal microfarad and voltage rating. If the capacitor shows no visible sign of failure, proceed to the next step.

STEP 2

Set multimeter to OHM setting. Place meter leads on each capacitor terminal. The battery in the meter should charge the capacitor and the ohm reading on the meter should fluctuate up and down. The meter should end up reading the value of the bleed resistor. **If the meter does not change reading, replace the start capacitor** with one of equal microfarad ratings. Voltage rating may be equal or greater than the original rating.

Testing a Run Capacitor for Proper Microfarad Rating

Do not do this test on a start capacitor.

Tools: Screwdriver w/ Insulated Grip
Multimeter

STEP 1

Disconnect power to the outdoor unit. Discharge the run capacitor.

Field Service Guide: Compressors

STEP 1

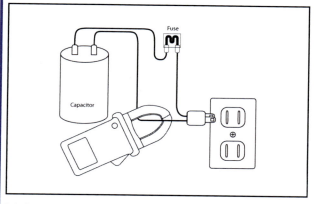

Make a wire rig for the capacitor check. Attach the rig to a discharged capacitor. Plug in the wire rig to a wall outlet. With power applied to the capacitor, measure the amp draw to the capacitor and multiply by 2650.

STEP 2

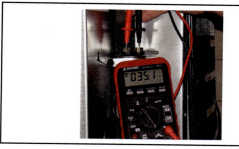

Most multimeters used by HVAC technicians have a capacitance measuring function built into them. Place meter leads across discharged capacitor. The multimeter will display the measured microfarad level of the run capacitor. If the measured microfarad is more than 10% different than the value specified on the capacitor case, replace it with one of equal microfarad rating. Voltage rating may be equal or greater than the original rating.

Testing a Run Capacitor with a "Power On" Test

Caution: DO NOT PERFORM THIS TEST ON A START CAPACITOR.

BEFORE PERFORMING THIS TEST MEASURE RESISTANCE FROM EACH CAPACITOR LEAD TO THE CAPACITOR CASE. IF A SHORT CIRCUIT IS FOUND, DO NOT PERFORM THIS TEST. INJURY OR DEATH COULD RESULT.

If you do not have a multimeter with a microfarad reading capability, a simple test rig can be constructed from a power cord and a 5 amp automotive type fuse. The rig is attached to the capacitor and power is applied to the rig.

Tools: Screwdriver w/ Insulated Grip
Multimeter

STEP 2

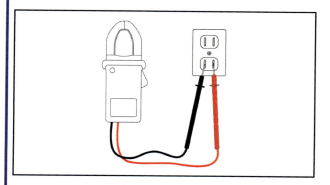

Measure the voltage applied to the capacitor.

35

STEP 1

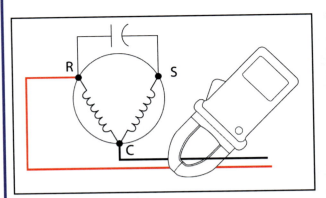

Run the system in <u>first</u> stage cooling and allow pressures to stabilize. Connect (ammeter) to the common lead of the compressor motor. Measure the running amps.

STEP 2

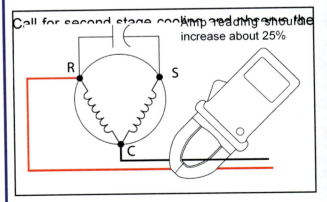

Call for second stage cooling and note the amp reading. When the compressor loads to second stage, the amp draw should increase by around 25%. The increase in amps indicates

Amp reading should increase about 25%

(continued)

STEP 3

EXAMPLE:

Amps = 4
Voltage Applied = 110VAC

Solution MFD = $\frac{2\,(2650)}{110}$ = $\frac{5300}{110}$ = 48MFD

Apply this formula to find the microfarad rating of the capacitor:

Microfarad = $\frac{\text{Amps times 2650}}{\text{Applied voltage to capacitor}}$

Troubleshooting a 2 Step Compressor to Determine if it is Loading and Unloading

A 2 step compressor uses a standard single speed PSC motor, so testing of the motor is identical to any single phase compressor motor test. However, the unloading solenoid should be tested to ensure it is working properly.

Testing the Unloading Solenoid of a 2 Step Compressor

Tools: **Ammeter**

Field Service Guide: Compressors

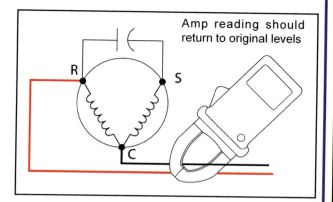

Amp reading should return to original levels

STEP 4

the compressor has loaded to 100% capacity. Remove the call for second stage cooling and the amp reading should decrease to around earlier levels.

If the amps do not change, continue.

STEP 3

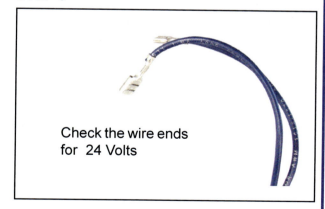

Check the wire ends for 24 Volts

Check to ensure 24 volts is present to the molded plug or to the rectifier chip. If 24 volts is not present, find the cause and make corrections. If 24 volts is present, continue.

Set voltmeter to read DC VOLTS. Measure the voltage at the plug solenoid terminals. 15-27 VDC should be present with 24 volts applied to the plug. (RECTIFIER ALSO) If there is no output voltage at the plug, the internal bridge rectifier circuit has failed. Replace the plug. (REPLACE RECTIFIER CHIP ON MODELS WITH EXTERNAL CHIP)

End the call for cooling and disconnect line voltage to the condensing unit. Remove the molded plug from the compressor. The 24 volt call for cooling should still be energized by the indoor air handling unit. Make sure there is 24 volts to the molded plug. (Second stage cooling call)

Field Service Guide: Compressors

If there is the proper DC voltage at the terminals on the plug, and the compressor does not load and unload, the compressor internal solenoid may be burned out, or the compressor may have internal mechanical failure. In either case, the compressor must be replaced.

NOTE: The compressor unloader solenoid can be burned out or damaged by applying voltage to the solenoid when there is inadequate charge in the system. Systems using the 2 step compressor have a low pressure switch that opens 24 volt power circuit when there is low refrigerant pressure. Jumping this control out to get the system to operate without proper pressure will likely cause the solenoid to be destroyed.

Checking a Reciprocating Compressor for a Damaged Valve Plate

If a compressor has tried to compress liquid or sludge, one of the compressor valves may have broken. Typically, the suction valve is damaged. When a compressor operates with a broken valve, the compressor cannot operate at proper refrigeration pressures. The system will have higher than normal suction pressure and lower than normal discharge pressure.

To confirm a failed compressor valve plate, a pump down is usually performed where the liquid line service valve is closed while the compressor is running. When the service valve is closed, the compressor will try to pump all of the refrigerant charge into the condenser coil. The refrigerant can't escape the condenser coil with the liquid line service valve closed unless the refrigerant circulates back through the compressor valve plate assembly. If the refrigerant does circulate through the compressor, the pressures will equalize. The equalizing pressures indicate there is some leakage occurring through the valves of the compressor. This test is not universally accepted by all compressor manufacturers as some compressors were never designed to hold a pump down cycle.

At no time during a pump down test should a reciprocating residential compressor be allowed to operate at any pressure below 0 PSIG. This test should also never be performed on a scroll compressor as the compressor may be damaged. (Scroll compressors do not have valves!)

Field Service Guide: Compressors

Testing for a Damaged Valve Plate (Reciprocating Compressors Only)

Tools: **Refrigeration Gauges**

STEP 1

Attach refrigeration gauges. Run the system.

STEP 2

With the compressor running, close the liquid line service valve. Pressures will fall. When the suction pressure reaches 1-2 PSIG, shut power off to the condensing unit.

DO NOT PUMP THE SYSTEM INTO A VACUUM!

STEP 3

Watch the suction gauge. The gauge pressure will typically rise slightly and then stop rising. This is an indication that the valves are capable of holding back the refrigerant charge in the condenser coil.

However, if the pressures quickly equalize, this is an indication of leakage of refrigerant through the valve plate. Remember, some compressors were never meant to hold a pump down.

Field Service Guide: Compressors

STEP 4

If there is indication of a broken or damaged valve plate, contact the compressor manufacturer to determine if the compressor should be replaced.

If the compressor passes the test, open the liquid line service valve and allow pressures to equalize before restarting the system.

> NOTE: A SMALL RISE IN SUCTION PRESSURE MAY OCCUR AFTER THE COMPRESSOR IS SHUT DOWN DUE TO SOME REFRIGERANT REMAINING IN THE SUCTION SIDE OF THE SYSTEM. THIS SMALL RISE IN PRESSURE DOES NOT INDICATE BAD COMPRESSOR VALVES.

Checking a Single or Three Phase Scroll Compressor for Mechanical Failure

When higher than normal suction pressure and lower than normal liquid pressure are present, many technicians begin to assume that the compressor is bad. In fact, there are other causes of high suction pressure and low liquid pressure other than compressor failure. These causes include:

- Bypassing or oversized metering devices
- Leaking heat pump indoor check valve assemblies
- Heat pump reversing valve leakage

Since valve plate leakage on compressors

has been the primary suspected cause of high suction pressure and low liquid pressure, there is a problem with assuming that a scroll compressor is the problem. This is due to the fact that scroll compressors do not have valve plates.

To elevate the suction pressure and lower the liquid pressure, scroll compressors would have to allow some of the discharge gas to leak back into the suction side of the system. This condition is highly unlikely to occur with scroll designs. Many scroll compressors feature discharge line check valves that hold the discharge gas outside of the compressor shell. This discharge line check valve is not leak proof.

One area that can point to mechanical damage to a compressor is the amp draw of the compressor. If there is any additional drag within the compressor body due to mechanical friction, you should be able to detect it with an ammeter. The measured amperage would be higher than the published amps at the combination of indoor air heat load and outdoor air temperature. Unfortunately, many systems you work on will not have this data available at the job site, and in fact many systems will not have the correct indoor air volume present to reference the required amps.

Testing a Scroll Compressor for Proper Pumping Capability

Tools:

| Refrigeration Gauges |
| Amp Meter |

Field Service Guide: Compressors

STEP 1

Attach refrigeration gauges. Run the system.

STEP 2

Assuming a proper charge level, the suction pressure should drop and the discharge pressure rise. If the pressures do not reach proper levels, check for an improperly sized metering piston or properly operating expansion valve. If these are OK, and the pressures do not reach normal levels, the compressor may be bad.

STEP 3

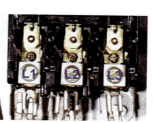
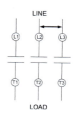

3 Phase Models

To change direction, switch any two incoming line power phases (L1, L2, L3).

SHUT OFF LINE VOLTAGE TO THE UNIT BEFORE REVERSING THE POWER LEADS OR INJURY/ DEATH MAY OCCUR.

Make sure the compressor is running in the proper direction. (three phase models)

If the compressor is running backwards, it will be excessively noisy and will not pump.

STEP 4

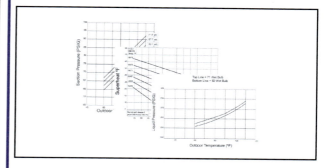

Obtain performance tables from the compressor manufacturer website. Compare the operating pressures against compressor amp draw charts. If the compressor is not operating within range specified by the compressor manufacturer, replace the compressor.

Field Service Guide: Compressors

Detecting Compressor Bearing Damage

Compressor bearings can be damaged by liquid refrigerant diluting oil, by copper plating, and by overheating. Compressors that are operating with damaged bearings will operate at higher than specified electrical amps for the operating refrigerant pressures. Comparing operating amps against performance tables provided by the compressor manufacturer is a valid method of detecting bearing damage.

Compressors operating with damaged bearings may have symptoms such as problems starting, excessive vibration, and metallic sounding operation.

Testing for Damaged Bearings

STEP 1   Tools: **Refrigeration Gauges
Ammeter**

Attach refrigerant gauges and run the system.

STEP 2

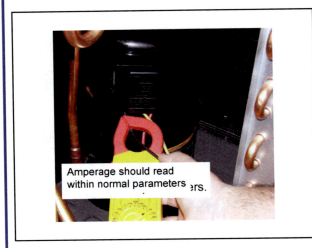

Amperage should read within normal parameters ers.

Measure compressor amps at the common motor lead.

STEP 3

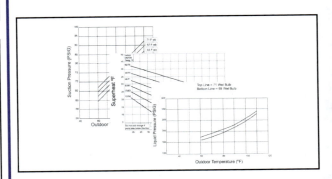

Compare operating amps against performance data table information for the specific compressor. If the amps are 15% greater than specified by the data table, the compressor may have damaged bearings. Confirm diagnosis with compressor manufacturer. (Performance tables may be obtained at compressor manufacturer websites or through service schools.)

Diagnosing a Seized Compressor-Single Phase

Determining if a compressor is seized requires that you eliminate all other possible causes before condemning the compressor as seized.

Symptoms

A potentially seized compressor will try to start, hum, and then open its internal overload. The compressor will draw Locked Rotor Amps (LRA) as it tries to start. Electrical causes must be eliminated as a potential problem before condemning the compressor. Electrical problems that could cause a compressor to fail to start will make a compressor act as if it is seized. These problems include:

- Low line voltage
- A pitted set of contactor points
- A broken wire between the compressor and run capacitor or contactor
- A failed run capacitor
- Un-equalized system pressures when the compressor tries to start

Before beginning the electrical test sequence, make sure the compressor is not trying to start against **Unequalized system pressures**. If it is in fact the compressor trying to start against Un-equalized pressures, check for refrigeration circuit restrictions or short cycling conditions.

Seized Compressor-Single Phase

Tools: Ammeter
Multimeter
Ohmmeter/Capacity Tester

STEP 1

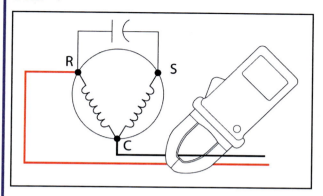

Remove power to the outdoor condensing unit. Place an ammeter onto the common motor winding lead of the compressor. (Typically the BLACK WIRE coming from the compressor motor terminal cover.) Restore power to the condensing unit and call for cooling. Check the

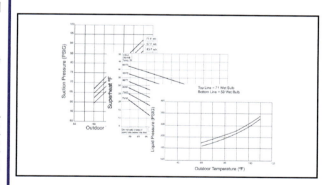

ammeter to be sure you are drawing LRA. If the compressor is trying to start, it should hum and then shut off on its internal overload. If the compressor does not try to start, the internal overload may be open. Allow time for it to reset. Once you have confirmed that the compressor is trying to start, proceed to Step 2.

Field Service Guide: Compressors

STEP 2

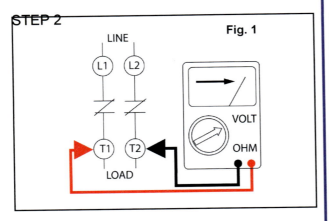

Fig. 1

Measure the voltage at the compressor contactor while it is under a load. Make sure you have the correct line voltage level at the LOAD SIDE TERMINALS (**Fig. 1**) of the compressor contactor. Typically this level must not be below or above 10% of the unit nameplate voltage

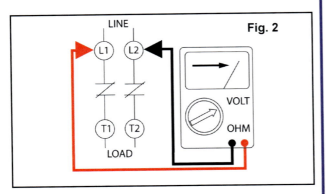

Fig. 2

rating. If the line voltage is too low at the LOAD TERMINALS, check the voltage to the LINE TERMINALS (**Fig. 2**) of the contactor. If the voltage is low at these terminals, there is a problem with the electrical supply to the condensing unit. If the line voltage is normal, but is low at the LOAD TERMINALS, check voltage across the contactor points (**Fig. 3.**), with the

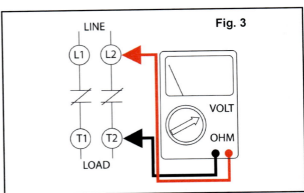

Fig. 3

contactor energized. You should measure 0 volts. If you measure voltage across the electrical points of the contactor, there is either pitting or an obstruction at the contactor. Correct the problem and then retry starting the compressor. If the voltage level at the contactor is within proper tolerance, continue on to Step 3.

STEP 3

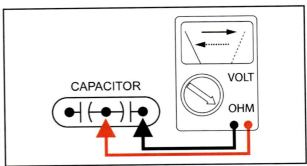

Disconnect power to the condensing unit and discharge all capacitors. Remove the wires from the run capacitor. Using either an ohmmeter or a capacitor tester, check to ensure that the run capacitor is operating properly. (See "Checking a Capacitor.") If it is not, replace it with one of equal value. If the capacitor is OK, continue on to Step 4.

Field Service Guide: Compressors

STEP 4

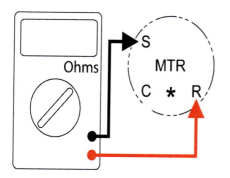

⚠ The leads have been removed from the compressor for clarity. Always perform this check on the wire leads.

With power to the unit still off, perform a motor winding test to check for an open run or start winding. (See "Motor Winding Test") If either winding is open, replace the compressor. If the windings are OK, proceed to Step 5.

STEP 5

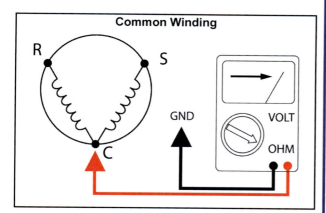

Check for a grounded compressor motor. (See "Checking for a Grounded Motor.") If any terminal is shorted to ground, replace the compressor. If the motor is not shorted, proceed to Step 6.

STEP 6

If everything checks out good electrically, and the compressor is not trying to start against Unequalized pressures, add a hard start kit. If the compressor fails to start, replace the compressor.

Performing a Single Phase Motor Winding Test

This test procedure will determine if a PSC compressor motor has failed due to an open motor winding. This test will also detect a possible open Internal Overload (IOL).

Symptoms

A compressor with an open winding will fail to start. The compressor may not do anything, or may in fact hum as it tries to start and then trip off on its internal overload. If the IOL is open, the compressor will not try to start.

Single Phase Motor Winding Test

Tools: **Multimeter**

45

Field Service Guide: Compressors

STEP 1

Remove power to the outdoor condensing unit and discharge all capacitors.

STEP 2

Set your ohmmeter to read very low ohms. (Down to ½ of an ohm may be read.) Place one ohmmeter lead to the Start Terminal and the other ohmmeter lead to the Common Terminal. (Fig 1) You should measure a low resistance. If you measure a low resistance, the Start winding is not open. Next measure the resistance between

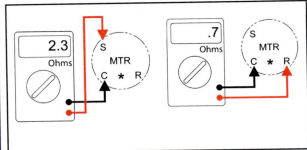

Figure 1 **Figure 2**

the Run terminal and the Common terminal (Fig 2), you should measure a small resistance. If you do, the compressor does not have an open winding.

If you measure infinite resistance between Common and either the Start or Run terminal, there is an open winding. Infinite resistance to both Start and Run terminals indicate an open IOL.

STEP 3

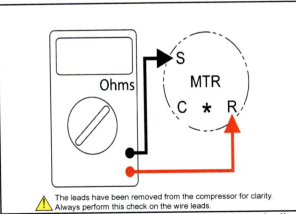

⚠ The leads have been removed from the compressor for clarity. Always perform this check on the wire leads.

To determine if the problem is an open winding or an open IOL, check the resistance between the Run terminal and the Start terminal. If you measure resistance, the IOL is open. Allow up to four hours for the IOL to re-close. If the IOL does not re-close, replace the compressor.

(continued)

Field Service Guide: Compressors

Three Phase Motor Winding Test

Tools: **Multimeter**

STEP 1

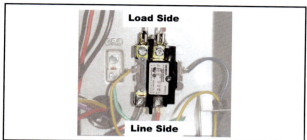

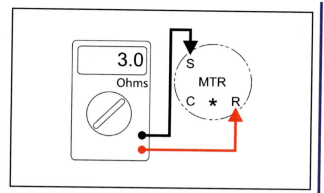

If you do not measure resistance between the Run and Start Terminals, there is an open winding. Replace the compressor.

Remove power to the outdoor condensing unit. Disconnect the three wires to the compressor 1, 2, and 3 motor terminals at the LOAD SIDE TERMINALS on the compressor contactor.

Load side terminals are the terminals that connect the compressor motor to the contactor. NOT THE INCOMING LINE VOLTAGE.

STEP 2

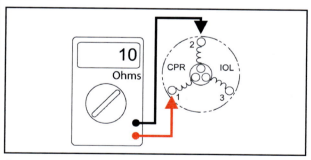

Performing a Three Phase Motor Winding Test

This test procedure will determine if a three phase compressor motor has failed due to an open motor winding. This test will also detect a possible open Internal Overload (IOL).

Symptoms

A three phase compressor with an open winding may fail to start. In some cases, the motor may run on one phase. The compressor may not do anything, or may in fact hum as it tries to start and then trip off on its internal overload. If the IOL is open, the compressor will not try to start.

Set your ohmmeter to read very low ohms. (Down to ½ of an ohm may be read.) Check resistance between all combinations of motor terminals. For example, between terminals 1 to 2, 1 to 3, and 2 to 3. You should measure equal resistance between all terminal combinations. If you do not measure resistance between any terminals, the IOL may be open. Allow time for the motor to cool down and the IOL to re-close.

(continued)

Field Service Guide: Compressors

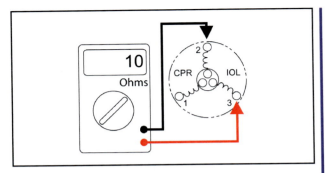

This may take up to four hours. If the IOL does not re-close, replace the compressor.

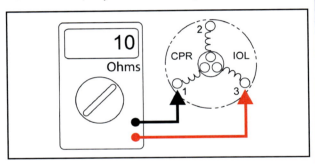

If you measure infinite resistance between any combination of 2 terminals, yet have resistance between the other terminals, the compressor has an open winding. Replace the compressor.

NOTE: SOME THREE PHASE COMPRESSORS HAVE SEPARATE TERMINALS FOR THE IOL. CHECK THE SCHEMATIC DRAWING TO DETERMINE WHICH ELECTRICAL CONFIGURATION YOU ARE WORKING WITH.

Detecting a Three Phase Voltage Imbalance

When three phase power is supplied to a commercial building, electricians take off power from different phase legs to power up 230 volt single phase equipment. If the same leg is used for the majority of the single phase power requirements, one three phase leg may drop its voltage too far below the other legs. In practice, a maximum of a 2% voltage imbalance is all that is allowed. This is due to the fact that voltage imbalances generate excessive heat in a three phase motor winding, such as those found in expensive three phase compressors.

We can determine the voltage imbalance present at a job site by performing the following test.

Calculating Voltage Imbalance

Step 1

Tools: Calculator
Multimeter

Leg 1 = 235   Leg 2 = 227   Leg 3 = 229

Run the condensing unit and measure the voltage being supplied to the compressor contactor on all three legs. Make sure the compressor is running.

Field Service Guide: Compressors

STEP 2

Add the three measured voltages and divide by three. You now have the average voltage.

$$(L1)235 + (L2)\ 227 + (L3)\ 229 = 691$$

$$691 \div 3 = 230$$

STEP 4

$$5 \div 230 = .0217 \times 100 = 2.17\%$$

Divide the largest difference by the average voltage and multiply the result by 100.

STEP 5

The result is the percentage of difference from

STEP 3

L1 =	L2 = 227	L3 = 229
235	-230	-230
-230	-3	-1
5		

Identify the leg with the largest difference from the average.

L1 = 2.17%

This imbalance creates an increase in the temperature of the winding in the phase where the L1 phase is connected.

the average. Please note that a maximum percentage of 2% is all that is allowed.

49

Field Service Guide: Compressors

STEP 6

To correct the problem, try moving the lines forward on the compressor contactor lugs, such as L1 to L2, L2 to L3, and L3 goes to L1, and then recheck the voltages. If the problem is not corrected, move the lines forward one more position and retest. If the problem is still not corrected inform the building owner to have an electrician analyze the buildings load distribution.

Failure to correct this type of problem will create the potential for premature motor failure at the compressor and indoor blower motor.

ECM and PSC
Motors

**ECM and PSC
Motors**

Field Service Guide: Motors

Chapter

ECM Motor Operation and Troubleshooting

The information in this chapter is provided courtesy of Regal-Beloit Corporation

Table of Contents

Overview of ECM Technology 2

    ECM Motor Diagnostics 3

Motor Not Running: Step By Step 4

Motor Running: Step By Step 5

Troubleshooting the ECM Motor using the GE ECM™ TECMate PRO: Step By Step 7

Replacing the ECM Control Module: Step By Step 10

Replacing the ECM Motor Module: Step By Step 12

Final Checks 15

Field Service Guide: Motors

Overview of ECM Motor Technology

What is ECM technology? ECM (Electronically Commutated Motor) technology is based on a brushless DC permanent magnet design that is inherently more efficient than the shaded-pole and permanent-split-capacitor (PSC) motors commonly found in air handlers, furnaces, heat pumps, air conditioners and refrigeration applications throughout the HVACR industry. By combining electronic controls with brushless DC motors, ECM's can maintain efficiency across a wide range of operating speeds. Plus, the electronic controls make the ECM programmable, allowing for advanced characteristics that are impossible to create using conventional motor technologies.

PSC Motor

ECM Motor

Early HVAC literature listed these motors as **ICM (Integrated Control Motor)**, meaning that a control was integrated or used in conjunction with a motor to control its operation. This was later changed to **ECM (Electronically Commutated Motor)** as they are typically referred to today. The definition of commutate is to reverse the direction of an alternating electric current (the means by which all electric motors rotate). In an ECM this process is controlled electronically by a microprocessor and electronic controls, which provides the ability to program and control the speed and/or torque of the motor.

The GE ECM™ motor, currently used by most residential HVAC systems is a brushless DC, three-phase motor with a permanent magnet rotor. Motor phases are sequentially energized by the electronic control, powered from a single-phase supply. These motors are actually made of two components, a motor control (control module) and a motor, sometimes called a motor module.

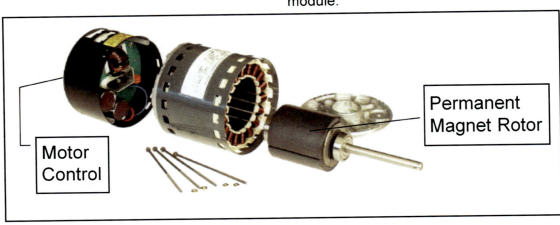

Motor Control

Permanent Magnet Rotor

The information in this chapter is provided courtesy of Regal-Beloit Corporation

Field Service Guide: Motors

The **motor control** is the brains of the device, where single phase (1Ø) 120 or 240 VAC 60 cycle (Hertz/frequency) power is connected. The control then converts AC power to DC power to operate the internal electronics, thus the name DC motor. The microprocessor in the motor control is programmed to then convert DC power (by means of electronic controls) to a three phase (3Ø) signal to drive the motor, thus the name Three Phase Motor. It also has the added ability to control the frequency (which controls the speed in revolutions per minute) and the amount of torque (current/power) it delivers to the motor.

The **motor** is essentially a three phase motor with a permanent magnet rotor. The permanent magnet rotor contributes to the electrical efficiency of the ECM and also to its sensor-less ability to control the rpm (revolutions per minute) and commutation (when to alternate the cycle). Typical DC motors require brushes to provide the commutation function. This is where the motor gets the name brushless DC motor.

The benefit of all of this technology is increased electrical efficiency and the ability to program more precise operation of the motor, over a wide range of HVAC system performance needs, to enhance consumer comfort.

ECM Motor Diagnostics

When servicing ECM blowers, do not automatically assume that the ECM motor has failed. Follow these step to test the ECM motor and ECM motor control before replacing these components.

> **WARNING:** *Working in the motor with power connected may result in electrical shock or other conditions that may cause personal injury, death or property damage.*
>
> **WARNING:** *On Models 2.0/2.3/2.5 always disconnect power from the HVAC system and wait at least 5 minutes before opening the motor, i.e. removing the two bolts from the motor control (end bell) and disconnecting the 3-pin plug to the motor. This to allow the capacitors to dissipate for safety.*
>
> **WARNING:** *Always disconnect the power from the HVAC system before removing or replacing connectors, servicing the motor, removing the high voltage plug, and before reconnecting.*
>
> **WARNING:** *Disconnect AC power from the system and make sure the blower wheel has come to a complete stop.*
>
> **WARNING:** *Do not operate motor without blower wheel attached. Such operation will cause motor to oscillate up and down.*
>
> **WARNING:** *You must have the correct replacement module from the manufacturer that is a direct replacement for the failed module. USING THE WRONG MODULE VOIDS ALL PRODUCT WARRANTIES AND MAY PRODUCE UNEXPECTED RESULTS.*

The information in this chapter is provided courtesy of Regal-Beloit Corporation

Field Service Guide: Motors

Tools: **Multimeter / TECMate PRO**

Before troubleshooting the ECM motor, check these system basics:

1. Confirm that the correct thermostat input and ONLY the correct input voltage is present at the main control board on the furnace/air handler. Loose or broken low-voltage wires are also potential problem areas and can cause intermittent problems. Use the manufacturer's guide to confirm proper demands (heat or cool), especially on multi-stage systems. Use Sequence of Operation charts and thermostat wiring diagrams to confirm proper wiring and operation.

2. Check the setting of the jumper pins or DIP switches on the manufacturer's control board. Do not assume they are correct; use the manufacturer's guide to select the proper airflow, delays, and profiles. Always disconnect the main power to the unit when making these adjustments.

3. Check all terminal/plug connections both at the furnace/air handler control board and at the motor. Always disconnect power to the system before disconnecting and reconnecting plugs. Look for loose plugs and/or loose pin connections in the plug, and for burnt, bent or loose pins or seats.

4. Confirm there are no limits, rollouts, or safeties tripped. Also check for any fault codes present on the furnace/air handler control boards. If fault codes are present, follow the manufacturer's recommendations to resolve the problem.

5. It is normal for the motor to rock back and forth on start up. Do not replace the motor if this is the only symptom identified.

Motor Not Running

STEP 1

On 120VAC systems there should be a jumper between terminals 1 and 2. On 240 VAC systems, the jumper should be removed. If a motor is operating at 240VAC with the jumper in place, the motor will be permanently damaged.

Check for proper high voltage and ground at the 5-pin connector at the motor. These are dual voltage motor capable of operating in 120 or 240 volt systems. Input voltage within +/- 10% of the nominal 120VAC or 240VAC is acceptable. Correct any voltage issues before continuing.

STEP 2

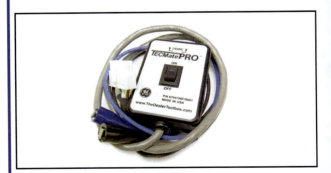

If the motor is a 2.0/2.3 motor and has proper high voltage and ground at the 5-pin connector, go to following section "**Troubleshooting the ECM Motor using the GE ECM™ TECMate PRO.**" If the motor is a 2.5 motor and has proper high voltage and ground, reference the equipment manufacturer's manuals for further check procedures.

Tools: **Multimeter / TECMate PRO**

Field Service Guide: Motors

Motor is Running

If the system is excessively noisy, does not appear to change speeds in response to a heat or cool demand, or is having symptoms during the cycle such as a tripping limit or freezing coil, Follow these steps:

STEP 1

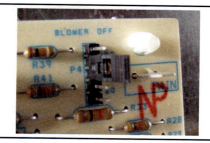

Wait for programmed delays to time out. If delays are too long, then reset them using the manufacturer's charts.

STEP 2

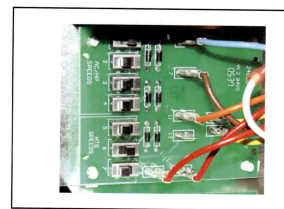

Ensure the airflow settings are correct for the installed system using the manufacturer's charts. Remember that the change in airflow between continuous fan and low stages of operation may be very slight depending on the size of the system.

STEP 3

Remove the filter and check that all of the dampers, registers, and grills are open and free flowing. If removing the filter corrects the problem, replace with a clean or less restrictive filter.

STEP 4

Also check and clean as needed the blower wheel, secondary heat exchanger (if applicable) and evaporator coil (if applicable).

5

Field Service Guide: Motors

STEP 5

Check the external static pressure. If it is higher than the manufacturer's recommendations, correct the airflow restriction

STEP 6

If the motor does not shut off at the end of the cycle, check the delay times and wait for the delays to time out. Also, make sure that there is no call for "Continuous fan" on the "G" terminal. This motor may take a while to come to a complete stop with selected delays and the normal ramp down.

STEP 7

On 120VAC systems there should be a jumper between terminals 1 and 2. On 240 VAC systems, the jumper should be removed. If a motor is operating at 240VAC with the jumper in place, the motor will be permanently damaged.

Check for proper high voltage and ground at the 5-pin connector at the motor. These are dual voltage motor capable of operating in 120 or 240 volt systems. Input voltage within +/- 10% of the nominal 120VAC or 240VAC is acceptable. Correct any voltage issues before continuing.

STEP 8

If the motor is a 2.0/2.3 motor and has proper high voltage and ground at the 5-pin connector, go to following section "**Troubleshooting the ECM Motor using the GE ECM™ TECMate PRO.**" If the motor is a 2.5 motor and has proper high voltage and ground, reference the equipment manufacturer's manuals for further check procedures.

Field Service Guide: Motors

Troubleshooting the ECM Motor using the GE ECM™ TECMate PRO (for 2.0/2.3 motors only)

The GE ECM™ TECMate PRO is designed to assist field service technicians by troubleshooting GE ECM™ 2.3 motors independently of the HVAC system. Analysis of field returns shows that quite often the GE

ECM™ is misdiagnosed as faulty. This is due in large part because of the unavailability of effective troubleshooting tools for the GE ECM™ motor. The TECMate PRO is designed to isolate a motor failure from other HVAC system controller failures. GE ECM™ motors are used in one of two modes: Thermostat Mode and Variable Speed Mode. Thermostat Mode is controlled by a 24VAC signal usually from a thermostat, whereas Variable Speed Mode is controlled by a Pulse Width Modulating (PWM) signal. In either mode, the TECMate PRO is capable of identifying a motor failure versus other HVAC controller failures.

Tools: TECMate PRO
Socket Wrench/Sockets
Multimeter

STEP 1

CAUTION: Disconnect AC power from the furnace, air handler, or system being serviced.

STEP 2

Remove the 16-pin connector from the motor, and connect the 16-pin connector from the TECMate PRO to the motor. Do not disconnect the 5-pin AC power connector from the motor.

Field Service Guide: Motors

STEP 3

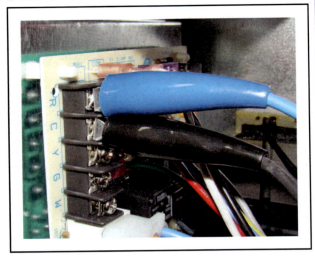

Connect the two alligator clips from the TECMate PRO to 24VAC.

STEP 4

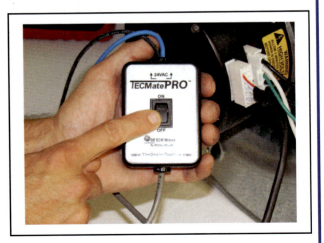

Place the switch on the TECMate PRO in the off position.

STEP 5

Reconnect AC power to the system.

STEP 6

Place the switch in the on position and observe the motor. If the motor starts up, the motor is good.

Field Service Guide: Motors

STEP 7

If the motor passes the test, then some other component in the HVAC system is faulty.

STEP 8

If after this test, the motor does not start, then proceed to replace the motor control. NOTE: Before replacing the control, test to insure the motor is not damaged: (1) check for insulation, and (2) check for mechanical integrity by rotating shaft by hand. The following steps describe this test.

STEP 9

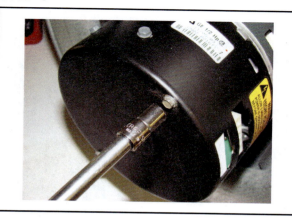

Remove the control by locating and removing the two standard ¼" bolts from the back of the control. The control module is now free of mechanical attachment to the motor endshield but is still connected by a plug and three wires inside the control.

STEP 10

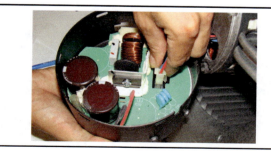

Carefully rotate the control to gain access to the plug at the control end of the wires. With thumb and forefinger, reach the latch holding the plug to the control and release it by squeezing the latch tab and the opposite side of the connector plug and gently pulling the plug out of the connector socket in the control. DO NOT PULL ON THE WIRES. GRIP THE PLUG ONLY. The control module is now completely detached from the motor.

Field Service Guide: Motors

STEP 11

Verify with a standard ohmmeter that the resistance from each connector pin (in the motor plug just removed) to the motor shell is >100K ohms. (Measure to unpainted motor end plate).

STEP 13

Rotate the motor shaft to test for rubbing and/or mechanical defect.

STEP 12

Verify with a standard ohmmeter that the resistance from each connector pin to the other two connector pins, is similar and < 20K ohms.

STEP 14

If any connector pin fails this test and/or the shaft doesn't spin easily, THE MOTOR AND CONTROL IS DEFECTIVE AND MUST BE REPLACED. CONTACT YOUR DEALER FOR A REPLACEMENT MOTOR. If the motor passes this test, but failed the Thermostat and Variable Speed Mode tested by the TECMate PRO, THEN THE CONTROL ONLY NEEDS TO BE REPLACED. CONTACT YOUR AUTHORIZED DEALER FOR A REPLACEMENT CONTROL.

Field Service Guide: Motors

Replacing the ECM Control Module

STEP 1   Tools: Screwdrivers, Socket Wrench/Sockets

After the system AC power has been off for 5 minutes, unplug the 16-pin connector and the 5-pin connector from the motor control.

STEP 2

Remove the blower assembly from the HVAC system and remove the two hex-head screws from the back of the control.

STEP 3

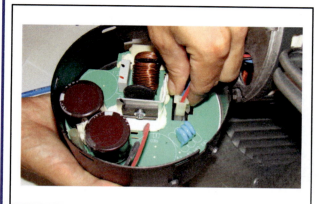

Unplug the 3-pin connector from the inside of the control by squeezing the latch and gently pulling on the connector.

STEP 4

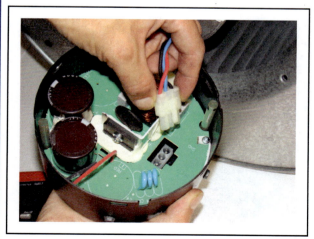

Insert the 3-pin connector into the new control module. A slight click will be heard when inserted properly. This connector is keyed for proper connection.

Field Service Guide: Motors

STEP 5

Orient the new control to the motor's endshield with connectors facing down, insert bolts and tighten. If replacing an ECM 2.0 control with an ECM 2.3 control, insert plastic tab into perimeter of replacement control and align tab with mating hole in the endshield. Use the new shorter bolts provided to ensure a secure attachment. Orient the control connectors to the endshield between 4 and 8 o'clock positions

STEP 6

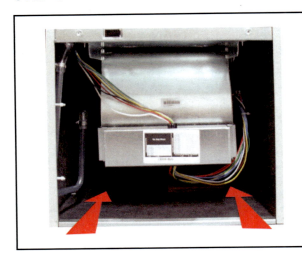

Reinstall the blower/motor assembly into the HVAC system by following the manufacturer's guidelines.

STEP 7

Plug the 16-pin connector and 5-pin connector back into the motor. The connectors are keyed. Observe proper orientation.

STEP 8

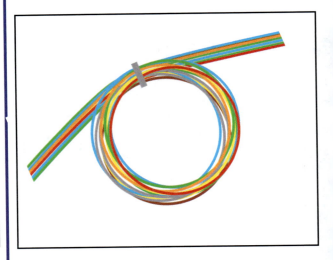

Be certain to form a drip loop so that water cannot enter the motor by draining down the cables.

Field Service Guide: Motors

Replacing the ECM Motor Module

STEP 1 Tools: Screwdrivers, Socket Wrench/Sockets

After the system AC power has been off for 5 minutes, unplug the 16-pin connector and the 5-pin connector from the motor control.

STEP 2

Remove the blower assembly from the HVAC system and remove the two hex-head screws from the back of the control.

STEP 3

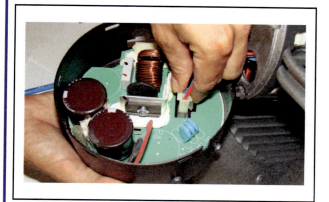

Unplug the 3-pin connector from the inside of the control by squeezing the latch and gently pulling on the connector.

STEP 4

Loosen the bolt securing the blower wheel to the motor shaft

Field Service Guide: Motors

STEP 5

Loosen the bolt securing the belly band around the motor.

STEP 6

Carefully remove the motor from the belly band and blower wheel.

STEP 7

Slide the new motor module into the belly band and through the blower wheel. Make sure the belly band is not covering any shell holes.

STEP 8

The motor module does not have a specific orientation, however, the motor control does. Make sure the three-wire plug will reach the motor control when it is oriented properly before tightening the belly band.

Field Service Guide: Motors

STEP 9

Tighten the belly band and secure the blower wheel to the motor shaft.

STEP 10

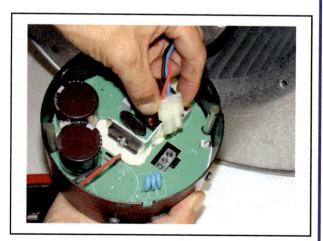

After installing the new motor module, reinstall the motor control as described previously in "**Replacing the ECM Control Module**"

Final Checks

☐ Check all wiring and connections, especially those removed while servicing.

Ensure the system is set up as follows:

☐ Verify the condensate drain is not plugged or clogged.

☐ Reconnect the AC power to the HVAC system and verify that the motor is working properly.

☐ Check and plug leaks in return ducts and equipment cabinet.

☐ Verify that the system is running quietly and smoothly, in all modes (heating, cooling, and continuous fan) and all stages (if applicable).

☐ Return all thermostat settings to the customer's preference.

If this is a repeat failure, it is important to check the following:

☐ If any evidence of moisture, correct the issue.

☐ If the area is subject to high amounts of lightning strikes, then use of additional transient protection may be helpful.

15

Field Service Guide: Motors

Chapter
PSC Motors

Table of Contents

PSC Blower Motors 2
    Introduction 2
    Operating Characteristics of a PSC Motor 2
    PSC Motor Failures 2
        Bearing Seizure 2
        Electrical Failure 3
Testing for Electrical Failure: Step By Step 3
Checking a Run Capacitor with a Capacitor Test Mode on a Multimeter: Step By Step 3
Checking for an Open Motor Winding (Open Internal Overload): Step By Step 4
Checking for an Electrically Grounded Motor: Step By Step 5
    What to Check when a Problem Occurs 6
    Summary 6

1

PSC Blower Motors

Introduction

Permanent Split Capacitor (PSC) blower motors are the most common type of motor found in residential HVAC systems. These motors are used to power compressors, condenser fan assemblies, and indoor air blower assemblies. The motors used in residential systems are fractional horsepower motors.

Indoor fan assemblies feature multi-speed PSC motors that are directly coupled to the blower wheel. These motors are called direct drive motors and consist of the motor and matching run capacitor.

Operating Characteristics of a PSC Motor

Permanent split capacitor motors have two internal motor windings, a run winding and an auxiliary start winding. The two windings when energized create a powerful magnetic field that rotates around the rotor of the motor. The magnetic field alternately pushes and pulls the motor rotor in a circular motion to turn the motor shaft.

The run capacitor discharges voltage in time to the voltage coming into the motor. When the AC sinewave changes polarity, the capacitor charges and discharges. The discharged voltage generates the best alignment of magnetic fields that increases motor power. The run capacitor is selected by the motor manufacturer to have a microfarad rating range that will get optimum performance out of the motor.

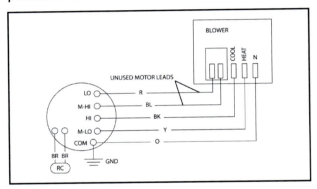

In this illustration, a typical PSC blower motor circuit is shown. The motor has various speed taps that can be energized to change blower speeds. Be aware that when the blower is running, or when voltage is applied to the motor, all of these taps will have voltage present!

PSC Motor Failures

Bearing Seizure

PSC motors could have bearing seizure if excessive strain is placed on the motor due to blower wheel problems or excessive dirt. If the motor has a bearing problem, the bearings are not replaceable, the motor will need to be replaced.

The run capacitor is attached to the left of the motor on this blower assembly.

Field Service Guide: Motors

To quickly test for a bearing problem with the motor, turn power off to the furnace. Reach into the blower housing and spin the blower wheel. The wheel should freely spin. If the motor does not spin, make sure the blower wheel is not dragging on the blower housing. If it is, repair the problem.

If the blower wheel is OK and the motor will not spin or makes grinding noises as it turns, replace the motor.

Electrical Failure

PSC motors can have an electrical failure of the motor windings. One of the windings could open, or the internal overload could open and not reset. The motor could have an electrical winding short to ground. The run capacitor could also fail which would cause the blower to run slow or go off on internal overload.

Testing for Electrical Failure

STEP 1   Tools   Multimeter

Check for proper line voltage to the motor as it tries to start. Voltage should be close to 120VAC. If voltage is not correct, find the cause of the problem. It is likely to be in the furnace control board. If proper voltage is present at the motor yet the motor hums and goes off on internal overload, remove power to the furnace.

Checking a Run Capacitor with a Capacitor Test Mode on a Multimeter

STEP 1   Tools   Multimeter

Remove power to the furnace. Discharge the capacitor with a insulated handled screwdriver.

Remove the two brown wires that attach to the run capacitor. Set multimeter to the Capacitor Test mode. In this mode, the measured microfarad rating of the capacitor will be displayed on the meter.

3

STEP 2

Place a meter lead on each capacitor terminal. Read the microfarad level of the capacitor. It should be within 10% of the rating printed on the capacitor. If it is, the capacitor is good. If it is out of range, replace it with one of equal rating and try running the motor. If the reading is within 10% of microfarad rating, the capacitor is good.

Checking for an Open Motor Winding (Open Internal Overload)

STEP 1 Tools **Multimeter**

Remove power to the furnace and discharge the run capacitor. Remove the wires from the run capacitor.

STEP 2

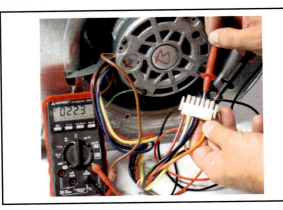

Set the multimeter to read OHMS. Look at the motor label to find the wiring diagram. Identify the two wires that are connected to line voltage. In this case, they are the orange wire and the black wire. The black wire is the high speed motor winding. The orange wire is the common

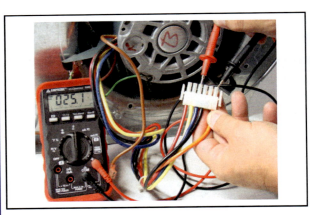

connection of the motor. Read the resistance from the common motor winding wire to all of the motor speed tap wires. The resistance will go up as the speed tap measured goes down. Black will have lower resistance than red low speed tap.

Field Service Guide: Motors

Checking for an Electrically Grounded Motor

Tools **Multimeter**

STEP 1

Remove power to the furnace and discharge the run capacitor. Remove the wires from the run capacitor.

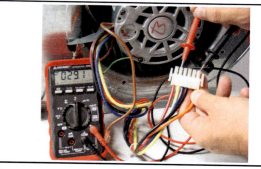

If there is an infinite resistance read through any winding, replace the motor. If the motor windings all check out with proper resistance, go to the next step.

If there is infinite resistance to all motor winding speed taps, the internal overload inside the motor may have opened. Allow time for the motor to cool down. If the motor is cool, replace the motor.

STEP 2

Measure the resistance between each motor wire to the chassis of the motor. Infinite resistance should be measured from each lead to the motor ground. If there is measurable resistance from any motor speed wire to ground, replace the motor.

STEP 3

Find the two brown wires. Measure the resistance from each wire to the common wire identified in STEP 2. One wire will read a short between the common wire and brown wire. The other wire is the start winding. Read the resistance from this brown wire to common. Resistance should be measured. If infinite resistance is measured, the winding is open. Replace the motor.

Field Service Guide: Motors

What to Check when a Problem Occurs

Motor hums tries to start, then goes off on internal overload.
- Improper line voltage
- Mechanical failure of the motor or binding blower wheel
- Bad run capacitor.
- Motor winding open.
- Grounded motor.

Motor runs slow.
- Improper voltage to the motor.
- Excessive duct static pressure.
- Bad run capacitor.

Motor does not try to start, proper voltage is applied to motor.

- Open motor winding
- Open internal motor overload protector. (Allow motor to cool down.)

Motor trips circuit breaker to air handler/furnace.
- Motor winding short to ground
- Capacitor short to ground

Summary

Check for proper voltage to the motor first.

Check run capacitor's for proper microfarad range.

Read the motor schematic to find the common and run winding taps.

Check all wires for grounding to the motor case.

Air Volume
Measurement

**Air Volume
Measurement**

Field Service Guide: Air Volume Measurement

Chapter
Air Volume Measurement

Table of Contents

Air Volume Measurement **2**
    Introduction 2
    Air Volume Requirement 3
    Temperature Rise Method 4
    Temperature Rise Method (Gas Heat) 4
    Determining BTUH Output of a Gas Furnace 4
To find the BTUH Output of the Furnace by Clocking the Gas Meter: Step By Step **5**
Determining Temperature Rise: Step By Step **8**
    Applying the Temperature Rise Method to Determine Air Flow 8
    Temperature Rise Method (Electric Heat) 10
Determining BTUH Output on Electric Heaters: Step By Step **10**
Determining Heat Rise: Step By Step **11**
    Three Phase Heaters: Formula for BTUH Output 13
    Summary 13
External Static Pressure Method **13**
    How to read each Duct Static Pressure Independently 15
    Using Static Pressure to find Air Volume 15
    Air Performance Charts: External Static Pressure 16
Measuring Total External Static Pressure with a Gas Furnace: Step By Step **17**
Measuring Total External Static Pressure with an Air Handler: Step By Step **18**
    When Measured External Static Pressure is Excessively High 19
    When Excessive External Static Pressure is Present 19
    Finding Static Pressure Loss Across Duct Components 19
    Summary 19

Air Volume Measurement

Introduction

Many service technicians and installers have never actually measured how much air a blower assembly is moving. An HVAC system that is serviced without having had an air volume calculation done operates with improper charge, unknown operating characteristics, unknown efficiency, uncertain capacity, and uncertain reliability.

Here is a simple technical explanation of why an air conditioner's air volume level must be known:

The evaporator coil sits in the air stream at the indoor blower assembly. The refrigerant circulates through the evaporator and absorbs heat from the air. If the air volume is low, the coil will absorb less heat than it should. Since heat changes pressure and superheat, the system will operate at a pressure level that is not high enough. The natural tendency of the technician servicing the system will be to add refrigerant in an attempt to raise pressure. The system will now operate with excessive charge and a lack of heat.

The operating characteristics of a system charged without enough air volume and excess refrigerant will include problems such as compressor starting problems, capacity complaints, premature failure, poor efficiency, and poor reliability.

Measuring air volume takes about 10 minutes of time. If not done, the system cannot function properly.

There are two methods of air volume measurement that can be easily performed by a qualified service technician. The two methods are **Temperature Rise Method** and **External Static Pressure Method**. Both methods of air volume measurement will be discussed.

In the *temperature rise method*, the heating section of the system is operated with the indoor fan speed set to cooling speed. The temperature of the air entering and leaving the air handler or furnace is measured to find the temperature rise. A formula is computed and air volume determined.

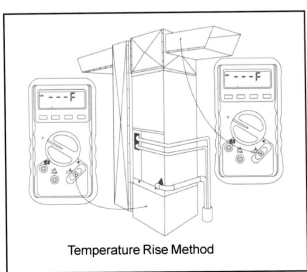

Temperature Rise Method

In the *external static pressure method*, a differential manometer is used to measure the air pressure at the inlet and outlet of the indoor blower assembly. The measured air pressure is compared to charts provided by the equipment manufacturer to determine how much air volume is flowing in cubic feet per minute. (CFM)

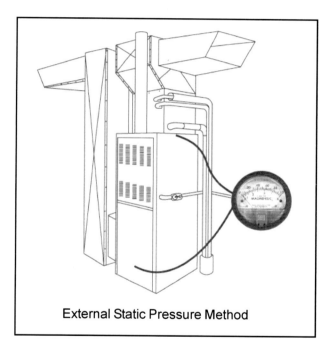

External Static Pressure Method

has weight. Every pound of air carries so many btu's of heat in it. When the systems are engineered by the manufacturers, the amount of air is set and the heat in the air is measured. This is important to understand as a system can only absorb as much heat as is available. There are two ways the amount of heat fluctuates, by the amount of pounds of air flowing and by the heat in the air. If the heat in the air falls, the system capacity falls. If the amount of pounds of air falls, the system capacity falls.

By setting up the air volume properly, the system will always receive the proper amount of air in pounds. However, as the room temperature changes in the home, the amount of heat in each pound of air will fluctuate. Not a problem as the amount of heat in the air is measured in direct relationship to wet bulb temperature of the air. Manufacturer charging charts always plot wet bulb temperature as a requirement because it tells them how much heat is in each pound of air. The charts ASSUME that indoor air volume has been properly measured and adjusted so the evaporator coil always receives the proper amount of heat based upon the wet bulb temperature of the return air.

Air Volume Requirement

Air conditioning systems are engineered with a specific amount of indoor air passing across the surface of the evaporator coil. The amount of air is measured in cubic feet per minute. (CFM) Residential air conditioning systems typically require 400 CFM of indoor air for every 1 ton of cooling capacity. For example, a 2 ton unit would need 800 CFM of indoor air since 2 times 400 equals 800. For every cubic foot of air, the air

Field Service Guide: Air Volume Measurement

In summary, capacity changes with the amount of heat that is absorbed at the evaporator coil. Manufacturers have established a relationship between indoor air wet bulb temperature and heat in a pound of air. By setting up the indoor blower to deliver the specified amount of indoor air in CFM, the system will have a fixed constant that allows for wet bulb temperature to be referenced to system suction pressure. <u>If wet bulb is measured and used to plot required operating pressures and air volume is wrong, the charging chart is basically useless.</u>

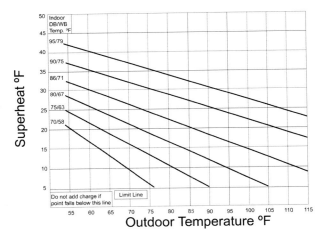

Temperature Rise Method

Determining how much air is flowing through a blower assembly can be done by checking the temperature rise that occurs during heating operation of an electric heat air handler or a gas furnace.

The BTUH Output of the heating system must be found to perform this measurement. There are two separate methods for determining BTUH Output, one for gas furnaces and the other for electric heat air handlers. If the system does not have any heat option, this method will not work.

The formula for finding CFM is:

$$CFM = \frac{BTUH\ OUTPUT}{Temp\ Rise\ (ACF)^*}$$

*Altitude correction factor below 1000ft = 1.08

Temperature Rise Method (Gas Heat)

Two steps are performed by the technician performing this procedure: determine BTUH Output of the furnace, and measure air temperatures. Each step requires the furnace burners to be operating.

Determining BTUH Output of a Gas Furnace

In this series of steps it is necessary to know the heat content level of the natural gas being delivered to the home. The heat contained in a cubic foot of natural gas can range from somewhat below 1050 BTU/cubic foot to slightly above 1050 BTU/cubic foot. To obtain the heat content of the natural gas in your area, contact the local gas provider.

If it is not possible to obtain the heat content of the gas from the gas provider, the furnace nameplate BTUH input should be used to determine the BTUH output of the furnace. Be aware that calculated air volume will not be precise. (Deviation will be due to fluctuations in heat content of the fuel.)

If the furnace nameplate lists BTUH Input, multiply the BTUH input of the furnace by the efficiency of the furnace, for example 100,000 BTUH Input times .80 Efficiency = 80,000 BTUH output.

Field Service Guide: Air Volume Measurement

```
CATEGORY 1 FORCED AIR FURNACE FOR INDOOR INSTALLATION ONLY IN A BUILDING
CONSTRUCTED ON-SITE
INSTALLATION
ELECTRIC 115 V.   60 HZ   1 PH,   MAXIMUM TOTAL INPUT  8.5 AMPS
FACTORY EQUIPPED FOR NATURAL GAS
EQUIPPED WITH NO. 45 DRILL SIZE ORIFICE
HOURLY INPUT RATING  MANIFOLD PRESSURE  NATURAL GAS PROPANE
BTUH/H  (KW)          INCHES W.C. PO/ (KPA)  INCHES W.C. (KPA)
80,000  (23.44)         3.5                 (87)
MAXIMUM PERMISSIBLE GAS SUPPLY PRESSURE TO FURNACE
MINIMUM GAS SUPPLY PRESSURE FOR PURPOSES OF INPUT ADJUSTMENT
LOW INPUT
LIMIT SETTING
DESIGN MAXIMUM
```

Furnace Nameplate

In this example Input BTUH 80,000 BTUH times .80 efficiency = 64,000 BTUH OUTPUT. (Estimated)

To find the BTUH Output of the Furnace by Clocking the Gas Meter

This method is the most accurate way of determining the BTUH Output of a gas fired furnace. The furnace will be operated to determine how many cubic feet of natural gas enter the furnace burners. The input will then be multiplied by the efficiency of the furnace to determine BTUH Output.

The heat content of a cubic foot of gas should be found by contacting the local gas company. If this cannot be done, use a default rating of 1050 BTU per cubic foot of natural gas.

In this procedure, all other gas appliances in the home should be off. Keep pilot lights lit. The furnace should be operating at proper manifold pressure as stated on the furnace nameplate. (See above.) The furnace should be calling for heat with all stages of capacity firing.

Tools: **Gas Pressure Manometer**
Watch/Timing Device

STEP 1

Find out the BTUH content of a cubic foot of natural gas. This information is available from your local gas company. The default average used in generating air volume tables is 1050 BTU per Cubic Foot.

It may be very difficult to obtain this information from the local gas company as the heat content of 1 cubic foot of natural gas fluctuates from day to day. If the heat content of the fuel can be determined by making a phone call it is well worth the effort as accurate BTUH Input of the gas furnace can be found.

If the actual heat content of the gas cannot be obtained, use a default value of 1050 BTU/cubic foot of natural gas for your calculations. Be aware, there will be some inaccuracy in your calculations performed in this procedure.

STEP 2

Shut off all gas appliances in the home. Do not shut off the pilot lights to any appliances. The only gas appliance that should be operating in this test is the gas furnace.

Set the blower to operate at cooling speed during heat mode operation.

Field Service Guide: Air Volume Measurement

STEP 3

Install a gas pressure manometer onto the furnace manifold pressure tap.

STEP 4

```
CATEGORY 1 FORCED AIR FURNACE FOR INDOOR INSTALLATION ONLY IN
A BUILDING
CONSTRUCTED ON-SITE
INSTALLATION
ELECTRIC 115 V.   60 HZ   1 PH,   MAXIMUM TOTAL INPUT  8.5 AMPS
FACTORY EQUIPPED FOR NATURAL GAS
EQUIPPED WITH NO. 45 DRILL SIZE ORIFICE
HOURLY INPUT RATING MANIFOLD PRESSURE     NATURAL GAS PROPANE
BTUH/H    (KW)           INCHES W.C. PO/ (KPA)    INCHES W.C. (KPA)
80,000   (23.44)              3.5           (87)
MAXIMUM PERMISSIBLE GAS SUPPLY PRESSURE TO FURNACE
MINIMUM GAS SUPPLY PRESSURE FOR PURPOSES OF INPUT ADJUST-
MENT
LOW INPUT
LIMIT SETTING
```

Call for heat. Make sure all furnace stages are calling for heat and the burners are operating at high fire rate. Check manifold pressure versus the nameplate requirement. Make adjustment as needed.

STEP 5

With the furnace operating at high fire rate, go to the home's gas meter. Time the number of seconds it takes for the gas meter small scale to complete one revolution on the dial.

STEP 6

Determine the scale of the dial on the gas meter. The scale needs to be found so that total cubic feet of natural gas entering the home can be found using the chart on the next page.

Field Service Guide: Air Volume Measurement

STEP 7

GAS FLOW IN CUBIC FEET PER HOUR 2 CUBIC FOOT DIAL							
Sec.	Flo	Sec.	Flo	Sec.	Flo	Sec.	Flo
8	900	29	248	50	144	82	88
9	800	30	240	51	141	84	86
10	720	31	232	52	138	86	84
11	655	32	225	53	136	88	82
12	600	33	218	54	133	90	80
13	555	34	212	55	131	92	78
14	514	35	206	56	129	94	76
15	480	36	200	57	126	96	75
16	450	37	195	58	124	98	73
17	424	38	189	59	122	100	72
18	400	39	185	60	120	104	69
19	379	40	180	62	116	108	67
20	360	41	176	64	112	112	64
21	343	42	172	66	109	116	62
22	327	43	167	68	106	120	60
23	313	44	164	70	103	124	58
24	300	45	160	72	100	128	56
25	288	46	157	74	97	132	54
26	277	47	153	76	95	136	53
27	267	48	150	78	92	140	51
28	257	49	147	80	90	144	50

Plot time measured on the chart to determine cubic feet of gas being burned by the furnace per hour.

For 1 Cu. Ft. Dial:
Gas Flow CFH = Chart Flow Reading divided by 2

For ½ Cu. Ft. Dial:
Gas flow CFH = Chart Flow Reading divided by 4

For example if it took 36 seconds for 1 revolution of the gas meter dial and the dial was a 1 cubic foot dial, the cubic foot used is 200 divided by 2 = 100 cubic feet of fuel per hour.

STEP 8

36 seconds = 200 cubic feet per hour/2

36 seconds = 100 cubic feet per hour

100 x 1050 = 105,000 BTUH Input

Multiply the cubic feet of gas burned per hour by the heat content value obtained from the gas supplier. (1050 BTU default average) The answer is BTUH INPUT to the furnace.

For example, lets say we timed 36 seconds per revolution on a 1 Cu. Ft. dial, the furnace is an 80% furnace.

STEP 9

Assume an 80% efficient furnace.

105,000 BTUH Input x .80 = 84,000
                                   BTUH Output

Multiply BTUH Input obtained in step 7 by furnace efficiency to determine BTUH Output.

Field Service Guide: Air Volume Measurement

Now that BTUH Output is known, the temperature rise that occurs across the gas furnace can be taken with the furnace operating in heating mode. The indoor blower motor must be running at the cooling speed during this portion of the procedure. Place the blower speed tap to operate at cooling speed during heat mode operation by switching motor leads at the indoor furnace control board terminals for fan speed selection.

Determining Temperature Rise

A temperature rise must be taken by the technician. It is recommended to use the same thermometer for measuring supply air and return air temperatures. The supply air temperature should be taken out of direct sight of furnace heat exchangers. (18 inches away from supply air plenum). The temperature difference between the supply air and return air temperatures is called the Delta T.

STEP 1   Tools: | **Thermometer** |

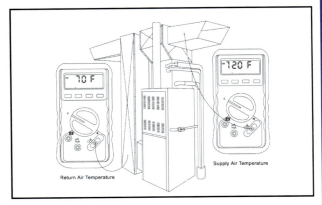

Configure the furnace to run at cooling speed in the heating mode. With all stages of heat calling, measure the return air and the supply air temperature. Take the supply air temperature reading out of direct sight of heat exchangers. A good rule is 18 inches away from the supply air plenum.

STEP 2

| **Return Air = 70°F** |
| **Supply Air = 120°F** |
| **Delta T = 50°F** |

Determine the temperature difference between the return air and supply air. This difference is called the Delta T.

Applying the Temperature Rise Method to Determine Airflow

With all information gathered properly (BTUH output & temperature difference), the indoor air volume in CFM may be determined.

The altitude correction factor must be found to complete the information gathering needed to find CFM. The table is shown here. It lists altitude correction factors for various altitudes above sea level.

Altitude	Correction Factor
<1000	1.08
1000	1.04
2000	1.00
3000	0.97
4000	0.93
5000	0.90
6000	0.86

To determine CFM, divide the BTUH Output divided by (Temperature Difference Times Altitude Correction Factor (ACF))

$$CFM = \frac{BTUH\ Output}{Temp.\ Diff.\ x\ ACF}$$

Lets use our previous examples to find the amount of air volume being produced by a gas furnace.

In our examples we had a furnace that had an input of 105,000 BTUH operating at 80% efficiency. The BTUH Input of the furnace was multiplied by the efficiency which indicated:

Furnace output = 84,000 BTUH

The supply air was 120°F and the return air was 70°F.

Temperature Difference = 50°F

The altitude is 600 ft. From the altitude correction table we find a correction factor of 1.08.

Multiply the temperature difference by the altitude correction factor. For this example we are at an altitude of 600 ft. The altitude correction factor from the table is 1.08.

Temperature Difference = 50°F x 1.08 = 54

The air volume being produced by the furnace is found by performing this simple math equation:

$$\frac{84,000}{54} = \textbf{1556 CFM}$$

NOTE:

If the air volume is too high or too low

It is highly unlikely that measured air volume will exactly match the 400 CFM per 1 ton of cooling capacity requirement. Acceptable ranges of air volume are between a low of 350 CFM - 450 CFM per ton of cooling capacity.

If air volume is too high, select the next lowest fan speed and recalculate temperature rise to find the new CFM. If the air volume is too low, increase the fan speed and repeat the temperature rise portion of the equation and find new CFM.

If the fan speed taps are at their highest setting and air volume is too low, diagnose the cause of low heat load on the evaporator coil in the *Diagnostic Chapter*.

Field Service Guide: Air Volume Measurement

Temperature Rise Method (Electric Heat)

We can measure the amount of air being delivered by an electric heat air handler by taking the temperature rise through the air handler with the electric heaters and indoor fan assembly energized. <u>The formula is the same as gas furnaces.</u>

To perform the measurement, the heating output of the electric heaters in the air handler in BTUH output per hour must be measured. It is very easy to determine the heating output of the single phase electric heaters.

The formula for finding BTUH Output is:

BTUH Output = Volts * Amps * 3.413

Determining BTUH Output of Electric Heaters

Tools: Multimeter, Ammeter

STEP 1

Set the blower fan speed for Cool Mode speed. The blower must run at cooling mode speed during heat mode operation.

STEP 2

First, run the air handler in the heating mode of operation by calling for heat. Make sure to energize all of the heaters if the heater section has more than 1 stage of capacity. When the heaters are all on, measure the voltage to the heaters. For example, let's say we measured 200 volts.

STEP 3

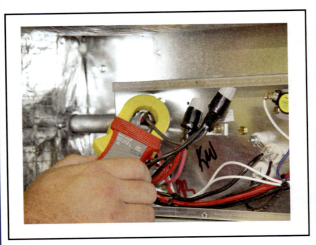

Measure the amps being drawn by the heaters. Let's say we measure 50 amps.

Field Service Guide: Air Volume Measurement

STEP 4

Solution:

200 V * 50A = 10,000

10,000 * 3.413 = 34130 BTUH Output

Apply your readings to the formula:

BTUH Output = volts x amps x 3.413

We now know the BTUH Output of our electric heater.

Determining Temperature Rise

STEP 1   Tools: Thermometer

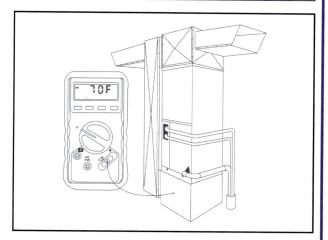

Once you have calculated the heating output of the air handler, measure the return air temperature. Let's say we measure 70° F.

STEP 2

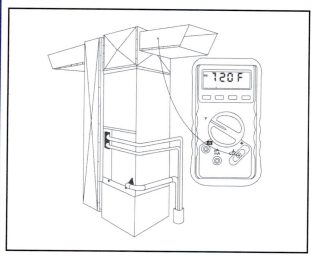

Next, measure the supply air temperature out of direct line of sight from the heaters. Let's say we measure 120° F.

STEP 3

Supply Air Temperature (120°F)
- Return Air Temperature (70°F)
Temperature Rise (50°F)

To get the temperature rise subtract the Return Air Temperature from the Supply Air Temperature.

11

Field Service Guide: Air Volume Measurement

STEP 4

Altitude	Correction Factor
<1000	1.08
1000	1.04
2000	1.00
3000	0.97
4000	0.93
5000	0.90
6000	0.86

From Chart ACF= **1.08**

From the chart we can see that the Altitude Correction Factor for 600 ft above sea level is 1.08.

STEP 5

From Chart ACF= **1.08**

50°F * 1.08 = 54

Multiply the ACF by the temperature rise of 50°F

STEP 6

BTUH OUTPUT = 34130
ACF = 1.08
Temp Rise = 50°F

$$\frac{34130}{54} = 632 CFM$$

Solve for CFM

NOTE:

If the air volume is too high or too low

It is highly unlikely that measured air volume will exactly match the 400 CFM per 1 ton of cooling capacity requirement. Acceptable ranges of air volume are between a low of 350 CFM - 450 CFM per ton of cooling capacity.

If air volume is too high, select the next lowest fan speed and recalculate temperature rise to find the new CFM. If the air volume is too low, increase the fan speed and repeat the temperature rise portion of the equation and find new CFM.

If the fan speed taps are at their highest setting and air volume is too low, diagnose the cause of low heat load on the evaporator coil in the *Diagnostic Chapter.*

Field Service Guide: Air Volume Measurement

Three Phase Heaters: Formula for BTUH Output

Although not found in residential homes, you may encounter a 3 phase heater and wish to calculate BTUH Output. The formula is slightly different than single phase heaters.

Volts * Amps * 3.413 * 1.73 = BTUH OUTPUT

Summary

Temperature Rise Method

The formula for both methods is the same.

The method of determining BTUH Output is different.

Clocking the meter and just multiplying BTUH input times efficiency to determine CFM for gas furnaces is not an exact measurement.

Take temperature measurements on the supply air side out of direct sight of heaters. (18 in from air supply plenum)

External Static Pressure Method

External static pressure is a measurement of the air pressure at the inlet and outlet of the indoor air blower assembly. This pressure is the same pressure a balloon has pushing against its internal walls. Air blowers have this same type of pressure at their inlet and outlets.

Manufacturers place special probes called static pressure probes into the ducting at the inlet and outlet of the air handlers and furnaces. These probes have holes drilled into them that are used to sense the static pressure of air in that area.

Static Pressure Probe

The static pressure probes are connected to a differential pressure meter such as a Magnehelic gauge made by Dwyer. This gauge has two ports, a high pressure port and a low pressure port. The scale on the gauge should read a maximum of 1" of water column. Higher scales cannot be used for air pressure readings common in residential homes.

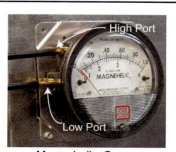
Magnehelic Gauge

13

Field Service Guide: Air Volume Measurement

The amount of static pressure at the fan inlet and outlet will have a direct impact upon how much air volume the fan can deliver. As the static pressure across the fan goes up, the ability to move air goes down. This static pressure at the inlet and outlet of the fan blower when added together is called *total external static pressure*.

To measure the total external static pressure, the probe that goes to the HIGH PORT of the pressure gauge is inserted into the supply air side of the fan blower. The probe that goes to the LOW PORT of the pressure gauge is inserted into the return air inlet to the fan. The probe is now reading total external static pressure.

As this graph shows, the higher the Static Pressure the less air will be able to be moved through the air handler. And the opposite holds true as well. The less Static Pressure that is present, the greater the ability to move air through the air handler.

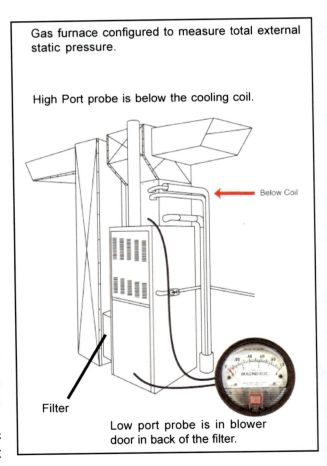

Gas furnace configured to measure total external static pressure.

High Port probe is below the cooling coil.

Below Coil

Filter

Low port probe is in blower door in back of the filter.

Anything that has resistance to air movement will cause a pressure drop. The total pressure drop in a supply duct can be measured at the outlet of the blower fan. The static pressure read at this point is the total static dropped from the furthest component in the ducting. When a static pressure probe is placed into a blower door at the inlet to the fan, the total static pressure losses of the return air duct components are measured. When these two static pressures are added together, the *total external static pressure* is known.

Field Service Guide: Air Volume Measurement

How to Read Each Duct Static Pressure Independently

The pressure gauge can be used to find the static pressure of the supply ducting or the return ducting. To measure the supply ducting static pressure, remove the probe from the return air and leave it exposed to atmosphere. Leave the supply air probe in its place.

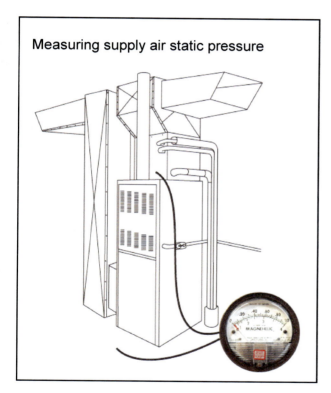

Measuring supply air static pressure

To measure return air ducting static pressure, insert the low port probe into the return air at the blower door by making a hole in the blower door or inserting into an available small opening. Remove the supply air probe and leave it exposed to atmosphere. The probe now reads return air static pressure. Add the two readings together and you will get total external static.

Make it easier, simply insert both probes into their respective positions and total external static will be displayed on the gauge.

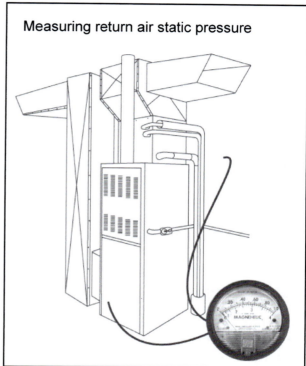

Measuring return air static pressure

This test is useful when trying to find out which duct may be causing high static pressure and low air volume levels. It may be both ducts or it may only be one. With the tool you can find which one may have excessive pressure drop that is hurting blower air delivery performance.

Using static Pressure to find Air Volume

Special tables are published by equipment manufacturers that will show how much air the system can deliver in CFM based upon the total external static pressure measured.

15

Field Service Guide: Air Volume Measurement

*DY080R9V3W - FURNACE COOLING AIRFLOW (CFM) AND POWER (WATTS) VS. EXTERNAL STATIC PRESSURE WITH FILTER											
OUTDOOR UNIT SIZE (TONS)	AIRFLOW SETTING	DIP SWITCH SETTING						EXTERNAL STATIC PRESSURE			
		SW 1	SW 2	SW 3	SW 4			0.1	0.3	0.5	0.7	0.9
3.0	LOW (350 CFM/TON)	ON	OFF	OFF	ON	CFM	1050	1050	1050	1010	800
						WATTS	235	295	340	350	290
	NORMAL (400 CFM/TON)	ON	OFF	OFF	OFF	CFM	1200	1200	1200	1040	840
						WATTS	335	385	410	365	310
	HIGH (450 CFM/TON)	ON	OFF	ON	OFF	CFM	1350	1350	1210	1070	900
						WATTS	455	480	435	390	345

NOTES: * First letter may be "A" or "T"
1. At continuous fan setting: Heating or Cooling airflows are approximately 50% of selected cooling value.
2. LOW airflow (350 cfm/ton) is COMFORT & HUMID CLIMATE setting;
NORMAL airflow (400 cfm/ton) is typical setting;
HIGH airflow (450 cfm/ton) is DRY CLIMATE setting.

This chart here is typical of charts found on gas furnaces. Notice the blower is capable of up to .9 inches external static pressure. This is a very high range. Typical total external static readings should range anywhere from about .15 - .65 e.s.p. The reason this table goes so high is because the system uses an ECM type blower motor which is very powerful. Notice the steady air volume produced over a wide range of static pressures. This would not be possible with a PSC blower system.

For static pressure readings to be accurate, the static pressure probes must be placed into the system at the proper positions. If placed incorrectly, the pressure drop of components such as return air filters will increase the total external reading and cause a misinterpretation of the information that is gathered from the static pressure tables.

Air Performance Charts: External Static Pressure

In this example of a CFM versus external static pressure chart, an air handling unit with a PSC blower motor is plotted. The chart requires the user to find the voltage to the blower motor and what speed tap the blower is operating at. Static pressure is then measured and plotted to find CFM. There are footnotes at the bottom of the chart that indicate for example whether the filter is included in the reading. This is important to note as it will affect where the low pressure port probe is placed into the ducting. If the filter is included, the probe is placed in front of the filter. If the filter is not included, the probe is placed after the filter. Making a mistake here will make the readings invalid, so be careful.

AIR FLOW PERFORMANCE TWE024P13,0A,FA												
EXTERNAL STATIC PRESSURE (INCHES OF WATER)												
	VERTICAL (See Notes)						HORIZONTAL (See Notes)					
	230 VOLTS			208 VOLTS			230 VOLTS			208 VOLTS		
CFM	HI	MED	LO	HI	MED	LO	HI	MED	LO	HI	MED	LO
300						0.65						
350						0.63						
400			0.61			0.6					0.66	0.64
450			0.59		0.55	0.54			0.69		0.64	0.59
500		0.61	0.55		0.53	0.48			0.63		0.61	0.52
550	0.6	0.57	0.5	0.71	0.55	0.4	0.63	0.56		0.6	0.55	0.43
600	0.58	0.52	0.44	0.65	0.45	0.31	0.6	0.57	0.48	0.59	0.49	0.34
650	0.55	0.47	0.36	0.58	0.38	0.2	0.58	0.51	0.4	0.56	0.41	0.22
700	0.52	0.4	0.27	0.51	0.29	0.08	0.55	0.43	0.3	0.53	0.32	0.1
750	0.47	0.32	0.17	0.44	0.18		0.51	0.35	0.19	0.48	0.21	
800	0.42	0.24	0.05	0.37	0.06		0.46	0.26	0.08	0.43	0.09	
850	0.36	0.14		0.3			0.4	0.16		0.36		
900	0.3	0.04		0.23			0.33	0.05		0.28		
950	0.22			0.16			0.25			0.19		
1000	0.14			0.09			0.16			0.09		
1050	0.05			0.01			0.06					

Courtesy of American Standard

NOTES:
Vertical: With filter, no horizontal drip tray. Small apex baffle. Subtract 0.06" W.G. for downflow.
Horizontal: As shipped but without filter. Subtract 0.05" W.G. for Horizontal left.

Measuring Total External Static Pressure with a Gas Furnace

Tools: **Magnehelic Pressure Probe Drill**

STEP 1

Make an access hole between the top of the furnace and the bottom of the cooling coil. DO NOT DRILL INTO THE CONDENSATE PAN OF THE COOLING COIL. If creating a hole is not possible, try using the hole where the main air limit is mounted. Insert the static pressure probe that is connected to the high port of the pressure gauge into this hole. Position the probe so the tip is facing into the air stream.

STEP 2

Drill a hole into the blower door of the furnace in a spot where no damage will occur. Insert the low port probe into this hole and position the tip to face into the flow of return air.

STEP 3

Call for cooling operation. When the blower motor comes up to speed, read the external static pressure.

Compare to charts to determine CFM.

STEP 4

Change the blower speed taps to get the desired CFM. If air volume is not high enough and the highest speed tap is being used, the cause of low air volume must be found. Check static pressure at the return and at the supply independently. If one of them has a high reading, find the cause of the air restriction.

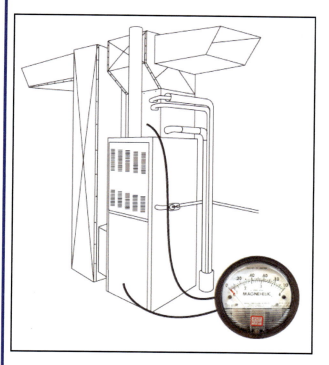

Field Service Guide: Air Volume Measurement

Measuring Total External Static Pressure with a Air Handler

Tools: Magnehelic Pressure Probe Drill

STEP 1

Make an access hole at the discharge supply air outlet area of the air handler. Insert the positive pressure probe into this hole. When inserting the probe, place the tip of the probe to face into the air stream.

STEP 2

Determine if the filter is included in the air performance data chart. If the filter is included, drill a hole where return air duct attaches to the air handler. If the filter is not included, drill a hole into the blower door of the air handler in a spot where no damage will occur and where the probe when inserted will not touch anything electrical. Insert the low port probe into this hole and position the tip to face the direction of return air.

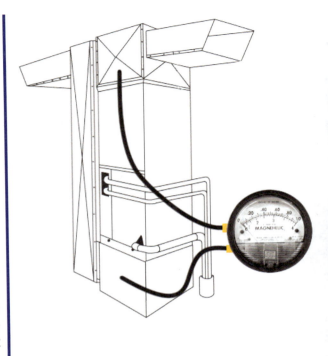

STEP 3

Call for cooling operation. When the blower motor comes up to speed, read the external static pressure on the gauge. Compare to charts (pg 16) to determine CFM.

STEP 4

Change the blower speed taps to get the desired CFM. If air volume is not high enough and the highest speed tap is being used, the cause of low air volume must be found. Check static pressure at the return and at the supply independently. If one of them has a high reading, find the cause of the air restriction.

FILTER NOTE:

These charts, when including a filter in the data, are specifying a factory installed filter, not a high efficiency add on filter! If a high efficiency filter has been added to the air handler, remove the factory installed filter and measure return air static via a hole in the air handler door.

Field Service Guide: Air Volume Measurement

When Measured External Static Pressure is Excessively High

What is too high? What is considered too high will depend upon what type of motor is in the air handling component. If it is a variable speed ECM type motor, about .9" external static pressure is the limit. If the blower is a PSC type blower, above .50" is typically too high, if the blower is not oversized for the cooling system. In other words, if a 3 ton system has a 4 ton air handler, the air handler can usually deliver 1200 CFM for a 3 ton at external static pressure that is above .50". If the system is a gas furnace with a 3 ton blower, 1200 CFM will usually be achieved at .50" external static pressure. Anything above that will typically cause air volume to be below required levels.

When Excessive External Static Pressure is Present

Check the static pressure in the supply duct by removing the probe from the return air. Next, check the static pressure in the return air by inserting the probe back into place and then removing the supply air probe.

The duct with the higher reading should be investigated for air volume restrictions and proper duct dimension sizing. Make duct corrections as needed. It may be necessary to remove components from the duct system such as high efficiency filters.

Some high efficiency air filters can drop over .2" of static pressure. This is almost half of the available pressure from a gas furnace using a PSC blower motor.

Finding Static Pressure Loss Across Duct Components

When trying to determine how much a duct component such as a filter is contributing to total static pressure loss, a pressure drop can be taken across the component. The high port probe is placed in front of the component in the direction of entering air into the component. The low port probe is positioned where the air leaves the component. The pressure drop is displayed on the pressure gauge.

Summary

Total external static pressure is the return and supply air static added together.

Static pressure is measured with special probes. (Available from Dwyer.)

Pressure drops across components can be measured.

Be careful of small print on CFM charts. (Check if filter is included.)

Do not drill a hole into an air handler or furnace door without checking clearances.

ECM type motors can deliver required air at higher external static pressures than PSC type motors. (Unless grossly over-sizing furnace/air handler blowers.)